A PLACE MORE VOID

**Cultural Geographies
+ Rewriting the Earth**

Series Editors
Paul Kingsbury, Simon Fraser University
Arun Saldanha, University of Minnesota

A PLACE
MORE VOID

Edited by Paul Kingsbury and Anna J. Secor

University of Nebraska Press | Lincoln

Library of Congress Cataloging-in-Publication Data
Names: Kingsbury, Paul (Paul Thomas), editor. |
Secor, Anna Jean, editor.
Title: A place more void / edited by
Paul Kingsbury and Anna J. Secor.
Description: Lincoln: University of Nebraska
Press, [2020] | Series: Cultural geographies +
rewriting the earth | Includes bibliographical
references and index.
Identifiers: LCCN 2020021094
ISBN 9781496222633 (hardback)
ISBN 9781496223661 (paperback)
ISBN 9781496224354 (epub)
ISBN 9781496224361 (mobi)
ISBN 9781496224378 (pdf)
Subjects: LCSH: Geography—Philosophy. |
Nothing (Philosophy)
Classification: LCC G70 .P57 2020 |
DDC 910.01—dc23
LC record available at
https://lccn.loc.gov/2020021094

Designed and set in Minion Pro by L. Auten.

Contents

Illustrations

Acknowledgments

Heartfelt thanks to the book's contributors, whose patience and hard work ensured our editorial tasks went swimmingly. We also gratefully acknowledge the contributions of all those who participated in the five (!) "Into the Void" sessions at the 2017 Annual Meeting of the American Association of Geographers in Boston, Massachusetts. We would also like to thank the anonymous reviewers and Arun Saldana for their insightful comments on an initial draft of the manuscript; Bridget Barry at University of Nebraska Press, for her guidance and support throughout the process; and Sam Brawand and Jane Curran for their thorough copyediting.

Finally, we thank our families, friends, and colleagues in the Departments of Geography at Durham University, Simon Fraser University, and the University of Kentucky, whose constant love, motivation, and counsel enabled us to joyfully plunge into *A Place More Void*.

A PLACE MORE VOID

Introduction

Into the Void

Paul Kingsbury and Anna J. Secor

It is about the ninth hour in Rome, and a Soothsayer has one last chance to warn Julius Caesar about the Ides of March and impending harm before he reaches the Senate. But there is a problem: the narrow streets will soon be jammed with senators, judges, and common petitioners. And it is going to get so crowded that the frail Soothsayer realizes that he might be crushed to death. His plan? To get "to a place more void" where he can intercept and speak to Caesar.[1] The result? The Soothsayer succeeds in meeting Caesar but is ignored yet again, and the would-be Roman king is famously stabbed to death by rebellious senators.

It is about the ninth month of the year, and we need to submit a CFP for the 2017 American Association of Geographers Annual Meeting in Boston. There's a problem, though: the Listservs will soon be chock-a-block with CFPs enticing faculty, students, and other researchers with issues of substance, pressing matters, and important stuff. Our plan? To entice geographers to eschew such weighty things, to consider these materials as simple solids, and to get "Into the Void" (the title of the proposed session) by offering a forum for anyone engaged in theoretical, empirical, and/or methodological research that examines how holes, voids, chasms, lacks, gaps, nothingness, and other empty or unfathomable entities (de)structure spaces, places, landscapes, and other geographical phenomena. It is an invitation to a place more void. The result? We succeeded in holding five sessions that addressed the following types of voids: invisible, chimerical, supernatural, absent, and disintegrated. Even though the back-to-back sessions started at 8 a.m. and ended at 7 p.m., no one was harmed (at least not intentionally or to our knowledge). Another result, of course, is this book that you now hold in your hands or behold on the screen.

Unlike the soothsayer we did not foresee these outcomes. But perhaps we should have, given the attention that has already been directed toward voids of all sorts inside and outside of geography. We address both of these domains below, but before we do so, let us briefly address the various meanings that comprise our central notion of the void. To begin with, the term *void* is complex, and this very complexity directly informs the contents and organization of the book. A void can be an adjective, predicative, or noun. As an adjective, according to the *Oxford English Dictionary* (OED), a void refers to something that is "completely empty" and as a predicative, as in the phrase "void of," it refers to being "free from" or "lacking" something. As a common noun, the void designates "a completely empty space" or an "unfilled space in a wall, building, or other structure," as well as "an emptiness caused by the loss of something." There is also another connotation of the void, which refers to something that is "not valid or legally binding" or, in the context of speech and action, something that is "ineffectual; useless" (OED 2019). For quantum field theory the void is a generative and destructive field: the vacuum of our universe is turbid, roiling with creation and annihilation, while for string theory there are 10^{500} *different* ways for there to be nothing in the universe.

The void, then, is inherently mutable: it sprawls in its various connotations of description, quality, and thing. Furthermore, there are certain degrees of "voidness" in the void, ranging from the extreme void of a black hole from which no matter, radiation, or even light can escape, to the void of a simple hole wherein something is hollowed out and filled with another element such as air. And then there is the void as absence, which might incur a sense of presence in terms of an absent presence. There's also the void of silence, which might weigh heavily as an awkward pause or stretch on endlessly as a broken heart. Another void concerns the collapse or fraying of a realm that demarcates a limit or boundary. As John Lennon sings in the trippy song "Tomorrow Never Knows," which closes the 1966 album *Revolver*, the void is not necessarily a realm of charred opacity or deadness; it can be a prismatic field of spangling possibility and even enlightenment: "it is shining, it is shining."[2] That said, the song's lyrics, which draw on the eighth-century text the *Bardo Thödol* (known in the West as the *Tibetan Book of the Dead*), recognize that such Enlightenment demands a "surrender to the void" (see epigraph) so as to embrace the loss and fulfillment of Ego death.

Keeping all the above elements of the void in play is one of the main goals of this book, not simply as an affirmation of an ethics of difference or multiplicity, but also as a testament to the void's spaciousness, that is, its various splits, fissures, frays, fragments, and dispersals that already define it and its voiding as such. And so, in order to address the above lacunae, in what follows, we stage an encounter with the (physical and metaphysical) void before attempting to create a non-uniformly expanding, non-orientable, internally wounded map of the void's appearances and pressure points in the various fields of study that comprise the discipline of geography.

Missed Encounters with the Void

Any discussion of the void is a discussion about no(one)thing. Subsisting in the vortices of culture, religion, mathematics, science, philosophy, and aesthetics, the void is manifold. To enter the terrain of its paradoxes, we can begin with the story of zero as it travels from East to West. This is a story that shows how the void, as an object of knowledge and speech, is bound up with geographical and historical contingency. In the telling, we will slide along the incorporeal edge of the empty space and its signifier (zero), traversing time and space in an effort to orchestrate an encounter with the void, that most notorious of no-shows.

Our story begins in 300 BC, when Babylonians started using a placeholder to mark an empty column on an abacus. These two wedges were not yet a number; they had no specific place on the number line, no meaning of their own, but merely made it clear that a position was unoccupied. While the Greek and Roman number systems remained cumbersome without it, zero blossomed into numeracy both in Mayan civilization during the first century BC and several centuries later in India, where Hinduism and Buddhism had made emptiness and nonexistence key spiritual concepts. In contrast, in ancient Greece neither the void nor infinity was permitted to perturb a cosmology in which the earth was at the center of a finite set of spheres whose motion was of divine origin. Finally, it was Islamic scholars of the ninth century, spiritually undaunted by the void (as that from which creation ensued), who challenged the Christian refusal of zero. The Indian zero (*sifr*) spread throughout the expanding Islamic empire, and by the eleventh century Islamic leaders declared the Aristotelian system (which admitted neither infinity nor the void) blasphemy (see Seife 2000).

Zero was a fearful proposition to the Greeks for good reason. Not only does it come trailing a whiff of the grave, but zero exhibits some odd behavior. Multiplying by zero turns all quantities to dust, crushing the number line to a mere point. Dividing by zero calls forth the unfathomable: How much nothing composes something? How many parts of no-part does it take to make a part? The result is nonsense, the defeat of mathematical logic. The problem is simple to demonstrate: If 6 x 0 = 0, then by the procedures of algebra it should be that 6 = 0 / 0. But it simply does not—or even if it does, this equivalency is equally true of any other number. All things can be proved to be equal to 0 / 0, and thereby to be equal to each other—and equal to zero. In short, dividing by zero, all numeracy trails off to infinity or slips back into the void. It is like a black hole, condensing anything in its vortex to a single point. And what is lost is irretrievable. Zero not only undermines the expected properties of multiplication (expansion) and division (contraction) but also undermines the *relationship* (inversion) between them. Once we multiply a number by zero, we must not try to resurrect that number with division. Division by zero is akin to necromancy and is strictly forbidden (it never turns out well).

Despite its capacity for nihilism, eventually zero conquered the West through trade. Demonstrating its most practical side, zero proved its worth. Taking its place in the number line (before one, after minus one), zero opened the door for the emergence of calculus, perspectival painting, and modern physics. What had begun as the mark of absence became an integer.

Today, we would miss zero if it were not there. With zero, we finally have something there to tell us that there is nothing there. And yet, instead of bringing us closer to the void, by standing in for emptiness, it is as though zero effectively covered over the void, blocked it from view, replaced it with *something*. Perhaps in refusing zero, what the Greeks eschewed was not the void as such but rather its signification. The goddess of Parmenides's poem says that only that which exists is there to be thought or spoken of: "For you could not know what-is-not (for that is not feasible), Nor could you point it out" (translation by Gallop 1984). The Parmenidean injunction against speaking of the nonexistent assumes that to speak of what-does-not-exist *existing* is to say that *nothing is something*—and that is clearly nonsense, irrational, and morally suspect (like dividing by zero). So the Greeks decided that the only way to hold "being" apart from "nonbeing" was to refuse the possibility of the latter's signification. We may now have zero, a modern-day goddess might say, but we should refuse this offering. For, following Lacan (2018, 72), what is offered is not that which appears as the offering (the spoken) but that which falls out of speech: "*this isn't it*" (emphasis in the original). Zero is not nothing; it is its simulacrum.

One could simply say that the void is that which cannot be signified, that which resists all symbolization, and leave it at that. Case closed. Court dismissed. We might conclude like Ludwig Wittgenstein (1992), "Whereof one cannot speak, thereof one must be silent" (108). But it turns out that the void generates as much speech as silence. If the problem of an empty spot gave rise to zero, then perhaps we can also say that the problem of the nonexistent is precisely what gave rise to all of this speaking and thinking. The contradiction with which Parmenides struggles—our inability to signify nonexistence without ontologizing it—signals an impossibility that inheres in language itself. Language depends on something missing or excessive in the relationship between words and things in order to function. According to Jacques Lacan, the slide of signification depends on there being a missing signifier, an unsayability, a void around which chains of signifiers connect and circulate. Like the empty square in a sliding tile puzzle, this void is what gives us a little bit of "play," what allows movement, speech, desire, and the emergence of something new. It is not simply that the void cannot be signified, but that this impossibility is the hole from which all signification issues. In short, if there were no void (no gap, no remainder, no excess) in what is thinkable or sayable—if we could speak what cannot be spoken, if when we spoke everything was said—we would not speak at all.

To become speaking beings, we must enter a symbolic order that disperses our being and instantiates bits of nonbeing. Lacan defines such an entry in terms of alienation and castration, which far from scarring or snipping off possibilities, actually creates them by transforming us into desiring subjects. But given that desire "crawls, slips, escapes, like the ferret" (Lacan 1998, 214) and that "desire may register itself *negatively* in speech" (Copjec 1994, 14; emphasis in the original), our wanting to talk may express itself as a silence, as a wanting not to speak at all. As speaking beings, we are always at risk of not speaking, of not writing, of halting our writerly flows with abrupt inactivity that interrupts our eager advances. One possibility, then, of our wanting to speak or write is to give the Other nothing: to scream a mute silence or scrawl out a page intentionally left blank. The desire to offer silence or a blank page might inoculate us against a terrifying encounter with not doing anything at all or, worse still, in the editorial space of an introduction, the horror of desiring not to do anything at all. Here we are in good company with Friedrich Nietzsche (1989) and his exhortation that rather than embrace the void of nihilistic passivity in terms of an editorial dereliction of duty, we "would rather will *nothingness* than *not* will" (97; emphasis in the original). And, if we're honest, that is, if we take seriously our experiences of writing beyond this page, all those journal articles, book chapters, emails, and so on, does not any act of writing confront the fine line of wanting to write and not wanting to write? Or, conversely, to write in order to avoid the horror of not wanting to write? Perhaps the marks of these very words are the result of inscribing a difference between wanting to do something and wanting to do nothing. At any rate, this anxious "scriptural economy" (de Certeau 1984, 131–53) caught between writing something and nothing even pricked Sigmund Freud's (2002) conscience when he wrote: "With none of my writings have I had such a strong feeling as I have now that what I am describing is common knowledge, that I am using up pen and paper, and shall soon be using the services of the compositor and the printer, to say things that are in fact self-evident" (Freud 2002, 54).

In our attempt to locate the edge between speech and silence, the difference between writing something and nothing, we encounter the void as a missed encounter, that is, as a something that does not happen. Arguably, we miss our encounter with the void because of its own lack of self-correspondence; each time we reach for it, we find that what we catch *isn't it*. Where we had sought an empty place, we find a numeral (0); when we speak of it, we call it into being; instead of nothing, we find ourselves with *something*. Perhaps the problem that Parmenides stumbled into is that nothing *is not* nothing: it is that which differentiates *something* in the place of nothing. The void is missing from itself! Indeed, the void in the context of physics turns out not to be the opposite of something but a particular configuration of it. In electromagnetic theory, for example, the "zero field" is the same as two waves moving in opposite directions so that their peaks and troughs cancel one another out; we might reasonably wonder, "Is that two things or no things?" (Weatherall 2016, 113). And in quantum field theory, the vacuum is precisely where "something" and "nothing" are not mutually exclusive, but where matter and antimatter (electrons and positrons) are spontaneously created and annihilated (Weatherall 2016). As an immaterial condition that upholds the possibility of materiality and its reverse, the (quantum) void is thus what the Stoics called an "incorporeal": it does not exist but *subsists* (Deleuze 1990; Grosz 2017). The void thus operates in terms of what Deleuze (1990) calls the "paradoxical element," the immaterial frontier that articulates the difference between "nothing" and "something" at the same time as it traces the impasse of their indistinguishability. As Deleuze puts it, "everything happens at the border" (9).

Admittedly, not everyone is willing to vacate to a place more void. Some will beg the question and say there is no such thing. Others will point out that because this place more void is so generative and capacious it cannot be a void at all. Still others might object that, despite our invitation, the void remains utterly inaccessible; they might sternly remind us that "there is no conceivable encounter with the void" (Badiou 2005, 56). It hardly matters. Whether it appears as a lack or a surplus, a grave or a womb, an empty place or its mark, what is in play is paradox: the unresolvable itself. Certainly, there have been attempts at "resolution"—attempts to disentangle, dichotomize, foreclose, ontologize—but we are beyond those here. We are suspicious of stitched up syntheses and petrified outcomes. Our interest is in the void's deadly liveliness and the many names under which its acrobatics take place: remainder, surplus, event, aporia, *différance*, death drive, impasse, nonrelation, kenon, spacing, to name quite a few moves. Our interest is also in how these names-of-the void populate and pump the heart of the geographical project in both its earthy and cosmic incarnations.

Writing the Earth, Writing the Void

Every good undergraduate knows that the discipline of geography gets its name from the ancient Greek words for "earth" (*gē*) and "writing" or "description" (*graphia*). Very few of these students, however, are likely to realize the importance of the void for ancient Greek understandings of space and place. Atomists, Aristotelians, Epicureans, Pythagoreans, Stoics, and other philosophical camps argued at length over the centuries about whether or not the void (*kenon*)—variously understood as simply space, empty space or place, and an empty thing or an empty part of thing—existed at all and what the consequences were for asserting that the nonexistent exists (as we saw in Plato's Parmenides; see also Algra 1995). Debates also swirled around questions about the location of the void in terms of whether it was confined to earth or whether it encompassed an infinite extent of space beyond the realm of what was referred to as "heaven," that is, beyond the atmosphere that enveloped the earth. Thus, two distinct kinds of voids emerged in early Western thought: "The true Void came to be distinguished from air. Anaxagoras, in the fifth century, demonstrated by experiments with "empty" wineskins and waterclocks that the spaces we call empty are really filled with air, which is something since it resists pressure. By proving the substantial existence of air he thought he was disproving the existence of any true Void" (Cornford 2014, 12).

Even before and beyond the Ancient Greeks' codifications of geography's epistemologies and ontologies, the void was relevant to the writing of the earth and indeed the cosmos in terms of their genesis or coming into being. Writing (in the appropriately titled) *Abysmal*, Gunnar Olsson (2007) observed that the

> *Enuma elish*, the oldest creation epic yet to be discovered . . . takes place at a time "when there was no heaven, no earth, no height, no depth, no name" (Heidel 2009, tablet 1, 1–8). No nothing, not even, as in the younger Genesis, an earth without form and void. In the conception of the Babylonian poet a void was consequently a void-in-an-of-itself, not merely a void of form. Then (as well as now) it was through the practice of naming that shapeless matter (more precisely fluid water rather than solid earth) changed into meaning-filled meaning. (Olsson 2007, 3)

Olsson highlights how the making of the earth and cosmos is not just an inherently geographical process; rather, it *is* geography insofar as it involves the working with and transforming the earth and void. The writing of the earth—its *geo-graphos*—is central to the making of the earth and would become a prominent feature of the many forms of geographical regimes of power and knowledge that derived from Babylonian and ancient Greek and stretched across the Medieval, Renaissance, and Modern eras. As Victor Burgin (1996) notes:

> *Horror vacui* was central to Aristotelianism. In classical cosmologies, space was a plenum. Similarly, in the medieval world, God's creation was a fullness without gap. In quattrocento [fifteenth-century Italy] perspective the subject first confronts an absence in the field of vision, but an absence disavowed: the vanishing point is not an integral part of the space of representation; situated on the horizon, it is perpetually pushed ahead as the subject expands its own boundary. The void remains abjected. In later, non-Euclidean geometry we find the spherical plenum of classical cosmologies collapsed upon itself to enfold a central void. (Burgin 1996, 55–56; emphasis added)

Horror vacui, that is, the fear of empty space, became a cartographic symptom in European Renaissance maps of empire and colonialism that announced "Hic sunc dracones!": here be dragons and other weird creatures that fill the even more monstrous *Terrae Incognitae!* (Van Duzer 2013). The void thus cannot be separated from the creative operations and energies of geography: the writing of the earth and void are co-constitutive. So much so that it would not be inappropriate to consider a history of geography in terms of its history as a form of kenography, that is, void writing. As Patrick McGreevy (2001) notes, "the world and the void, like reason and madness, come as a pair. It is the act of creation, of division—though the boundary line may be arbitrary, leaky, and false—that brings into existence not only the world but also the void" (254). Returning to Burgin's observation about the importance of *horror vacui*, Marcus Doel (1999) has suggested that we can discern "at least three holes. The first hole is the *peep hole* of representation, exemplified in the egocentric apex of the cone of vision. The second hole, the *vanishing point*, structures the field whilst withdrawing from it. The third hole, the *point of flight*, deconstructs the orderly lineaments of Euclidean, non-Euclidean, and *n*-dimensional spaces" (Doel 1999, 70–71; emphasis in the original).

All three of these holes have informed geographical knowledge: at times geographers have claimed for their mappings a "God's eye view," while at other moments they have sought to grasp the unseen forces of topographical differentiation; there are even instances of geographers cutting and twisting their maps to produce non-orientable topological surfaces. Geographers (like mathematicians, semioticians, philosophers, speleologists, sub-atomic physicists, artists, and all manner of burrowing creatures) are not without their own (missed) encounter with the void—but what can be said of the void in geographical scholarship today?

Geography's Holey Places

For both modern geographers and the Ancient Babylonians and Greeks, the void is that which demarcates the limits and possibility of geographical ontology and epistemology. To situate the void at the heart of geography is not difficult. After all, if we follow the Stoics, the void is the counterpart to a central geographical concept: the void is the limit of *place* (a dichotomy that our invitation to "a place more void" knowingly undermines). Echoing the Stoics, who defined the void and place in relation to the lack of bodies in one and the presence of bodies in the other, Edward S. Casey (1997) writes that "what void and place share is the common property of being *the arena for the appearance of bodies. . . .* But while a place is the immediate arena for such appearance . . . the void is the scene for this kind of place" (18; emphasis in the original). Thus, the void is that which lacks a body but which, if occupied, becomes a place: "If the void is not itself a place, it must become one" (16; see also Grosz 2017). It is a neat demarcation: the void (or space) seems to stand outside of place; it is empty but capacious, a zone of anticipated habitation. Place is full, sensual, immersive; it is the habituation of bodies, of presence.

And yet, the void is more contaminant than container: a sense of loss creeps into humanistic geography, and "place" becomes something from which we are alienated, a plenitude to which we can never return—a sign of something missing (Rose 1993). If the void is the limit of place, it is a (dis)placed limit, one that—like the border in recent work in political geography (Bigo 2008; Mezzadra and Neilson 2012) or the state of exception (Agamben 1998, 2005; Belcher et al. 2008)—is everywhere and nowhere, the unlocalizable principle that makes all localization possible, drawing the boundary between exterior and interior at the same time as it expresses the impossibility of maintaining such a distinction (see also Kapoor 2018). This has political possibilities too in that "undocumented persons, by using their politically absent yet physically present bodies as vehicles for practicing dissensus, can find possibilities for recognition and action in public space" (Sigvardsdotter 2013, 523; see also Amir 2013; Derickson 2017; Bennett and Jackson 2017).

The tremors of the ancient void extend beyond the botheration of place. Those seemingly antiquated debates between Plato and the Pythagoreans who designated space as an abstract concept of geometrical figures directly underpin the dichotomy between field and entity that is often adopted in twenty-first-century GIS (geographic information system) practices (see Clementini 2017). In addition, GIS users have to negotiate the 3D representations of voids qua openings in building elements (Zlatanova 2017). And that seemingly stuffy idea about the void lurking above the realm of "heaven" is actually at work in our contemporary geographies of outer space in terms of "the cosmic void between planetary and other cosmic bodies, drawing on notions of absence, vacuity or nothingness" (Dunnett et al. 2017, 2).

If one of the earliest understandings of the void concerned its air-like and empty qualities, then we find the study of this kind of void throughout modern physical geography. Physical geographers, earth scientists, geomorphologists, and so on have explored vesicle formation in smectite clays, interconnected bubble and tube voids in karst and lava rocks that transmit the underground flow of water, the weathering processes in the cracks of ice wedge polygons, infiltration and the absorption capacity of fine-textured soils. We can also see the airy void as an object of study in the research on cave genesis (speleogenesis), mine spoils, which are composed of strange large voids that distinguish them from naturally occurring soils. In addition, the empty liquid void of the sea that awaits being conquered by capitalism illustrates how the void is capable of uniting physical and human geography (Steinberg 2001).

One of the most important topics in human geography—the built environment—is another domain that is perforated by the void, especially in terms of the issue of vacancies. Notably the notion of "void" is etymologically derived from a dialect variant of the Anglo-Norman and Old French word *voide*, which in turn, is related to Latin for "vacate" (*vacare*). Robert Smith and Stephen Merrett (1987) identify vacant private housing and void rates in the United Kingdom. In some instances, where accounts are sent out while the property is unoccupied, the void may be first identified by the rate demand being returned by the post office, perhaps marked "gone away." Alternatively, if rates are paid in instalments by direct debit or credit transfer, instead of half yearly, then any cancellation of this arrangement by the former occupier may indicate a void (787). Echoing our previous assertion that "nothing" is not the other of "something" but the impasse that is inherent to its structure, void rates point toward other impasses of the void in capitalism. Rather than act as an impediment to its "normal" functioning, vacancies, empty brownfields, derelict buildings, industrial ruins, and so on are necessary impasses, or more accurately internal contradictions that provide fodder for capitalism's next spatial fix and attempt to restructure itself (see also Edensor 2013; Meier 2012).

Geography's Elsewheres

In addition to the above airy and empty ontological voids, we find epistemological voids or concerns over gaps of knowledge bubbling away in modern geography. A groundbreaking essay here is John K. Wright's prescient 1946 AAG Presidential Address. For Wright, the world's unknown lands or terrae incognitae, though diminished in size and number, should "appeal . . . to the imaginative faculties of geographers and others and the place of the imagination in geographical studies" (Wright 1948, 1). Such imaginative faculties were incited by the "Sirens of *terrae incognitae*"; for example, "in the contemplative mood that mountain tops induce, we have brooded over the view, speculated on the lay of the land, experienced a pleasurable sense of the mysterious—perhaps felt even a touch of the sinister. We have heard the Sirens' voices" (2). What is striking about Wright's address is the emphasis on the "deep-seated distrust of our artistic and poetic impulses" (7), as well as wonder, objectivity and subjectivity, aesthetic imagining (6). Countering these suspicions, Wright affirms the practice of what he calls "geosophy," or "the study of geographical knowledge from any or all points of view" (12). In so doing, he extends an invitation to the void.

In the final sentence of Wright's address (1948), which prefigures humanistic geography (and evinces the masculinist discourse of the discipline), he asserts that "perhaps, the most fascinating *terrae incognitae* of all are those that lie with the minds and hearts of men" (15). Yet despite the turn toward questions of human consciousness and creativity that Wright's call presaged, for a long time the psyche as it appeared in human geography remained void-like, an unspoken set of "underlying assumptions about . . .

undisclosed, undynamic 'black boxes' [of mental processes], which ultimately could only produce static descriptions of overt spatial behaviour" (Pile 1996, 34). Drawing on Wright's essay, Steve Pile (1996) suggested that psychoanalysis, with its emphasis on the dynamic unconscious, could provide a rich conceptual framework for charting "the *terrae incognitae* of people's hearts and minds" (9). Of course, like all attempts to make the unknown known, this is a fraught expedition. As Felicity Callard (2003) argued some years later, those dimensions of the unconscious that are most unpalatable and intractable still tend to recede, leaving intact the self-image of critical geography. One could say that, like the number zero, the unconscious arrives in geography to both mark and cover over the terra incognita that troubles it.

And this trouble runs deep. The geographical imaginary is structured by the void of all that which exceeds or does not signify within its discourse. Subsumed within the binaries of Western ontology, made present in such a way that the real of what is unassimilable is foreclosed, sexual and racial difference have been what Jacques Derrida would call the "constitutive outside" of geographical thought (see Dixon and Jones 1998). As Gillian Rose (1993) argued, "various forms of white, bourgeois, heterosexual masculinity have structured the way in which geography as a discipline claims to know space, place and landscape" (137), making all "others" present in particular (binarized) ways while leaving no ground for feminist, queer, or black geographies as political and intellectual projects. By pulling the curtain on the gendered, sexed, and racialized binaries that demarcate(d) the field of geographical knowledge—culture/nature, abstract/concrete, rational/emotional, public/private, space/place among many others—Rose (1993) exposed how the edifice of masculinist geographical knowledge relied upon a traditional ontology of essentialized and binarized sexual difference.

Importantly, it is not that "woman" or the feminine *is* the void in this masculinist geographical imagination (though certainly the vagina and the womb have both at times been nominated for that role [for example, see Irigaray 1985]). On the contrary, fleshy and concrete, woman is figured to be more "place" than "void" and made to appear on the side of the *corporeal*—though sexual difference (as a kind of "ontological negativity" [Zupančič 2017, 37]) is not anymore present for all that. Thus, what Rose (1993) advocated was a kind of "paradoxical space" in which "the subject of feminism" occupies two positions at once: one within the represented (masculinist) discursive space and one in what Teresa de Lauretis (1987) calls "the space-off, the elsewhere of those discourses" (26; qtd. in Rose 1993, 139). This paradoxical space might rightly be called a "demonic ground"—a space from which it becomes possible to show how geographical knowledge is genealogically bound up with what it has rendered historically and spatially unrepresentable (McKittrick 2006, xi). What comes to trouble geographical knowledge is thus not difference as it is inscribed within gendered and racialized dualisms, but that which these binaries seek to obscure: an elsewhere that is more paradox than foundation, a difference that is neither complement nor opposite—a nonrelation.

Back from the Dead

There are also those who have invited the demon void to cross geography's threshold and held open the door for that which is not to enter. Not unlike Anaxagoras's empty wineskin or the potter's vase, such present absences often take a particular form. Rather than an edgeless void, they appear as a hole in the shape of someone or something lost or deceased, ruined or decayed. These are the specters and the memorialized departed, the afterimages of bygone episodes, the ghost towns and the industrial ruins where the past is tangibly present (DeLyser 2005; Edensor 2005; McCormack 2010; Maddrell 2013; Bartolini, MacKian, and Pile 2017a, 2017b). Spectral geographies "tangle up the string of temporal linearity," engage experiences of the uncanny, and unsettle the presumptions of the living (Maddern and Adey 2008, 292; see also Pile 2005). While hauntings often (re)materialize the past, some ghosts arrive from the future, such as the malicious demons of imminent disaster (Anderson 2010). Others belong to a disavowed present. As Emilie Cameron (2008) argues, "ghosts allude to the presence of that which has been excluded, marginalized, and expelled" (283), and as such the discourse of haunting has a political valence when applied to indigenous and colonized peoples, who are not departed but actively being erased.

Thus it is often the comingling of presence and absence that has solicited the attention of cultural geographers, perhaps because, as Lars Frers (2013) argues from a phenomenological perspective, the absence of what is past or lost is itself *not nothing*: such an absence is sensed and experienced as a material presence. From a more Derridean perspective, the specter that haunts the living is the impasse of the trace (Wylie 2007; Derrida 1994). Just as there can be no full presence or self-coincidence, "erasure is equally never complete," but rather "leaves a mark, or trace—an absence of presence" (Wylie 2010, 108). The trace or the ghost appears, like the signifier, as something that is ambiguously there in the place of nothing; the ghost is not itself "absence," but rather the sign of the nonpresence that besets every present thing (see also Bartolini, MacKian, and Pile 2017a, 2017b).

One could worry that there is no room for such unspeakable (non)beings in the field of a "re-materialized geography" that has followed trends in the humanities and social sciences to emphasize "what is present, observable, tangible and measurable" (Meier, Frers, and Sigvardsdotter 2013, 423). Indeed, geographers have contributed greatly to the *new materialisms*, from feminist materialisms to object-oriented ontologies and practice philosophies. This turn toward biophilosophy and (in some cases) vitalism might appear to sideline concerns with, as Paul Harrison (2007) puts it, "distance, withdrawal, and disappearance" (592). And yet, as the work of many geographers attests (see, among others, Dewsbury 2007; Clark, Massey, and Sarre 2008; Anderson and Wylie 2009; Braun and Whatmore 2010; Shaw and Meehan 2013; Clark and Yusoff 2014), the most productive materialisms do not attempt to excise what complicates or recedes from matter (the ideal, the incorporeal, the nonrelational) but instead attend to its "aporetic demands" (Harrison 2007, 593; see also Harrison 2009). In fact, an emergent strength of the new materialisms may be their capacity to *take on* the void or the incorporeal within a nonbinaristic ontology that does not rely on untrammeled Being for its consistency (Barad 2007; Žižek 2012; Grosz 2017).

This introduction has covered a lot of ground and slipped into many voids. It would be tempting to keep going and chart more spaces of geography's voids. . . . Perhaps we are haunted by our own editorial *horror vacui*. Whatever the case, we believe our brief tour from the Babylonians to Badiou not only represents a significant slice of geography's engagements with the void so far but also shows how the ideas, practices, and passions that comprise geography are not without the void. Indeed, we find that a generative and annihilating void "into which all polarity is cast in order to be annulled" continues to percolate through human geography (Doel 1999, 94). We should also note that, to date, there has been no deliberate or orchestrated attempt to directly theorize, empirically explore, or simply consider geography's various voids. And this is precisely another key goal of our book: to create a place more void that sparkles with "new intervals and interstices whose void ever craves fresh food" (Shelley 1977, 488).

Into *A Place More Void*

Partly as a result of the various characteristics that unite and divide the above voids, and partly as a result of the commonalities and differences that animate each of the chapters, we decided to structure *A Place More Void* in terms of the following four parts: Holes, Absences, Edges, and Voids. The purpose of this partitioning is not to create a neat and tidy arrangement, but rather to bring into focus some overlapping problems, arguments, and concepts that unify the various chapters.

By way of troubling the (im)materiality of the void, we open the volume with part 1: "Holes." The holes that appear in these chapters—urban gaps, earthly caves, spiritual vortices, and immersive spaces—are at once actual and virtual, material and immaterial. In the first chapter, "Urban Renewal and the Actuality of Absence: The 'Hole' (*Trou*) of Paris, 1973," Ulf Strohmayer examines the geographies of a hole in Paris. For Strohmayer, the material becoming of an absence in the heart of the city demonstrates how the logic of forgetfulness entailed by Derrida's "dangerous supplement" is at work in urban planning. Taking us underground in chapter 2, Kai Bosworth's "'The Crack in the Earth': Environmentalism after Speleology" considers how caving exposes the crack in the environmental subject. Bosworth argues that caving practices, by centering disconnection and incommensurability, complicate the ontological propositions of new materialisms. Chapter 3, by Keith Woodward and John Paul Jones III, "The Vortex and the Void: Meta/Geophysics in Sedona," begins by examining the historical narratives that swirl around and discursively constitute Sedona's vortex sites and then turns to explore the tensions and limitations between, on the one hand, various vorticists or subjects of the void such as spiritualists, scientists, tour guides, and pilgrims; and, on the other hand, the realm of vorticism in terms of its theorizations of the ontology of the vortex. Much of their argument concerns identifying the overlaps between vorticism (especially ideas espoused by Pete A. Sanders) and enduring philosophical problems such as the mind/body split that churns away in the works of Hegel, Lacan, and Descartes. Closing part 1 is an atmospheric invitation to a tactile and enlivened experience of the void by way of Flora Parrot and Harriet Hawkins's art project, "Six Voids."

Part 2, "Absences," turns our attention toward that which is missing: the silent, the vanishing, or withdrawn. In these chapters, the void as absence—whether the absence of sound, the enigmatic dimension of the sign, the unsaid of the archive, or the retreat of a landscape—seems to pull the subject along in the wake of its implacable withdrawal. The part begins with chapter 5, Morgan Meyer's "Tracking Silence: Place, Embodiment, and Politics," wherein we read of two differently positioned trackers of silence: Bernie Krause, a soundscape ecologist, and the sound tracker Gordon Hempton. Working through the practices of these two artists of silence, Meyer builds on his "relational ontology of absence" to show how silence (like other absences, voids, or holes) is encountered, materialized, measured, and qualified—at the same time as it eludes the grasp of the "tracker." But what is it that draws people to "track silence" or plumb the depths of the void? In chapter 6 Mitch Rose addresses the pull of the void in "The Void and Its Summons: Subjectivity, Signs, and the Enigmatic." For Rose, what beckons and pulls the subject forward is that which withdraws and remains remote from it: what Rose calls the "enigmatic dimension of the sign," or the void at the heart of signification. For Rose, if language is what we use in our attempt to lay claim to that which language itself steals away, then representation is perhaps less powerful and oppressive than it is "haunted and desperate." That the discipline of geography itself is haunted by undeparted oppressive forces is the topic of chapter 7 by Alison Mountz and Kira Williams, "Derwent's Ghost: The Haunting Silences of Geography at Harvard." Tracing the inconsistencies, intimacies, and absences that riddle the archive, Mountz and Williams conjure the ghost of geographer Derwent Whittlesey, restoring his humanity and historical context to the narrative of the geography program at Harvard and its demise. Finally, the perpetual vanishing of both the watcher and the watched, entangled in a disconcerting reversibility, becomes the central motif of chapter 8, the final chapter 8 in this part, "'It Watches You Vanish': On Landscape and W. G. Sebald," by John Wylie. Wylie takes the reader phrase by phrase through a short, untitled poem by the German writer Sebald and thereby leads us to the point where it feels like we can almost, but not quite, grasp the notion of landscape as it passes us by (or we pass it)—to the cusp of its disappearance and our own.

Part 3, "Edges" addresses the dynamics of the void in terms of its various movements and circumventions. An edge concerns the external limits of objects, areas, and surfaces, as well as far-flung parts and places that are removed from central points. In terms of dynamics, the part covers the shifting circumscriptions of the void's outer extremities: its enfoldings, metamorphoses, impasses, and elevations. In chapter 9, "*enfolding*: An Experimental Geographical Imagination System (gis)," Nick Lally and Luke Bergmann propose a project for mapping "holey spaces, relational spaces, blank spots on the map, the unknown and the uncertain, the unmappable (and that which should not be mapped), the dreamscape, and other spatial concepts that are unworkable." Opening topological rifts, wormholes, and spaces of disconnection or betweenness, Lally and Bergmann show how their experimental platform, *enfolding*, produces spatial figures that express an immanent relationality. Such spatiality finds a specifically feminist inflection in chapter 10 by Carmen Antreasian, "Beyond the Feminine Void: Rethinking Sexuation through an Ettingerial Lens." Unfolding the often-erased space of the womb, Antreasian's contribution focuses on "matrixial metramorphosis," or the passage of the becoming subject through the vagina into the symbolic realm, to mark the limits of Lacanian phallogocentrism. Meanwhile, in chapter 11, "Politics for the Impasse," Jess Linz and Anna J. Secor attempt to hold open the void, to occupy an edgy impasse, and to pick up the tools they find there. For Linz and Secor, this is a political project to dig out a paradoxical, demonic, or minor territory where strange kinships and imperfect solidarities are possible. Taking the void to another level, part 3 closes with chapter 12, "Raising Sasquatch to the Place of the Cryptozoological Thing" wherein Oliver Keane and Paul Kingsbury consider the centrality of sublimation in the conference-based construction of the non-empirical object of Sasquatch. Such an object straddles the edge between conventional science and cryptozoology, that is, the study of cryptids or hidden animals. According to Keane and Kingsbury, attendees of the Sasquatch Summit maintain a paradoxical (non) relationship to Sasquatch as the elusive and compelling Thing, that is, the materialization of an alluring void, whose very possibility of existence is marked by its impossibility.

Part 4 of the book, "Voids," addresses the void as such wherein all the swirling guises and movements of holes, absences, and edges swirl and get stitched up into nominal designations of "void." The primary focus here is on the doings and the potentialities of the void: its subtractions, productive and positive capacities, and ability to assemble, materialize, and connect. These activities and possibilities are situated in the interrelated domains of poetry, psychoanalysis, political economy, and philosophy. The part begins in the most appropriate way possible, with a poem in chapter 13: "O(void): Excerpts from *Lot*, a Long Ethnopoetics Project about the Colonial Geographies of Haida Gwaii" by Sarah de Leeuw. The poem is a work of the ovoid, an egg shape. Words appear, disappear, reappear: flashes of violence and of home. The o(void) subtracts the void by adding it to a couplet, a pair of islands, bringing the reader to a place neither barren nor excessive but both. "A force of openness— . . . a groundless (an-archic) reservoir of plenitude for things to emerge," is how Mikko Joronen characterizes Heidegger's "ontological void" in chapter 14, "Playing with Plenitude and Finitude: Attuning to a Mysterious Void of Being." Joronen explores how attunement to the void creates a capacity for play, for a positive engagement with the impotentiality of being and its groundless plenitude. Chapter 15 extends another bridge across the chasms of thought. In their chapter, "In the Void of Formalization: The Homology between Surplus Value and Surplus *Jouissance*," Ceren Özselçuk and Yahya M. Madra work through and across the different ways in which Louis Althusser and Lacan locate the void as the constitutive impossibility of the (capitalist, desiring) subject. They conclude with an argument for recognizing both the homology between analytic and capitalist discourse and that which it displaces: perhaps most critically, the historical contingency of capitalism. Chapter 16, the closing chapter in part 4, affirms the void's place as the immaterial kernel at the heart of a materialist geography. Lucas Pohl's essay, "Localizing the Void: From Material to Immaterial Materialism," argues for an understanding of the void as that which both allows space to assemble and disturbs its materialization. For Pohl, it is not a question of "absent matter" but of *absence mattering*.

Ending the book is our "Coda: A Void More Placed." In many ways, a coda is an extended cadence (from the Latin *cadentia*, "a falling"). We enlist a trialogue (two first persons that comprise us as individuals and third person as coeditors) that falls toward, falls with, and then finally falls apart in a way that elaborates on the book's epistemological contributions and eschatological ramifications. We not only consider how the book better situates the cultural geographies of the void but also address our desire for where the book might take its readers. Our wager is that the only way to end a book on the void is to take seriously the void's intimate and arguably inescapable relationships with eschatology. Specifically, we unabashedly speculate on the issues of death, judgment, and the final destinies of the book's readers, contributors, and coeditors.

Notes

1. Shakespeare ([1623] 2000), *Julius Caesar*, act 2, scene 4, line 39.
2. John Lennon and Paul McCartney (1966), "Tomorrow Never Knows," *Revolver*, Sony.

References

Agamben, Giorgio. 1998. *Homo Sacer: Sovereign Power and Bare Life*. Translated by Daniel Heller-Roazen. Stanford CA: Stanford University Press.

———. 2005. *State of Exception*. Translated by Kevin Attell. Chicago: University of Chicago Press.

Algra, Keimpe. 1995. *Concepts of Space in Greek Thought*. New York: E. J. Brill.

Amir, Merav. 2013. "The Making of a Void Sovereignty: Political Implications of the Military Checkpoints in the West Bank." *Environment and Planning D: Society and Space* 31, no. 2: 227–44.

Anderson, Ben. 2010. "Preemption, Precaution, Preparedness: Anticipatory Action and Future Geographies." *Progress in Human Geography* 34, no. 6: 777–98.

Anderson, Ben, and John Wylie. 2009. "On Geography and Materiality." *Environment and Planning A: Economy and Space* 41, no. 2: 318–35.

Badiou, Alain. 2005. *Being and Event*. Translated by Oliver Feltham. London: Continuum.

Barad, Karen. 2007. *Meeting the Universe Halfway: Quantum Physics and the Entanglement of Matter and Meaning*. Durham NC: Duke University Press.

Bartolini, Nadia, Sara MacKian, and Steve Pile. 2017a. "Spirit Knows: Materiality, Memory and the Recovery of Spiritualist Places and Practices in Stoke-on-Trent." *Social & Cultural Geography* 20, no. 8: 1114–37.

———. 2017b. "Talking with the Dead: Spirit Mediumship, Affect and Embodiment in Stoke-on-Trent." *Transactions of the Institute of British Geographers* 43, no. 2: 70–183.

Belcher, Oliver, Lauren Martin, Anna Secor, Stephanie Simon, and Tommy Wilson. 2008. "Everywhere and Nowhere: The Exception and the Topological Challenge to Geography." *Antipode* 40, no. 4: 499–503.

Bennett, Luke, and Amanda Crawley Jackson. 2017. "Making Common Ground with Strangers at Furnace Park." *Social & Cultural Geography* 18, no. 1: 92–108.

Bigo, Didier. 2008. "Globalized (In)Security: The Field and the Ban-Opticon." In *Terror, Insecurity and Liberty: Illiberal Practices of Liberal Regimes after 9/11*, edited by Didier Bigo and Anastassia Tsoukala, 10–48. London: Routledge.

Braun, Bruce, and Sarah J. Whatmore, eds. 2010. *Political Matter: Technoscience, Democracy, and Public Life*. Minneapolis: University of Minnesota Press.

Burgin, Victor. 1996. *In/Different Spaces: Place and Memory in Visual Culture*. Berkeley: University of California Press.

Callard, Felicity. 2003. "The Taming of Psychoanalysis in Geography." *Social & Cultural Geography* 4, no. 3: 295–312.

Cameron, Emilie. 2008. "*cultural geographies* Essay: Indigenous Spectrality and the Politics of Postcolonial Ghost Stories." *cultural geographies* 15, no. 3: 383–93.

Casey, Edward S. 1997. *The Fate of Place: A Philosophical History*. Berkeley: University of California Press.

Clark, Nigel, Doreen Massey, and Phillip Sarre. 2008. *Material Geographies: A World in the Making*. Washington DC: Sage.

Clark, Nigel, and Kathryn Yusoff. 2014. "Combustion and Society: A Fire-Centred History of Energy Use." *Theory, Culture & Society* 31, no. 5: 203–26.

Clementini, Eliseo. 2017. "Representation: Complex Objects." In *International Encyclopedia of Geography: People, the Earth, Environment and Technology*, edited by Douglas Richardson, Noel Castree, Michael F. Goodchild, Audrey Kobayashi, Weidong Liu, and Richard A. Marston. https://doi.org/10.1002/9781118786352.wbieg0876.

Copjec, Joan. 1994. *Read My Desire: Lacan against the Historicists*. Cambridge MA: MIT Press.

Cornford, F. M. 2014. "The Invention of Space." In *The Concepts of Space and Time: Their Structure and Their Development*, edited by Milič Čapek, 3–16, Dordrecht, Holland: D. Reidel.

de Certeau, Michel. 1984. *The Practice of Everyday Life*. Translated by Steven Rendall. Berkeley: University of California Press.

De Lauretis, Teresa. 1987. *Technologies of Gender: Essays on Theory, Film, and Fiction*. Bloomington: Indiana University Press.

Deleuze, Gilles. 1990. *The Logic of Sense*. Translated by Mark Lester, with Charles Stivale. Edited by Constantin V. Boundas. New York: Columbia University Press.

DeLyser, Dydia. 2005. *Ramona Memories: Tourism and the Shaping of Southern California*. Minneapolis: University of Minnesota Press.

Derickson, Kate Driscoll. 2017. "Taking Account of the 'Part of Those That Have No Part.'" *Urban Studies* 54, no. 1: 44–48.

Derrida, Jacques. 1994. "Spectres of Marx." *New Left Review* 205: 31–58.

Dewsbury, J. D. 2007. "Unthinking Subjects: Alain Badiou and the Event of Thought in Thinking Politics." *Transactions of the Institute of British Geographers* 32, no. 4: 443–59.

Dixon, Deborah P., and John Paul Jones III. 1998. "My Dinner with Derrida, or Spatial Analysis and Poststructuralism Do Lunch." *Environment and Planning A* 30, no. 2: 247–60.

Doel, Marcus. 1999. *Poststructuralist Geographies: The Diabolical Art of Spatial Science*. Lanham MD: Rowman & Littlefield.

Dunnett, Oliver, Andrew S. Maclaren, Julie Klinger, K. Maria D. Lane, and Daniel Sage. 2017. "Geographies of Outer Space: Progress and New Opportunities." *Progress in Human Geography* 42, no. 2: 314–36.

Edensor, Tim. 2005. *Industrial Ruins: Space, Aesthetics and Materiality*. Oxford: Berg.

———. 2013. "Vital Urban Materiality and fIts Multiple Absences: The Building Stone of Central Manchester." *cultural geographies* 20, no. 4: 447–65.

Frers, Lars. 2013. "The Matter of Absence." *cultural geographies* 20, no. 4: 431–45.

Freud, Sigmund. 2002. *Civilization and Its Discontents*. Translated by David McLintock. New York: Penguin.

Gallop, David. 1984. *Parmenides of Elea: A Text and Translation*. Toronto: University of Toronto Press.

Grosz, Elizabeth. 2017. *The Incorporeal: Ontology, Ethics, and the Limits of Materialism*. New York: Columbia University Press.

Harrison, Paul. 2007. "'How Shall I Say it . . . ?' Relating the Nonrelational." *Environment and Planning A* 39, no. 3: 590–608.

———. 2009. "In the Absence of Practice." *Environment and Planning D: Society and Space* 27, no. 6: 987–1009.

Heidel, Alexander. 2009. *The Babylonian Genesis: The Story of the Creation*. 2nd ed. Chicago: University of Chicago Press.

Irigaray, Luce. 1985. *Speculum of the Other Woman*. Translated Gillian C. Gill. Ithaca NY: Cornell University Press.

Kapoor, Ilan. 2018. *Psychoanalysis and the GlObal*. Lincoln: University of Nebraska Press.

Lacan, Jacques. 1998. *The Seminar of Jacques Lacan*. Book 11: *The Four Fundamental Concepts of Psychoanalysis*. Edited by Jacques-Alain Miller. Translated by Alan Sheridan. New York: W. W. Norton.

———. 2018. *The Seminar of Jacques Lacan*. Book 19: *. . . or Worse, 1971–1972*. Edited by Jacques-Alain Miller. Translated by A. R. Price. Cambridge: Polity Press.

Lennon, John, and Paul McCartney. 1966. "Tomorrow Never Knows." *Revolver*, Sony Records.

Maddern, Jo Frances, and Peter Adey. 2008. "Editorial: Spectro-Geographies." *cultural geographies* 15, no. 3: 291–95.

Maddrell, Avril. 2013. "Living with the Deceased: Absence, Presence and Absence-Presence." *cultural geographies* 20, no. 4: 501–22.

McCormack, Derek P. 2010. "Remotely Sensing Affective Afterlives: The Spectral Geographies of Material Remains." *Annals of the Association of American Geographers* 100, no. 3: 640–54.

McGreevy, Patrick. 2001. "Attending to the Void: Geography and Madness." In *Textures of Place: Exploring Humanist Geographies*, edited by Paul C. Adams, Steven Hoelscher, and Karen E. Till, 246–56. Minneapolis: University of Minnesota Press.

McKittrick, Katherine. 2006. *Demonic Grounds: Black Women and the Cartographies of Struggle*. Minneapolis: University of Minnesota Press.

Meier, Lars. 2012. "Encounters with Haunted Industrial Workplaces and Emotions of Loss: Class-Related Senses of Place within the Memories of Metalworkers." *cultural geographies* 20, no. 4: 467–83.

Meier, Lars, Lars Frers, and Erika Sigvardsdotter. 2013. "The Importance of Absence in the Present: Practices of Remembrance and the Contestation of Absences." *cultural geographies* 20, no. 4: 423–30.

Meyer, Morgan. 2012. "Placing and Tracing Absence: A Material Culture of the Immaterial." *Journal of Material Culture* 17, no. 1: 103–10.

Mezzadra, S., and B. Neilson. 2012. "Between Inclusion and Exclusion: On the Topology of Global Space and Borders." *Theory, Culture and Society* 29, nos. 4/5: 58–75.

Nietzsche, Friedrich. 1989. *On the Genealogy of Morals*. Translated by Walter Kaufmann and R. J. Hollingdale. *Ecco Homo*. Translated and edited by Walter Kaufman. New York: Random House.

Olsson, Gunnar. 2007. *Abysmal: A Critique of Cartographic Reason*. Chicago: University of Chicago Press.

Oxford English Dictionary (OED) *Online*. 2019. s.v. "void." https://www.lexico.com/en/definition/void (accessed September 16, 2019).

Pile, Steve. 1996. *The Body and the City: Psychoanalysis, Space and Subjectivity*. New York: Routledge.

———. 2005. *Real Cities: Modernity, Space and the Phantasmagorias of City Life*. Washington DC: Sage.

Rose, Gillian. 1993. *Feminism & Geography: The Limits of Geographical Knowledge*. Minneapolis: University of Minnesota Press.

Seife, Charles. 2000. *Zero: The Biography of a Dangerous Idea*. London: Penguin.

Shakespeare, William. (1623) 2000. *The Tragedy of Julius Caesar*. Edited by William Montgomery. London: Penguin.

Shaw, Ian G. R., and Katharine Meehan. 2013. "Force-Full: Power, Politics and Object-Oriented Philosophy." *Area* 45, no. 2: 216–22.

Shelley, Percy Bysshe. 1977. "A Defence of Poetry." In *Shelley's Poetry and Prose*, edited by Donald. H. Reiman and Sharon B. Powers, 478–508. New York: Norton.

Sigvardsdotter, Erika. 2013. "Presenting Absent Bodies: Undocumented Persons Coping and Resisting in Sweden." *cultural geographies* 20, no. 4: 523–29.

Smith, Robert, and Stephen Merrett. 1987. "Empty Dwellings: The Use of Rating Records in Identifying and Monitoring Vacant Private Housing in Britain." *Environment and Planning A: Economy and Space* 19, no. 6: 783–91.

Steinberg, Philip E. 2001. *The Social Construction of the Ocean*. Cambridge: Cambridge University Press.

Van Duzer, Chet. 2013. "*Hic sunt dracones*: The Geography and Cartography of Monsters." In *The Ashgate Research Companion to Monsters and the Monstrous*, edited by Asa Simon Mittman and Peter J. Dendle, 387–435. Burlington VT: Ashgate.

Weatherall, James Owen. 2016. *Void: The Strange Physics of Nothing*. New Haven CT: Yale University Press.

Wittgenstein, Ludwig. 1992. *Tractatus logico-philosophicus*. Translated by D. F. Pears and B. F. McGuinness. London: Routledge.

Wright, John K. 1948. "Terrae Incognitae: The Place of the Imagination in Geography." *Annals of the Association of American Geographers* 37, no. 1: 1–15.

Wylie, John. 2007. "The Spectral Geographies of W. G. Sebald." *cultural geographies* 14, no. 2: 171–88.

———. 2010. "Non-Representational Subjects?" In *Taking-Place: Non-Representational Theories and Geography*, edited by Ben Anderson and Paul Harrison, 99–117. Farnham, UK: Ashgate.

Žižek, Slavoj. 2012. *Less than Nothing: Hegel and the Shadow of Dialectical Materialism*. New York: Verso.

Zlatanova, Sisi. 2017. "Representation: 3-D." In *International Encyclopedia of Geography: People, the Earth, Environment and Technology*, edited by Douglas Richardson, Noel Castree, Michael F. Goodchild, Audrey Kobayashi, Weidong Liu, and Richard A. Marston. https://doi.org/10.1002/9781118786352.wbieg1157.

Zupančič, Alenka. 2017. *What IS Sex?* Cambridge MA: MIT Press.

PART 1 Holes

1 Urban Renewal and the Actuality of Absence
The "Hole" (*Trou*) of Paris, 1973

Ulf Strohmayer

Holes and absences are part of our everyday experience in many shapes and guises: from the loss of a loved one to the banal being there (or not) of material items, from the ozone hole to the hole that forms a doughnut, we engage with the world through differentiations of the "present/absent" kind. Science, the ongoing attempt to establish knowledge about the world, has amplified such dualist tendencies by insisting on the categorical character of epistemology, inviting us to seek similarities in the description of events, processes, things, and facts. Again, absences are part and parcel of such practices by being at work in the implied paired notion of "dissimilarities." Being categorically similar infers at least the presence of a partial sameness between two different items, which in turn requires the absence of such sameness between two other items. Historically, to use an example here, we relate different forms of mobility by relating them through relational sameness to notions of movement; for this to work, however, we already need to be able to separate movement from what it is not, a pause, inertia or idleness.[1] Similarly we identify a hole in a road from any road in question through dissimilarities attaching to what we consider to be nominally identical to roads without holes—their smooth, uninterrupted surfaces. If further proof were needed of the necessity of differentiations along a "present/absent" spectrum we need look no further than turn to Aristotle's well-worn dictum *horror vacui* (in book 4, section 8, of his *Physics*)—that "nature abhors a vacuum." In fact, the history of philosophy is littered with elaborations on the theme, as it presents us with attempts to structurally order its dynamic temporal aspects—with Hegel's (and other) forms of dialectics counting among the better-known endeavors to add a relational dimension capable of providing organizational directives to such differentiations.

And yet everyday experience and science are both equally well attuned to difficulties arising in the context of distinctions, seeing that states or categories are often encountered and materially present in gradual rather that binary or mutually excluding forms. We can differentiate between say hunger and its absence but would find it harder both to establish categorical similarity between different forms of hunger or to establish a clean and stable threshold between "being hungry" and "not being hungry." Equally, to recycle the example used earlier on, we know perfectly well that a road without holes is not, in fact, a road without *any* hole, but is "just" a road without a *specific kind of* holes. Something else intervenes, mediated between different states—notions of intensity, of ebbs and flows, of becoming or of depth.

Scholarship in philosophy and the social sciences during the last generation has paid homage to this latter experience of differentiating distinctions by engaging with notions of ever-present difference (christened "*différance*" in the writings of Jacques Derrida or "(*immanent*) difference-in-itself" in that of Gilles Deleuze) at work in affects, assemblages, or discourses on construction and maintenance more broadly. The present volume is testament to the analytical power of these and related modes of thinking and writing. But while we celebrate such insights born of engagements with different forms of absence (or of holes in part 1 of this volume), it is equally important to remember that the acknowledgment of difficulties attaching to differentiations has been a concomitant feature of scientific discourse and practice at least since the Enlightenment. Discussions about intensity, to use but one example, originated in the recognition of scalar or gradual difference (infused by absences) becoming a conceivable possibility within categorical presences in the first half of the eighteenth century. Intensities appear in the form of adverbs (*more, less*), adjectives (*weak, powerful, lively*), or comparisons (*best, most, largely*; for a wider discussion, see Kleinschmidt 2004, 23–24) and manifest themselves in everyday life as much as they matter in scientific discourse and practice. Arguably, the idea of intensity can even be extended to become a byword for the modern experience itself (Garcia 2016).

Recognizing the "intensity" of something (a color, a sentiment, a form of trust, or any form of "energy") is, of course, but one manner in which we have learned to appreciate that "world" presents itself to us in a nonbinary way. We could add other, related articulations of the presence/absence (or "hole"/"filled") continuum like that of the threshold (which never is quite a border), any notion of "force" or "power," or multiple states that could enter into some kind of equilibrium; but we shall leave matter here: the logical point has been made.

Materializing Absence

Instead of further abstract pursuits, this chapter charts the contours of an analytical engagement with urban space that acknowledges both the necessity and material existence of differentiations while critically appraising their stability and epistemological usefulness. It does so by tackling an absence, a loss even, which materialized in the midst of a well-known urban fabric. In so doing it aims to contribute to debates about material dimensions attaching to the relationship between presence and absence, between "being there," "not being there" and "partially being there (or not)"—an ambiguity deliberately ignored by urban planners everywhere. In fact, urban planning could well be defined as a set of adaptive discourses and practices aimed at securing the continuity of presences, following a twofold logic of addition (the rationale for a new presence) and substitution (the functionality of a new presence married to the recognized absence of same in what precedes that new presence). Crucially, these two presences coexist synchronically (*in time*) but evolve diachronically (*across time*) through the successive *morphing* of an additive logic into its substitutional accompaniment *with the event of substitution embodying the always potential birth of a new additive momentum (or presence)*. As a result good planning is anticipatory planning, solving problems before an existing spatial logic fails to deliver the outcomes welcomed by those in power. Bad planning, by contrast, materializes in the form of spatial configurations that no longer produce the kind of presences deemed useful within and for an existing societal logic. Urban wastelands, brownfield sites, abandoned sites born of a former logistic imperative, weeds inflicting tarmacadam urban surfaces—the list of failed or not materializing substitutions is potentially endless.

Readers attuned to the work of Jacques Derrida (1976) will discover the application of a well-known form of reasoning at work here—the at once beneficial *and* threatening materialization of "that dangerous supplement" (141). What we could call the "planning supplement" does not describe omnipresent practices of addition and substitution; rather, it articulates a principle underlying such practices aimed to ensure the compatibility between "what is" and "what will be." In and of itself, a "supplement" is thus nothing noteworthy, but it becomes everything in conjuncture with substitutional practices; these latter become motivated and sustained by it. It is well worth remembering in this context that Derrida's (1976) use of the term *supplement* carries connotations of both *supplémenter* (to add to) and *suppléer* (to substitute);. This chapter argues that both of these are "in play" in urban planning discourse and practice. Contextualized accordingly as a practice at work in urban planning, the "supplement" entails a logic of forgetfulness required for an underlying ordering impulse to unfold its hegemonic, normative force as part of what Jacques Rancière (2004) has called the taken-for-granted "distribution of the sensible," crucially legitimizing some urban presences ("when to do what where") while delegitimizing others.

But occasionally the supplementary logic of urban planning misfires, be it as a result of sheer incompetence, social activism (for example, "squatting"), adaptive needs not fully articulated (for example, infrastructural decay; see Strohmayer 2012), or disruption for other reasons. In these and related cases, *presence becomes absence* (or something else)—as it does forcefully in the material case that forms the centerpiece of this chapter: the *trou* or hole of Paris.

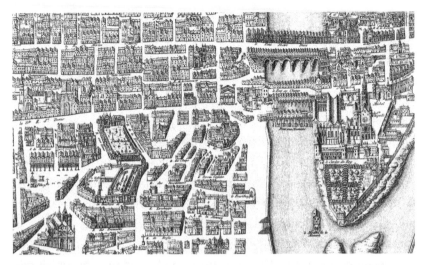

1. Extract from Plan de Saint-Victor, 1551. Source: https://upload.wikimedia.org
/wikipedia/commons/f/f2/Plan_de_Saint-Victor_vers_1550%2c_d%27après_la
_reprise_de_Dheulland_en_1756_-_aviary.jpg.

Approaching the Hole

The space in question, what has long since been referred to as the "Halles" district in the central first arrondissement in Paris, has been a formidable presence within the French capital at least since the late Middle Ages through the provision of market-related practices. Made famous as the belly or "venter" of Paris in Émile Zola's third *Rougon-Macquart* novel in 1873, the ongoing spatial history of "Les Halles" provides a good example of the "supplemental" logic of spatial configurations due to a continued realization of adaptive capabilities in situ. Key to these have been materializations of an economic logic: initially constructed as a market outside of Paris from 1137 onward, Les Halles were immediately included, in 1183, within Philippe-Auguste's fortification of Paris (see Robert and Tsikounas 2004).

However, it was only from 1590 onward that food-related items became part of the mix of activities. If thus for hundreds of years Les Halles embodied the traditional, additive rationality of urban development (warranting it the description of both a "palimpsest" and a "serial melodrama" in Wakeman 2007, 46, 50, respectively), it was gradually to become entangled in a supplementary logic in the course of the nineteenth century, the century when capital attached itself firmly to urban environments and began to shape them according to its own inherent logic (Harvey 1985; TenHoor [2007] thus deploys the language of biopolitics to analyze the transformative logics at work in the Halles district).

The resulting Haussmannian transformation of the area in question is a well-known ingredient of the radical makeover of Paris during the Second Empire (see Pinkney 1958; Strohmayer 1997). And while the supplementarity expressed in the construction of Baltard's well-known pavilions did not yet attach to a change in the economic logic of the Halles—"This was a brutal intervention right at the heart of the city, but—unlike the disaster of 1970—it did no more than perpetuate an old tradition, by which this quarter was periodically transformed without ever losing its role or its spirit" (Hazan 2010, 67–68)—in many ways Haussmann's overall idea and Baltard's well-known pavilion design articulated a series of fissures, of breaks with an existing logic of space. It did so through a number of concrete changes to spatially resonant practices: by embracing the notion of a centralized rather than spatially disjointed market, through its unified rather than fragmented architecture; by conclusively moving market-related practices to the "inside" of buildings, by embracing economies of scale; and finally by subjecting largely organic developments to a planned and forward-looking rationale (see Mead [2012] for a detailed analysis of the genesis and permutations attaching to Baltard's pavilions). In their Haussmannian form Les Halles delivered and organized those flows so central to the furthering of capitalist economies, in the process becoming an instrumental facilitator in the "annihilation of space with time" famously used by Karl Marx in his *Grundrisse* to characterize nineteenth-century advances in capitalism.

But once incorporated into this particular supplementary logic, the Halles would always be vulnerable to changes in or challenges to that logic. Four developments proved to require interventions in the postwar configuration of Paris (see Wakeman [2009]; McCall [2011] for concise overviews of how that configuration emerged): (1) the reinvention of produce traded in mar-

2. Photograph of the construction of Baltard's central Halles, around 1860. Source: AN 332/AP/26/E (fonds Baltard).

kets in the form of technologically rather than organically "fresh" produce due to the invention in 1925 and subsequent proliferation of refrigerated trucks; (2) the increasing congestion of inner-city Paris brought about by the success of the individualized motorcar and delivery trucks; (3) the desire of a new elite, following the creation of the Fifth Republic in 1958, to "modernize" France and make it fit for an increasingly globalized world; and (4) the gradual reemergence of the inner city as a space for (speculative) capital investments during the 1960s and the related removal of working-class residents from inner-city Paris. Following considerable debates, the key decision, on February 6, 1959, to relocate all market-related activities to a new central market at Rungis on the outskirts of Paris and (crucially) near the then only Parisian airport of Orly (accomplished by 1969), Baltard's Halles became part of a prolonged—and largely symbolic—battle between concerned citizens, urban planners, local residents, the French state, the city of Paris, and investors (see Michel 1988; Large 1992; the word *battle* picks up André Fermigier's use of the term in a series of interventions in *Le Nouvel Observateur* at the time; see Fermigier 1991). Baltard's pavilions and a whole way of life lost out in the eventual outcome: the pavilions were demolished in two tranches in 1971 and 1973. By 1979 the new "Forum des Halles" (designed by Georges Pencreac'h and Claude Vasconi) was inaugurated, combining a state-of-the-art underground transportation hub with sports and leisure-orientated activities and a major shopping complex. This development went hand-in-hand with the adjacent construction, on a site named the plateau Beaubourg (heretofore reserved for the parking of trucks serving the market at Les Halles), of Renzo Piano and Richard Rogers's Centre Pompidou (see Powell [2005] for a creative engagement with same), which not only changed urban architecture with a single stroke but also inaugurated another innovative absence in the context of the postwar, car-ready urban fabric: the absence of automobiles from an adjacent part of the city in the form of the pedestrianization of parts of the longest road in Paris, the rue Saint-Martin (see Hazan 2017, 100–101).

It would be tempting to fast-forward to the new millennium and note how an ever-accelerating supplementary logic induced yet another refurbishment of the Halles between 2004 and 2016, with final touches being added to the overall site as this chapter is written (see Fromonot [2005] for a summary discussion of early plans involved in this latest refurbishment; see also Wakeman 2007). Before we do so, however, it is incumbent upon us to pause for a moment. In so doing—by pausing—we mimic a key interruption that was to mark the transition from Baltard's Halles to the new Forum des Halles in the early 1970s. If with hindsight the decision to dismantle a part of the Haussmannian legacy, which a mere decade later would certainly have qualified for heritage and thus preservation status, seems patently absurd, not to say criminal, such reasoning seemed far and distant from the vantage point of the late 1960s, at least in a technocratically motivated and expert-led country such as the one France had been aiming to become since 1958.

Living with Holes

Not even the centuries-old French planning establishment (see Rabinow [1989] for an original account of its genesis) could prevent a cleavage between its differentiated ambitions, resulting in a prolonged interruption in the construction of the supplementary ensemble emerging at Les Halles. In fact, we had better speak of a twofold hiatus, the first of which was marked by the abandonment of market-related activities and the continued existence of some of Baltard's pavilions between 1969 and 1971, while the second manifested itself in the form of the "hole" that emerged when the first eight of those pavilions and about fifty-six houses were destroyed and plans for an underground transportation hub (incorporating the newly created RER, or regional rail system, alongside the Métro and new road infrastructures) required digging down to an unprecedented depth: Paris found itself staring into the abyss of a hole or *trou* for a number of years. The second interruption also owed its existence to a number of unplanned events, such as the 1973 oil crisis and the death of President Pompidou in 1974, resulting in the final scrapping of plans for a World Trade Center dominated by skyscrapers at Les Halles.[2]

Both absences caused by disruptions to a developing supplementary urban rationale proved to be harbingers of creative energy. The first of these, marking the absence of clearly defined activities from 1969 to 1971, set free a number of at best partially regulated cultural events:

> While debate on what to build at the site stagnated, many of the pavilions were converted for use as art galleries, theatre productions, public lectures, concerts, a circus, and even an ice-skating rink. Les Halles also hosted a special exhibition of the works of Picasso, an event that drew over 70,000 visitors to the pavilion. Although the idea of using Les Halles to build a new cultural space had been considered by the government, the people of Paris had shown that one could already exist in the old pavilions. New businesses even began to move in to cater to Les Halles' new clientele, including bookstores, antique dealers, cafés, and a range of fashionable boutiques.

3. The functionally emptied "Halles." Source: Archives de Paris.

The robust cultural resurgence that began to emerge at Les Halles gave the preservationist associations great hope for the future. (Kasten 2013, 53–54)

The destruction of the majority of pavilions toward the eastern end of the area starting on August 2, 1971, also marked an end to such spontaneous expressions of cultural energy and desires; if thirty years later the city of Berlin would know better how to harness urban creative impulses, France in 1971 was still haunted by May 1968, when an urban spontaneous revolt almost matured into a revolution. Clearly France's political elite was unwilling to cede even more ground to protest and uncontrolled expressions of cultural and political happenings. Instead of events, it had its eyes firmly set on the regulative power of consumption as the glue that would hold capitalist society together, "with non-consumption being constructed as a form of deviance at the same time as spaces of consumption eliminate public space in the city" (Sibley 1995, 95).

But for about two years the *trou* prevailed before the new spaces that were to become the Forum began to fill its emptiness with structures destined

STROHMAYER

4. The *trou* ("hole") of Paris. Source: Archives de Paris.

to lure shoppers into the heart of Paris. Eventually inaugurated in 1979, the Forum des Halles would do just that, with the ironic twist that saw it become the preferred meeting space especially for underprivileged and often immigrant youth from the banlieue, rendering obsolete almost overnight the ambitions of planners to create a space of high consumptive desires.

While it lasted, the *trou* marked its presence as an absence on daily activities (requiring detours) and became a reminder of a stalled form of planning in the eyes of many Parisians. But it also reimagined geographies by becoming the most unlikely stand-in for the US state of Montana in Marco Ferreri's absurd reimagining of Custer's Last Stand in his 1974 *Touche pas à la femme blanche* (*Don't Touch the White Woman!*) (Mickey 13 2017).

Filling a Hole

By 1974 the Italian anarchist filmmaker Ferreri was basking in the unexpected success of his previous film *La Grande Bouffe* (or *Blow Out*), a film about four friends literally eating themselves to death. This satire about the decadence of the bourgeoisie was followed by an equally star-studded transposition of the Battle of Little Bighorn into the *trou de Paris*. Starring Catherine Deneuve, Marcello Mastroianni, Ugno Tognazzi, Michel Piccoli, Philippe Noiret, and Alain Cuny, among others, the film was a flop at the box office and is often still described in a language bordering on derision: "*Don't Touch the White Woman* will prove a languorous and insipid viewing with little reward. It rather ranks amongst minor opuses in Ferreri's oeuvre owing to being superfluously Marxist and thus as antiquated as the Marxist ethos itself" (see Mickey 13 2017).

Whatever one's stance toward Ferreri's absurdist spectacle, it remains remarkable for its sheer chutzpah and for the remarkable use of an urban landscape out of circulation. The nonpresence that was the *trou* here becomes the conscious absence of any traditional mise-en-scène in the embrace of a (non-)artificial and decidedly urban context. It is these layered absences and their projection into a hole that allow for a variety of interpretations, ranging from a Rabelaisian parable in which George Armstrong Custer (Mastroianni) and General Alfred Terry (Noiret) observe the destruction of the surrounding urban landscape on their way toward "Montana" while muttering "C'est ça, le progrès" (That's progress), leading to a contemporary understanding of the film in which "the Indians are the former residents evicted from the center of Paris, and the cowboys are gunmen of the real estate speculators who try to exterminate them" (see Grup de treball 2010).

In another scene supporting such an urbane reading of the film, General Custer (Mastroianni) addresses Sitting Bull (Cuny), asking "Why did you leave your homes?" only to receive the response "Because you destroyed them."

But *Touche pas* also contains realistic allusions to the extermination of Native Americans and images reminiscent of the Holocaust (a group of Indian women and children being burnt to death inside a remaining pavilion leading to the collapse of an old chimney), the Vietnam War (images of President Nixon adorn many walls in the film), and the massacre of French-Algerians that took place on October 17, 1961, in Paris. Filling a gigantic *trou* with dead bodies, rather than the anticipated spaces of consumption, thus transforms the center of the modern city into a mass grave. In one extraordinary set of frames, a shop is turned into a display space for dead Indians, with the entrance fee ostensibly supporting widows of the wars, with the embalmed Indians being filled in turn with newspapers.

5. Film still from *Ne touche pas*.

Learning from Holes

The various interludes and events that took place during years marked by
a variety of different absences at Les Halles (which would warrant a more
extensive study than the one presented here in the space available) invite us
to reconsider the "supplementary logic" at work in urban planning. With
hindsight, it is easy to recognize the many ways in which absences provided
opportunities at Les Halles in the early 1970s as representing precursors to
the cultural and creative revival that was to become instrumental in urban
planning a mere decade later. If today urban development has learned fully
to embrace the creative industries across the scales (Vivant 2013; Scott
2014)—the success of Berlin to market itself as a hub of creative potential
and materializations count among the better-known examples today (see
Colomb 2012; van Schipstal and Nicholls 2014)—such thinking was not
yet fully developed in the early 1970s. Perhaps, then, the ideal of planning,
the neat and continuous succession of spaces that deliver accepted func-
tionalities and thus support a seamless "redistribution of knowledge and
truth" (Rancière 1989, 22) requires the occasional disruptive event. At its

best, the disruption of the capitalist logic of supplementarity that was the "*trou de Paris*" could thus be said to have created conditions of possibility for spontaneous forms of urban creativity among which Ferreri's film is but one expression. The sheer exuberance of the film, its spatial reconfigurations, and its open allusions astonish still. If the disruption, as this chapter argues, resulted from the lack of integrative capacities ordering the supplementary logic of urban planning but has since been incorporated into the very logic it sought to challenge, the notions of both "succession" and "nuances" that formed the opening gambit in these pages ought to be subjected to further scrutiny.

Part of such scrutiny could do well to analyze the complex relationship between "culture" and "capitalism" in a spatially resonating and thus materially present form. In the 1970s it was relatively easy to peg cultural work and expressions as antidotes against prevailing structures of exploitation and uneven forms of development—witness Fermigier's damning indictment of the battle for Les Halles:

> Qui a vendu les Halles? La Ville de Paris se comporte comme une entreprise privée soucieuse de tirer le maximum de profits des terrains qu'elle possède. (Fermigier 1971)

> (Who sold the Halles? The City of Paris acts as a private company concerned to make the most of the profits of the land it owns.)

Judged from the vantage points afforded by a new century, where an increasing number of cities act like enterprises across most of their engagements and with enterprises in turn fully embracing cultural forms of sponsorship, the distinction made by Fermigier in 1971 may be said to have disappeared for good. Ferreri's film, with all of the overt brittleness attaching to the "hole" within Paris, serves as a timely reminder of what is at stake in obliterating such differences.

At the same time, "learning from holes" ought not simply to include reflective labor on how they are filled but can perhaps profit from temporal considerations attached to the "when" of such developmental acts. Lengthening the time of the supplement is arguably part of the learning potentially derived from the *trou* of Paris, not only because it lasted longer than most urban absences but because the length of time led to a surprising diversity of events, activities, expression, and materializations, some planned, some not, that enriched the urban experience of those participating. In this way "learning" lost some of the directionality implied in traditional forms of pedagogy and tentatively embraced the conditions of possibility of different forms of learning, akin to the decidedly egalitarian form of engagement outlined in Rancière's (1991) *Ignorant Schoolmaster* in which an established supplementary form of pedagogy gives way to nondirective learning engagements. Translated into a spatial logic resonating with planners, the correspondence to Rancière's insistence on absolute equality between teacher and student can be located in the insistence on equality between supplementary and nonsupplementary spatial aspirations, dreams, desires, and solutions. Besides the planner who advocates for any particular supplement, perhaps we ought to imagine the one who waits, who does not immediately identify the growing of weeds as a sign of willful neglect (see Sauerwein 2010) and who is willing to supplement the supplement with a logic born of a longer-term sustainability, rather than short-term fit with presently identified societal needs. Here, spaces would be radically equal in their varied articulations of spontaneity and supplement, of disorder and structure simultaneously.

This train of thought should not be mistaken for a plea to freeze cities in whatever state of becoming they may find themselves at various sites or in certain places. Even the in-between of the cultural events at Les Halles in the early 1970s, writes Éric Hazan (2017), would not have lasted in situ: even the preservation of Baltard's pavilions would have eventually led to a musealization of sorts, akin to similar acts of preservation at Covent Garden in London, the docks in San Francisco, or elsewhere; "all the same, what happened in the 1970s between Saint-Eustache, the rue Saint-Honoré, the Bourse de Commerce and the boulevard Sébastopol is astounding" (80).[3]

Effectively, spaces beyond the supplementary logic have existed and continue to exist in virtually every city known to humankind. In Paris alone the vacant spaces of the "Petite Ceinture" have given birth to many different unplanned uses that presently enrich the French capital (see Strohmayer 2012), or consider the legendary Caribbean and gay raves held in the former Louxor Cinema just South of Barbès during the mid- to late 1980s or the "gare experimentale" that greeted me daily during my visits to the Archives de Paris in the nineteenth arrondissement, organizing the use of municipal spaces between the taking roots of officially agreed-on practices in such sites. Often such spaces have simply lost their acquired currency within the capitalist system and have not yet found or been given a new one (for examples, see Strohmayer 2018). The point is that planning conceptualizes such spaces as being in need of remedial action when, in fact, as this chapter argues, the absences that they create are vital for urban life, creative or otherwise.

Notes

I thank the *Fondation Maison des Sciences de l'Homme* for providing financing support during the writing of this chapter. Personal thanks are due to Éric Hazan for sharing coffee and insights on the ongoing reconstruction of the Halles district.

1. The sheer number of possible contrasts to "movement" alone suggests that categorical differentiations emerge in a relational rather than static form, thereby rendering any actual articulation of presences and absences that contribute to the formulation of a category instable at best.

2. As elsewhere, the supplementary logic at work at Les Halles worked in a contextual manner. The construction of skyscrapers in Paris suffered an arguably fatal blow following the highly contested construction, between 1969 and 1973, of the Tour Maine-Montparnasse in the Parisian fourteenth arrondissement. This building quickly became the most hated insignia of postwar architecture in Paris and paved the way for an abandonment of further plans for tall buildings in the central arrondissements in 1975 (see Chevalier 1993; Berstein and Rioux 2000).

3. Mention of the Bourse, a building that features prominently in *Touche pas*, illustrates the point in question: a building dating back to the 1760s that marks the westernmost extension of the Halles district, it housed the Parisan Chamber of Commerce since 2013 in a somewhat vain attempt to fill a remarkable space with some activity; in 2016 the building was handed over on a fifty-year lease to France's richest man, François Pinault, to showcase his collection of contemporary art from 2018 onward. Writing in the *Guardian* in 2017, Angelique Chrisafis notes that "the renovation of this neglected architectural treasure" is seen as the final act of Paris's attempt to "make

amends for what is seen as a shameful act of self-sabotage: the 1970s bulldozing of the 19th-century wrought-iron market pavilions at Les Halles and the creation, in their place, of an underground transport and shopping complex seen by some as a monstrous, mirror-glassed carbuncle" ("Former Paris Stock Exchange to Be Reborn as Major New Art Museum," *Guardian*, June 26, 2016, https://www.theguardian.com /world/2017/jun/26/former-paris-stock-exchange-to-be-reborn-as-major-new-art -museum).

References

Berstein, Serge, and Jean-Pierre Rioux. 2000. *The Pompidou Years, 1969–1974*. Translated by Christopher Woodall. Cambridge History of Modern France 9. Cambridge: Cambridge University Press.

Chevalier, Louis. 1993. *The Assassination of Paris*. Translated by David P. Jordan. Chicago: University of Chicago Press.

Colomb, Claire. 2012. *Staging the New Berlin: Place Marketing and the Politics of Urban Reinvention Post-1989*. New York: Routledge.

Derrida, Jacques. 1976. *Of Grammatology*. Translated by Gayatri Chakravorty Spivak. Baltimore: Johns Hopkins University Press.

Fermigier, André. 1971. "Qui a vendu Les Halles?" *Le Nouvel Observateur*, no. 348, July 12.

———. 1991. *La Bateille de Paris*. Paris: Gallimard.

Fromonot, Françoise. 2005. *La campagne des Halles. Les nouveaux malheurs de Paris*. Paris: La Fabrique.

Garcia, Tristan. 2016. *La vie intense: Une obsession modern*. Paris: Flammarion.

Grup de treball de l'institut català d'antropologia. 2010. "Barcelona's Colonia Castells and the 'Urban Renewal Syndrome.'" *Perifèries Urbanes*, October. http://periferiesurbanes .org/?m=201010&lang=en (accessed September 16, 2019).

Harvey, David. 1985. "Paris: 1850–1870." In *Consciousness and the Urban Experience*, by David Harvey, 63–220. London: Basil Blackwell.

Hazan, Éric. 2010. *The Invention of Paris: A History in Footsteps*. Translated by David Fernbach. London: Verso.

———. 2017. *Une traverse de Paris*. Paris: Seuil.

Kasten, Scott A. 2013. "Destroying the Mystique of Paris: How the Destruction of Les Halles Served as a Symbol for Gaullist Power and Modernization in 1960s and 1970s." Master's thesis, Georgia State University. http://scholarworks.gsu.edu/history_theses /70 (accessed September 15, 2019).

Kleinschmidt, Erich. 2004. *Die Entdeckung der Intensität: Geschichte einer Denkfigur im 18. Jahrhundert*. Göttingen: Wallstein.

Large, Pierre-François. 1992. *Des Halles au Forum: Metamorphoses au Coeur de Paris*. Paris: L'Harmattan.

McCall, Rachael. 2011. "Les Halles: A Series of Unfortunate Events." June. https://static1
.squarespace.com/static/50cd3652e4b0e1a121803a62/t/51ea5ec4e4b077fcc27a6dd4
/1374314180124/2011_rmcCall_LesHalles.pdf (accessed September 15, 2019).

Mead, Christopher Curtis. 2012. *Making Modern Paris: Victor Baltard's Central Markets and the Urban Practice of Architecture.* State College: Pennsylvania State University Press.

Michel, Christian. 1988. *Les Halles: La renaissance d'un quartier, 1966–1988.* Paris: Masson.

Mickey 13. 2017. Review of "Don't Touch the White Woman!" *Spaghetti Western Database* (*swdb*). Lasted edited March 28. https://www.spaghetti-western.net/index.php/Don
't_Touch_the_White_Woman!_Review_(Mickey13) (accessed September 16, 2019).

Pinkney, David H. 1958. *Napoleon III and the Rebuilding of Paris.* Princeton nj: Princeton University Press.

Powell, Hilary. 2005. "Recycling Junkspace: Finding Space for 'Playtime' in the City." *Journal of Architecture* 10, no. 2: 201–21.

Rabinow, Paul. 1989. *French Modern: Norms and Forms of the Social Environment.* Cambridge ma: mit Press.

Rancière, Jacques. 1989. *The Bights of Labor: The Workers' Dream in Nineteenth-Century France.* Translated by John Drury. Philadelphia: Temple University Press.

———. 1991. *The Ignorant Schoolmaster: Five Lessons in Intellectual Emancipation.* Translated by Kristin Ross. Stanford ca: Stanford University Press.

———. 2004. *The Politics of Aesthetics: The Distribution of the Sensible.* Translated by Gabriel Rockhill. New York: Continuum.

Robert, Jean-Louis, and Myriam Tsikounas, eds. 2004. *Les Halles: Images d'un quartier.* Paris: Publications de la Sorbonne.

Sauerwein, Berndt. 2010. "Morsche Brachen, wüste Fluren und Ruinen." In *Notizbuch der Kasseler Schule 81,* edited by H. Lechenmayr and K. Hülbusch, Kassel, 97–119. ag Freiraum und Vegetation Kassel. Available at https://www.researchgate.net/profile
/Bernd_Sauerwein/publication/272686642_Morsche_Brachen_wuste_Fluren_und
_Ruinen/links/54ec51300cf2465f532df4cb/Morsche-Brachen-wueste-Fluren-und
-Ruinen.pdf (accessed September 15, 2019).

Scott, Allen John. 2014. "Beyond the Creative City: Cognitive—Cultural Capitalism and the New Urbanism." *Regional Studies* 48, no. 4: 565–78.

Sibley, David. 1995. *Geographies of Exclusion.* New York: Routledge.

Strohmayer, Ulf. 1997. "Technology, Modernity, and the Restructuring of the Present in Historical Geographies." *Geographiska Annaler* 79b, no. 3: 155–70.

———. 2012. "Performing Marginal Space: Film, Topology and the *Petite Ceinture* in Paris." Artwork by Jipé Core. *Liminalities* 8, no. 4: 1–16.

———. 2018. "Dystopian Dynamics at Work: The Creative Validation of Urban Space." in *The Routledge Handbook on Spaces of Urban Politics,* edited by Kevin Ward, Andrew E. G. Jonas, Byron Miller, and David Wilson, 542–54. London: Routledge.

TenHoor, Meredith. 2007. "Architecture and Biopolitics at Les Halles." *French Politics, Culture & Society* 25, no. 2: 73–92.

van Schipstal, Inge L. M., and Walter Nicholls. 2014. "Rights to the Neoliberal City: The Case of Urban Land Squatting in 'Creative' Berlin." *Territory, Politics, Governance* 2, no. 2: 173–93.

Vivant, Elsa. 2013. "Creatives in the City: Urban Contradictions of the Creative City." *City, Culture and Society* 4, no. 2: 57–63.

Wakeman, Rosemary, 2007. "Fascinating Les Halles." *French Politics, Culture & Society* 25, no. 2: 46–72.

———. 2009. *The Heroic City: Paris, 1945–1958*. Chicago: University of Chicago Press.

2 "The Crack in the Earth"

Environmentalism after Speleology

Kai Bosworth

Contemporary liberal environmentalism relies on notions of wholeness, interconnection, and dynamic life to derive the moral certitude to contest resource extraction. An emergent strain of thought in the environmental humanities called new materialism has claimed to provide a more careful ontology *for* environmentalism that would recognize the interdependence and sublime enchantment of objects and bodies (Bennett 2010; Coole and Frost 2010). The central premise of new materialism contends that objects, materials, and natural spaces need not be understood only from anthropocentric perspectives but can and must be investigated in their dynamic and vital relations in themselves. Yet when confronted with the permeable spaces of the underground, we find not a world of interconnected vibrant objects, but unsettling confrontations with the fractured, the inorganic, and the limits of our corporeal and mental capacities. Underground spaces force us to reckon with the construction of our partial perspectives and fractured subjectivities, formed out of the gaps shared by our bodies and environs.

I argue that examination of caves and caving reveals the split in a constituted environmental subject, a subject too frequently elided by new materialism. Geographic scholarship has positioned caves and caving within tourism, adventure sports, or scientific mapping projects (Cant 2006; Pérez 2015; Edwards 2017). Geographers have investigated the cultural constitution of mystery and the phenomenologies of bodies underground (Cant 2003; della Dora 2011; Edensor 2013; Jaramillo 2016). But these accounts largely take caving as an *experience* with internal politics—for example, who caves, who knows about caves. More speculatively, I argue that caving might generate a novel environmental politics that flows beyond the activity of caving itself. I argue that the cramped, holey space of the cave offers what Jodi Dean (2016) has called an *anamorphic* environmental politics. Caving shows us the incomplete construction of our own subject position and offers that gap or wound as the condition of possibility for political opposition to extractive industries. I offer an account of what cavers in Wind and Jewel Caves in South Dakota take from the lack of knowledge, the crack of the subject, and the void in being that caving exposes: an *environmentalism after speleology*. In proposing a politics based on nonknowledge, constitutive wounds, and permeable bodies, caving disrupts the norms of interconnection, certainty, scar, and redress that have historically oriented American environmentalism and scholarly attempts to ground its material ontology.

Against Nature?

Two dominant schools of thought can be found in contemporary environmentalism and environmental theory. On the one hand romantic environmentalism imagines nature and humanity as separate realms. In this version of environmentalism, human progress and social development can only negatively affect the natural world, which should consequently be cordoned off and preserved as much as possible. The modern romantic approach has been roundly critiqued by geographers, scholars of science and technology, and environmentalists for its universalizing of Western and Christian modes of thought (Cronon 1996), for its chauvinistic approach to the study of non-Western modes of interacting with or imagining nature (Latour 1993), for the essentializing connotations of "naturalization" that have devastating consequences for women, people of color, and indigenous people (Haraway 1990; D. S. Moore, Kosek, and Pandian 2003), and for the way it ultimately imagines nature as an instrumental, valuable, and exploitable resource (J. W. Moore 2015).

The second school proposes to collapse the modern binary between nature and culture. This is the proposition of contemporary environmental thought, which largely follows the thesis for an "ecology without nature"

(Morton 2007). It is ecology that is positioned "against capitalism" (Foster 2002), an "ecology of things" (Bennett 2010) that all display liveliness, a "general ecology" of relationality that conditions all thinking (Hörl 2017). Ecology here might connote three particular kinds of connections: a general ontology of relationality as such, a particular epistemological stance for investigating relationality, and a normative political stance that affirms (1) the value of interconnection, (2) a view of systems as fundamentally open, (3) the relationship among things and systems can be characterized by life and vitality, and (4) that any severed connection is thus injurious and should be repaired. The relationship between an ecological ontology and its derived normative principles is the most important for this essay; I thus focus on how these four principles are taken to be derived in environmentalism and new materialism.

The interconnection of all things to every other thing is taken as a foundational ontological paradigm, one of the four informal "laws of ecology" of prominent American environmentalist Barry Commoner (1971, 33). As Frédéric Neyrat (2017) puts it, the thesis that everything is interconnected has become "the *principle of principles* of ecology" (101; emphasis in the original). Western environmentalism has long perceived the interplay of pollution, health, and well-being of living things across myriad scales. For example, Rachel Carson (1962) famously investigated the long-term health effects of the pesticide DDT, which through biomagnification has more intense effects upon apex predators. Her practice reveals webs of relationship that persist in and through human and more-than-human worlds, relations too frequently disregarded by economics and politics in the United States. Investigating the interconnection of all things would, it is argued, lead one to value the fragility of these relationships and thus to shy away from severing or disturbing organic interconnectivity (Connolly 2013).

Rather than the closed systems of second-order cybernetics and community ecology, the ecological stance suggests that systems are fundamentally *open*. The claim for open systems undermines the position that any social or ecological system is functionally determined by some other, larger system, such as a political, historical, or economic regime. More generally, the thesis upholds skepticism toward any concept of totality and large-scale determination. These tend to be seen as anthropocentric or merely nominalist. While various versions of the Gaia hypothesis could be accused of creating a transcendent image of the earth, proponents of this theory, from scientists such as Lynn Margulis to philosophers such as Isabelle Stengers and Bruno Latour are at pains to demonstrate Gaia is a name instead for the lively composition of nontotalizing worlds from the bacterial scales upward (Clarke 2017).

In demonstrating the openness yet interconnection of various actants, life is liberated from its confinement in living beings to become a general property of relationality. Rather than appearing as the soul of the body, life now cuts across and courses through all matter. Life becomes another word for force or activity. Life is relieved of its *telos* or purpose and becomes "a swarm of vitalities at play" (Bennett 2010, 32). As Claire Colebrook (2011) argues, it quite clearly "follows that man, then, ought to follow the ethic of this life, feeling and attuning himself to these relations rather than imposing them from without" (164). Vitalism promises a skepticism toward mastery and instrumentality. Instead, it replaces this orientation toward the world with one of experimentation and wandering contemplation.

But surely this kind of environmentalism, if it is to deserve such a name, must promise some manner of improving upon the contemporary catastrophe that the Anthropocene seeks to name? Although some have indeed taken new materialism to suggest a practice of wandering and wallowing in the ruins of capitalism, others elaborate upon John Dewey in promising redress to a public wounded by unforeseen ecological consequences of technical projects. Jane Bennett (2010) explains this political logic succinctly: "harmed bodies draw near each other and seek to engage in new acts that will restore their power, protect against future harm, or compensate for damage done—in *that* consists their political action" (101). Vital interconnectedness begets reciprocity among all beings for the wounds of the past, which are ascribed to the unruly nature of things (rather than the political and social forces that unleash them).

Recent explorations of the geologic and technic have challenged the ubiquity of the ecological principles of interconnection, open holism, life, and redress. While some, like Bennett (2010), have indeed paid attention to the geologic, it is only to reduce it to another player in life—now a "mineral or metallic life" (53). As Colebrook (2011) argues, "the consequences of this worldview are one loses sight of the more radical indifference that would characterize just those forms of technicity and monstrosity that mark the limits of life as it is conventionally defined" (164). The environmentalism of new materialism seems to instead follow Parmenides's statement that nature abhors a vacuum. In a world where everything is connected, there is no room for separation, which appears only as a fall from grace.

Caving practices, I argue, complicate the ontological assumptions and normative stances that new materialism proposes for environmentalism. Against a world where everything is interconnected, caving practices propose an "ecology of separation" (Neyrat 2017) by considering every interconnection to be founded on a crack, wound, or gap that precedes and articulates differences. This separation is different than the supposedly fundamental openness of a system to the environment as it instead exposes a kind of closure or incommensurability—"a before, a beneath, a beyond" that "cannot be fully coextensive with the human domain" (Clark and Yusoff 2017, 16). Against the ontology where an active life force courses through everything, caves expose a temporality and spatiality reserved beyond experience. To the extent that life exists here, it is of a character that challenges the very definition of life. Caves offer slow fracture and erosion, which offer no easy comfort nor normative foundation since "all life is a process of breaking down" (Deleuze 1990, 154). And while no precise politics can be grounded in this ontology, caves provide a situated vantage point or *detour* from which we can view not only the production of nature but also the constitution of our own partial perspectives.

The Earth Is Not Solid

In November 2013 Ken Steinken wrote an op-ed voicing his opposition to a uranium mine proposed in southwestern South Dakota. A high school teacher and caver, Steinken was not concerned with the usual range of not-in-my-backyard nor the well-founded environmental justice arguments. Instead, the central premise of his argument was, contrary to the experience of most, "the earth is not solid." The proposed Dewey-Burdock mine was to use in-situ recovery (ISR), a relatively new method (in North America at least) for extracting uranium. ISR requires little on-site human labor; instead of digging a pit or shaft, the mining is accomplished chemically. A solvent is pumped into boreholes in the earth and then removed after coursing through permeable spaces underground, thus dissolving uranium into its liquid. The uranium is then removed from the solvent, and waste-water is pumped back underground. The operation of ISR is premised on the fact that parts of the subsurface earth are permeable. Yet in order to present itself as operating an environmentally safe extraction process, the surrounding strata must be presented as confined or solid. Steinken (2013) exposed precisely this contradiction: "Of course, the mining company says that the layers of rock above and below the uranium-bearing strata are impervious, as dense as if they formed a triple-sealed, underground storage tank. How could anything leak out of solid rock? Then I think of Jewel Cave and its 166 miles of passages snaking underneath only six square miles of land, and the memory shoots holes through the 'solid rock' idea."

For more than a decade activists, geologists, lay people, and Native Nations in western South Dakota had been arguing the Dewey-Burdock project seemed to threaten the region's sparse groundwater resources, but the roots of this activism are long and run deep. Many of these same residents of western South Dakota had been fighting the remnants of past gold and uranium mining activities and proposals for new mines since the mid-1970s (Ferguson 2014; Grossman 2017; Husmann 2011). Waste from uranium mining in the 1960s was never properly cleaned up as a busted uranium market in the 1970s left companies bankrupt. The test boreholes and other remnants of incursion into the lithosphere added to the already highly permeable geology of the Black Hills to render more prevalent hydrologic communication of toxics among aquifers and surface waters (Bosworth 2017). These ruins of past extraction, only one component of a ruthless and ongoing settler colonialism, have drastically impacted the health of Lakota, Dakota, and Nakota people living downstream. Nonetheless, these Native Nations continue to contest not only extraction projects but also the supposed right of settler institutions to make decisions on the fate and fortune of land dispossessed only 140 years prior (LaDuke and Churchill 1985; Jarding 2011; Bosworth and Santella 2017).

Native activists with Women of All Red Nations (WARN) were central in the "discovery" of the circulation of postmining toxins nearly fifty years prior. The effects of mining practices wrought violence on bodies, especially on women and children (Thunder Hawk [2007] 2017). For a people for whom the Black Hills are of incredible importance (Ostler 2011) and for whom water is life (Young 1996), the proposition of a new uranium mine was a new offensive act in a long history of resource extraction and environmental violence. The company Powertech LLC, later bought by Azarga Uranium, continually flubbed basic environmental and cultural review processes and shunned consultation with Lakota people (see Tupper 2018). Instead, Azarga sought to prove that one three-dimensional subterranean territorial zone was uniquely protected from underground communication of water and contained nothing of cultural, spiritual, or scientific value.

Anticolonial and environmental justice concerns are sufficient normative grounds for collective opposition to the Dewey-Burdock project. Yet the legal proceedings of environmental review permitting, despite containing environmental justice analyses, rarely take as viable evidence the thousands of pages of impassioned political arguments of those who speak at their public hearings (U.S. Environmental Protection Agency 2017a). Rather, permitting processes attempt to garner testimony on very specific and cordoned-off aspects of a proposed project. These include, for example, water use and wastewater disposal or the permeability of underground materials. By doing so, public hearings can police the terms of knowledge and debate (Hébert 2016), limiting their interaction and communication with the public to the most basic kinds of informational exchange.

Yet even when institutions such as the EPA and Nuclear Regulatory Commission attempt to limit discussion to the most obtuse geologic knowledge and invisible spaces beyond human experience, the public finds a way to testify that the world is more complicated (see also Adam 1998). Elsewhere I have demonstrated that many individuals testifying in public hearings against this mine connected the permeability of the earth with that of their own (collective) bodies, seeing themselves and the landscape as, in the words of one woman, "a catacomb of tunnels" (qtd. in Bosworth 2017, 32). Here I want to demonstrate further that the prevalence of caves is central to this understanding of themselves and the geology of the Black Hills and that cavers have something to offer to our understanding of the relationship between the political and the geologic.

Jewel Cave and Wind Cave are currently the third and sixth longest caves in the world, and like almost all major caves, they display unique geologic formations found nowhere else. Wind Cave spans 142 miles of mapped caverns, unique for holding 90 percent of the planet's observed boxwork, a formation that looks something like corrugated cardboard. Wind Cave's narrow, crisscrossing passageways are packed within a mere one square mile of horizontal territory beneath Wind Cave National Park. About ten miles to the northwest, Jewel Cave features at least 181 miles of passageways and formations such as cave popcorn, cave bacon, balloons, a Cthulhu-like monster, and thousands of other cave oddities. As the cave explorers Herbert and Jan Conn (1981) described such formations, "some are pretty, some are grotesque, and some are incomprehensible" (151). Both caves feature strong airflow (as the namesake "Wind Cave" suggests), and scientists measuring the rate and volume of air at Jewel Cave suggest that the full volume of the cave could be some twenty times what has been explored to date. As an interpretive sign at the Jewel Cave National Monument visitor center poetically puts it, "what is known about the cave is dwarfed by what continues to be unknown."

Both Jewel and Wind Caves are national monuments, the latter among the first six signed into law by Theodore Roosevelt (although he never visited either cave). "Discovered" in the late 1800s by settlers flocking to the Black Hills searching for gold, the caves were quickly turned into tourist attractions. Yet cave tourism was not particularly lucrative, and the caves passed hands several times before eventually being purchased by the federal government. Both were taken to be small and uninteresting caves until the 1950s, when speleology began to grow as a leisure, adventure, and quasi-scientific practice in the United States. The National Speleological Society was formed in 1941 and grew throughout the country, organizing local groups of cave explorers called grottos. Organized locally and nationally to create standards for cave exploration, protection, and study, grottos provided a foundation for cave advocacy. The 1960s began the heyday for cave exploration in South Dakota as well, as Herb and Jan Conn added some sixty miles to Jewel Cave's mapped length. Although rarely mentioned in official histories of the caves, Wind Cave was also the site of a brief political occupation by American Indian Movement activists in 1981 (see Ostler 2011, 179).

As popularizers of caving, the Conns left a following of avid cavers in their wake, who with practical regularity add three to four miles of new passageways each year to this day. With GPS and other electronics useless underground, cave mapping remains a somewhat archaic practice, making use of only a clinometer, a laser distance meter, and one's eyeballs. Yet this also means that very few barriers to entry exist to becoming a caver. All one needs are clothes you do not mind getting covered with manganese, elbow and knee pads and a helmet, and a group of at least two others to journey along with you. Steinken is one of a handful of cavers—volunteer explorers, mappers, and enthusiasts—who for a few days every month plumb the depths of Jewel and Wind Cave systems plotting their subterranean extent, shape, and features. Cavers in the Black Hills generally take three- to four-day journeys on their expeditions to map new routes, the entire period of which will be spent underground.

Cavers in South Dakota have both an excitement and reverence for exploration. Although typical wilderness-style norms are in effect wherein you pack out everything brought into the cave (including four days of one's own feces and urine), ecological disturbance is unlikely as nothing except bacteria live far beyond the openings of South Dakota caves. This makes caving a truly isolating experience for living beings like ourselves.

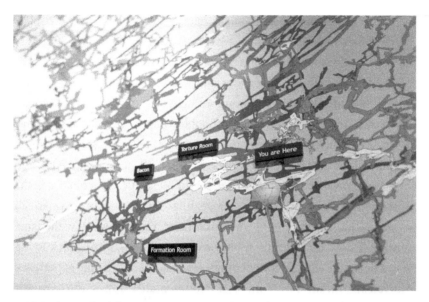

6. Map of myriad overlapping passageways at the Jewel Cave National Monument visitor center. Photo by the author.

Nearly all sound, light, and smell is brought underground with you. As one would imagine, caving requires frequent bodily contortion and exertion, and cavers often speak of a shift in their experience of their bodies as one of the most enjoyable aspects of caving. Many sections of Jewel Cave are named for the pain-inducing travails they entail—the Miseries, the Torture Room, the Calorie Counter, Monotonous Passage, Dungeon. Although there are fantastic features to behold, just as frequent are cramped, drab rock rooms covered in manganese. Absent underground are the lively networks or assemblages that populate contemporary materialism. Instead there are only strata, void, an occasional drip of water. These aspects of caving are what Nigel Clark (2017) (following Elizabeth Grosz) calls the "cosmological imponderables" of the earth. By this it is meant the spaces and strata "whose reach stretches far beyond any human collective" (229).

Does not caving and its attendant politics really just reproduce the romantic view of nature that contrasts with contemporary postnatural ecological politics? In some ways cave protection and management could seem to follow the norms of environmentalism; one should not expect complete determinism, after all. Most large cave systems in the United States are protected and managed by the U.S. National Parks Service (NPS), an institution built on colonial aspirations and whose mission seeks to balance preservation of sublime and unique aesthetics for tourism. The ecologies that exist in the mouths of caves, although composed of few and strange beings, are thought of in largely the same way as any other ecological system, in various states of equilibrium and disequilibrium, preservation and contamination. For example, a widespread issue in cave ecologies is the prevention of the spread of white nose fungus through North American bat populations, requiring that cave visitors refrain from wearing the same clothing if they venture into multiple caves. Although caves lack living beings beyond their surface openings, one could easily fit the experience of cave exploration into familiar environmentalist tropes: the drive for experience of the sublime, extremophilia, discovery of the new, the desire to name, and the adventure sports industry. What each of these discourses share with traditional environmentalism is an overall concern with the preservation of life and health at the risky adventurous frontier.

Yet cavers themselves are not beholden to follow this path, motivated less in my experience by exploratory heroism and more by curiosity, mental exertion, and intimacy with the planet. These emotions are drawn out in part by the perpetual void that they face in the longest caves on planet earth. The Conns describe this well in their 1977 Jewel Cave memoirs: every new feature or mapped and surveyed passageway brings with it "wonder and bewilderment at what remains. . . . Sometimes we find too many leads, while at other times we cannot find any. When we leave the cave in the evening, we are often tired, frustrated, and discouraged. Fortunately these feelings are quickly forgotten during the ensuing week, whereas curiosity lingers to lure us back" (Conn and Conn 1981, 64). With classic caver humor and rhyme, they remark that while bravery is required, "if you find you like it, chum, you have to be a little dumb" (65). This is hardly the "'tough' masculinities and . . . underground heroics over nature" (Cant 2003, 68) that one might expect. Instead, as Sarah G. Cant (2003) also finds, caving produces a kind of sensuous intimacy that "heightens awareness of the individual and subjective body," resituating it away from the masculine narratives of strength and adventure (79).

Despite the vast stretches of unknown passageways large and small that lead to caverns, formations, lakes, and rivers yet to be discovered, what *is* known through time spent underground enhances one's understanding of the permeability of the earth. For Steinken (2013), memories of meandering underground stir him to oppose uranium mining and "shoot holes through the 'solid rock' idea." Recalling as much a geophilosopher as a writer or earth scientist, Steinken (2013) argues: "Our planet is neither solid nor is its current form permanent. It's in a constant state of flux. It is subject to internal and external forces. Groundwater and gravity [will continue to] team up to exploit the tiniest crack or weakness in [what appears to be] an 'impenetrable' rock layer." This perspective has been reinforced by both expert and lay testimony, which time and time again has proven the confining layers in the Black Hills region to be perforated by both human and nonhuman intrusions. The testimony of the public gathered at an Environmental Protection Agency (EPA) hearing in May 2017 repeats the basic knowledge that we live on a dynamic planet and, more specifically, that the "porous aquifers and caves . . . are all intertwined and leak into each other" (U.S. Environmental Protection Agency 2017b, 80).

The spacing and stupefying nonknowledge that the never-ending void provides allows the political possibility of what Neyrat (2017) calls nature as *detour*—"a mediation allowing us to separate ourselves, even if only temporarily, from what we are doing . . . allowing us to measure the relations we produce and the material limits belonging to these relations" (121). As one caver explained to me, the experience of caving is a "simplified model" of how we can understand environmental impact, which can easily appear too complex for comprehension, as in the example of global warming. The detour of caving allows one to take a step back and assess the situated perspectives of human life embedded within earth processes.

The Fractured Subject

To paraphrase Gilles Deleuze (1990, 160), if one asks why holistic environmentalism does not suffice, why we must live with the crack in the earth, why the crack is even desirable, it is because only through the crack and its detours will new forms of thought and political action arise. In contradistinction to new materialism and contemporary environmentalism, Deleuze argues that the problem is that *all* life is in a process of breaking down or cracking up. No unwounded body, closed planet, or "full degree" of life can ever be attained or has ever existed. To act as if we are scarred by a historical fall from grace tends to produce not politics, but *ressentiment*. Instead, we might consider that life carries with it a constitutive wound that exists beyond the diachronic time of bodies and mixtures, instead in the quasi-synchronic time of the event. To the extent that cavers could be seen to reproduce romantic environmentalism, their practices simultaneously undo such a position through their drive to explore the crack of the earth. Theirs is beyond an ethic of everyday ecological management, instead pointing toward a politics derived from the event.

This kind of ethic presents a problem. Deleuze, drawing on Fitzgerald, asks: if the earth itself is cracked, "how could it not itself break up, how is it to be prevented from precipitating destruction?" (Deleuze 1990, 157). If life carries within it its own error, self-destruction, or void (Colebrook 2011, 2015), what is to prevent it from exhausting itself in that void? On what political grounds could one oppose planetary exhaustion if not life, health, and materiality? The possibility cavers offer is to speak not from the scars of personal experience that deserve redress, but to creatively turn the void into something else, what we might call the persistence of the truth of the event through the excess of its separation. The void of the cave attests that the beyond, beneath, and below of the earth exists as both a limit to human experience and an excess of earthly potential. This possibility Deleuze (1990) describes, now sounding something like a caver himself, as "all the more dangerous, more labyrinthine, and more tortuous" (165). It is something "that overthrows worlds, individuals, and persons, and leaves them to the depth of the ground which works and dissolves them" (168).

There are three consequences to this view of environmentalism through caving practices. First, cavers reinsert themselves as cracked subjects situated in and of the cave's inhuman geography. They are not "whole (complete) subjects" but "hole subjects." They are subjects of anamorphosis: subjects who begin to recognize and mobilize their fractured and partial nature. Anamorphosis is essentially the confrontation with an object that cannot be examined in full straight on (as a map or photograph, say) but appears coherent only when examined from the side, or partially. Using anamorphosis in the context of climate politics, Dean (2016) explains: "The perspective from which the hole appears is that of the subject—that is, of the gap that the shift to a partisan perspective opens up" (75). In attempting to view the entire ecosystem as a series of interconnected systems, environmentalism induces paralysis and evades politics. Caving induces anamorphosis: the event of caving is kind of a mind-warp that forces one to confront the inadequacy and partiality of perspective. It is no surprise that the cave paintings at Lascaux in France, the earliest in recorded human history, have been theorized as anamorphic paintings (Yusoff 2015).

Second, the void—or rather, voiding processes—are not just in the subject but also are reinserted back into the world, which ecology had taken for a whole complete meta-individual. The inhuman timescales of the underground are encountered in caving events, where cavers witness not necessarily sublime complexity and interconnection, but otherness, separation, and the lack of completion of the world itself. Caving encounters force thought to confront not only the void in itself—a lack of knowledge—but also the ungroundedness of the earth itself, the void in being. This is not just the particular physical or spatial presence of the void in caves, but a more general understanding of the incompletion, obduracy, and limits the earth poses in itself.

Finally, the cracked subject and crack in the world afford the possibility of recognizing our situated, partisan, and thus *political* perspectives through the detour of Nature. There are no guarantees in caving politics—as in any politics—but that simply means that like the void of the cave itself, the possibilities are never exhausted. As María A. Pérez (2016) demonstrates, the *yearnings* that caves produce can emerge from the absence of end or finality (spatially, temporally) as much as the presence of connections and encounters.

It would be all too easy to conclude that caving is a dark activity offering only contemplative reflection on death. But in writing the cave, as many cavers do—and as I am doing right now—one detaches its split nature and, allows it to speak through other concerns. This "splitting within being" opens a desire for the ethical and political (Copjec 2004, 36). When cavers and the public speak and write the cave's meanings for environmental politics, they are also contesting the understanding of the underground only as an extractive resource. Caving releases something about the inhuman forces into the political sphere, compelling many of us to examine the partiality of our perspective. In doing so, cavers augment the range of possible outcomes for environmental political action. Caving offers thus not a model for how to think about the whole planet, but a singular liberation of the forces of its holes. This is not a contamination of nature, but a contamination of us by the earth. Such a position would be an opening statement for an environmentalism after speleology.

References

Adam, Barbara. 1998. *Timescapes of Modernity: The Environment and Invisible Hazards.* London: Routledge.

Bennett, Jane. 2010. *Vibrant Matter: A Political Ecology of Things.* Durham NC: Duke University Press.

Bosworth, Kai. 2017. "Thinking Permeable Matter through Feminist Geophilosophy: Environmental Knowledge Controversy and the Materiality of Hydrogeologic Processes." *Environment and Planning D: Society and Space* 35, no. 1: 21–37.

Bosworth, Kai, and Julie Santella. 2017. "Dewey-Burdock Class III and Class V Injection Well Draft Area Permits—Public Comment." https://kaibosworth.weebly.com/uploads/5/6/1/7/56172587/bosworth_santella_public_comment_dewey-burdock_class_iii_and_class_v_injection_well_draft_area_permits.pdf (accessed September 15, 2019).

Cant, Sarah G. 2003. "'The Tug of Danger with the Magnetism of Mystery': Descents into 'the Comprehensive, Poetic-Sensuous Appeal of Caves.'" *Tourist Studies* 3, no. 1: 67–81.

———. 2006. "British Speleologies: Geographies of Science, Personality and Practice, 1935–1953." *Journal of Historical Geography* 32, no. 4: 775–95.

Carson, Rachel. 1962. *Silent Spring*. Boston: Houghton Mifflin.

Clark, Nigel. 2017. "Politics of Strata." *Theory, Culture & Society* 34, nos. 2/3: 211–31.

Clark, Nigel, and Kathryn Yusoff. 2017. "Geosocial Formations and the Anthropocene." *Theory, Culture & Society* 34, nos. 2/3: 3–23.

Clarke, Bruce. 2017. "Rethinking Gaia: Stengers, Latour, Margulis." *Theory, Culture & Society* 34, no. 4: 3–26.

Colebrook, Claire. 2011. *Deleuze and the Meaning of Life*. London: Continuum.

———. 2015. "Post-Phenomenology's Evil Cartesian Demon." In *Sex after Life: Essays on Extinction*, vol. 2, 49–74. Ann Arbor MI: Open Humanities.

Commoner, Barry. 1971. *The Closing Circle: Nature, Man, and Technology*. New York: Knopf.

Conn, Herbert, and Jan Conn. 1981. *Jewel Cave Adventure: Fifty Miles of Discovery under South Dakota*. St. Louis: Cave Books.

Connolly, William E. 2013. *The Fragility of Things: Self-Organizing Processes, Neoliberal Fantasies, and Democratic Activism*. Durham NC: Duke University Press.

Coole, Diana H., and Samantha Frost, eds. 2010. *New Materialisms: Ontology, Agency, and Politics*. Durham NC: Duke University Press.

Copjec, Joan. 2004. *Imagine There's No Woman: Ethics and Sublimation*. Cambridge MA: MIT Press.

Cronon, William. 1996. "The Trouble with Wilderness: or, Getting Back to the Wrong Nature." *Environmental History* 1, no. 1: 7–28.

Dean, Jodi. 2016. "A View from the Side: The Natural History Museum." *Cultural Critique* 94: 74–101.

Deleuze, Gilles. 1990. *The Logic of Sense*. Translated by Mark Lester, with Charles Stivale. Edited by Constantin V. Boundas. New York: Columbia University Press.

della Dora, Veronica. 2011. "Anti-Landscapes: Caves and Apophasis in the Christian East." *Environment and Planning D: Society and Space* 29, no. 5: 761–79.

Edensor, Tim. 2013. "Reconnecting with Darkness: Gloomy Landscapes, Lightless Places." *Social & Cultural Geography* 14, no. 4: 446–65.

Edwards, Jess. 2017. "'The Land to Forget Time': Tourism, Caving and Writing in the Derbyshire White Peak." *Landscape Research* 42, no. 6: 634–49.

Ferguson, Cody. 2014. "You Are Now Entering a 'National Sacrifice Area': The Energy Boom of the 1970s and the Radicalization of the Northern Plains." *Journal of the West* 53, no. 1: 69–78.

Fitzgerald, F. Scott. 1945. *The Crack-Up*. New York: New Directions.

Foster, John Bellamy. 2002. *Ecology against Capitalism*. New York: Monthly Review Press.

Grossman, Zoltán. 2017. *Unlikely Alliances: Native Nations and White Communities Join to Defend Rural Lands*. Seattle: University of Washington Press.

Haraway, Donna J. 1990. *Simians, Cyborgs, and Women: The Reinvention of Nature*. New York: Routledge.

Hébert, Karen. 2016. "Chronicle of a Disaster Foretold: Scientific Risk Assessment, Public Participation, and the Politics of Imperilment in Bristol Bay, Alaska." *Journal of the Royal Anthropological Institute* 22, no. s1: 108–26.

Hörl, Erich, ed. 2017. *General Ecology: The New Ecological Paradigm*. London: Bloomsbury.

Husmann, John. 2011. "Environmentalism in South Dakota: A Grassroots Approach." In *The Plains Political Tradition: Essays on South Dakota Political Culture*, edited by Jon K. Lauck, John E. Miller, and Donald C. Simmons, 239–66. Pierre: South Dakota State Historical Society.

Jaramillo, George S. 2016. "Miners' Lamp: Memory and the Underground through a Light Installation on Bonsall Moor." *cultural geographies* 23, no. 4: 727–33.

Jarding, Lilian Jones. 2011. "Uranium Activities' Impacts on Lakota Territory." *Indigenous Policy Journal* 22, no. 2. http://articles.indigenouspolicy.org/index.php/ipj/article/view /48.

LaDuke, Winona, and Ward Churchill. 1985. "Native America: The Political Economy of Radioactive Colonialism." *Journal of Ethnic Studies* 13, no. 3: 107–32.

Latour, Bruno. 1993. *We Have Never Been Modern*. Translated by Catherine Porter. Cambridge MA: Harvard University Press.

Moore, Donald S., Jake Kosek, and Anand Pandian, eds. 2003. *Race, Nature, and the Politics of Difference*. Durham NC: Duke University Press.

Moore, Jason W. 2015. *Capitalism in the Web of Life: Ecology and the Accumulation of Capital*. London: Verso.

Morton, Timothy. 2007. *Ecology without Nature: Rethinking Environmental Aesthetics*. Cambridge MA: Harvard University Press.

Neyrat, Frédéric. 2017. "Elements for an Ecology of Separation: Beyond Ecological Constructivism." In *General Ecology: The New Ecological Paradigm*, edited by Erich Hörl, 101–27. London: Bloomsbury.

Ostler, Jeffrey. 2011. *The Lakotas and the Black Hills: The Struggle for Sacred Ground*. New York: Penguin.

Pérez, María A. 2015. "Exploring the Vertical: Science and Sociality in the Field among Cavers in Venezuela." *Social & Cultural Geography* 16, no. 2: 226–47.

———. 2016. "Yearnings for Guácharo Cave: Affect, Absence, and Science in Venezuelan Speleology." *cultural geographies* 23, no. 4: 693–714.

Steinken, Ken. 2013. "A Uranium Mining Proposal Threatens Water Supplies: This South Dakota Project Claims Technology Will Trump Nature." November 5. http://www.hcn .org/wotr/a-uranium-mining-proposal-is-larded-with-snake-oil (accessed September 15, 2019).

Thunder Hawk, Madonna. (2007) 2017. "Native Organizing before the Nonprofit Industrial Complex." In *The Revolution Will Not Be Funded: Beyond the Non-Profit Industrial*

Complex, edited by INCITE! Women of Color Against Violence, 101–6. Cambridge MA: South End Press; repr., Durham NC: Duke University Press.

Tupper, Seth. 2018. "Court, Regulators Clash over Tribal Survey for Uranium Project." *Rapid City Journal*, August 5. https://rapidcityjournal.com/news/local/court -regulators-clash-over-tribal-survey-for-uranium-project/article_deac0d24-3a34-517d -ac68-830cc5ef54c1.html.

U.S. Environmental Protection Agency. 2017a. "Public Comments Regarding the EPA Region 8 Proposed Dewey-Burdock In-Situ Uranium Recovery Project Permitting Actions: Comments from Private Individuals." https://www.epa.gov/sites/production /files/2017-09/documents/epadewey-burdockcommentsreceivedfromprivateindividuals .pdf (accessed September 15, 2019).

———. 2017b. "Dewey-Burdock Public Hearing Transcripts." Announcements and Schedules. U.S. EPA. August 2, 2017. https://www.epa.gov/uic/dewey-burdock-public-hearing -transcripts (accessed September 15, 2019).

Young, Phyllis. 1996. "Beyond the Water Line." In *Defending Mother Earth: Native American Perspectives on Environmental Justice*, edited by Jace Weaver, 85–98. Maryknoll NY: Orbis.

Yusoff, Kathryn. 2015. "Geologic Subjects: Nonhuman Origins, Geomorphic Aesthetics and the Art of Becoming *In*human." *cultural geographies* 22, no. 3: 383–407.

3   The Vortex and the Void

Meta/Geophysics in Sedona

Keith Woodward and John Paul Jones III

Everything rotates.

—THOMAS PYNCHON, *Mason & Dixon*

Sedona, Arizona, it is widely claimed, is home to the most powerful vortexes in the Western Hemisphere, a product of the area's iron-rich sandstone formations of red mountains, mesas, buttes, spires, domes and canyons that house an array of "natural energetic power points" (Tierra 2008, n.p.), sites "where the Earth is exceptionally alive and healthy" (Andres 2000, 12).[1] If there is widespread debate about exactly what they are and how they work, most enthusiasts seem to agree that vortexes are amplified throughways—zones at which energy spirals into and out of the earth. Proclaiming Sedona a high-energy area of "sacred earth" (Mann 2004), the New Ageism movement nurtures a now decades-old mystical tradition that has spawned a thriving tourism industry of "Gaia's Pilgrims" (Ivakhiv 2001). Without doubt, tourists are also drawn to Sedona's landscape aesthetics, which offers scenery that is so visually "beautiful," "picturesque," and "sublime" that it threatens to short-circuit critical thought. Reclaiming that analytic edge could involve critical observations about the production of an aesthetics of landscape that relies on an epistemological separation—between nature and culture—*and* a second, parallel, human erasure (Willems-Braun 1997).

As if anticipating such concerns, local guides—though stubbornly grounding their reply not in historical contingencies but in universal humanism—invariably remark that the ancient and historical peoples of

Arizona did not actually live in Sedona but treated it as a sacred site, "so sacred that they did not live there" (Mann 2004, 3).[2] There a sense of cultural appropriation of Native Americans that such appeals to absence and mysticism too often seek to hide.[3] But beyond this the actual record is more complex and includes a palimpsest of peoples, including the Sinagua, who *did* inhabit the lower edge of the Colorado Plateau along the escarpment known as the Mogollon Rim and the Verde Valley into which it drains. Along with other tribes in the area, this pueblo culture was disrupted sometime in the fourteenth century. Two centuries later it was the Yavapai who crisscrossed the region, along with the Tonto Apache. We say "crisscross" because, as the guides suggest, it appears that the Yavapai did not actually live in Sedona. And yet they clearly hold it to be sacred: a tribal legend has it that "We come out at Sedona, the middle of the world" (Mann 2004, 11). But they were also nomadic people, thought to traverse a large area, and this may well account for Red Rock country's reputation as being too sacred to settle. Complicating the record even more is evidence that one of four branches of the Yavapai people had established a permanent base in the Oak Creek Canyon area just north of Sedona. The first archaeologist to visit there reported, in 1895, that the ruins reveal "aboriginal occupancy on all sides—ruins of buildings, fortified hilltops, pictographs and irrigating ditches—testifying that there was at one time a considerable population in this valley" (Fewkes, quoted in Mann 2004, 5).

Now we do not know for certain what J. W. Fewkes meant by "considerable," especially considering that the Yavapai were subjugated, massacred, and eventually forcibly resettled by the U.S. Army for over seventy-five years during the nineteenth century. After white settlers established Sedona—apparently named for the wife of the first postmaster—in the beginning of the twentieth century, its growth was slow, mostly marked by ranching, small-scale tourism, and visits by Hollywood movie productions (some sixty films were made in Sedona).[4] The town grew slowly until the 1970s, when it began its reputation as the "American capital of New Age spirituality" (Wolfteich 2009, 124). The Harmonic Convergence of August 1987 was a signature event popularizing the town. Even so, Sedona has always been small; today's resident population is under 11,000, a surprising number given the town's estimated 4.5 million visitors each year. Among these are hikers, photographers, and nature enthusiasts, but it is impossible to visit Sedona without seeing signs advertising a wide array of options available for alternative tourism, including Crystal Energy Healing, Lymphatic Drainage, Chakra Therapy, Hypnotherapy, Life Reading and Clearing, Herbology, Electro Dermal Screening, Biophoton Light Therapy, Psychic Channeling, and Hoop Therapy.[5] Sedona is also widely recognized as a favorite location for extraterrestrial flyovers, phenomena that are readily attested to by locals, some of whom offer sessions on Alien Abductee Regression. And in addition to its status as the headquarters for the harmonious earth movement, the city is purportedly a reception point for hybrid—that is, human/extraterrestrial—children and other more-than-human visitors.

It is with the recent New Age turn in Sedona's history that we concern ourselves here.[6] The germinal thinker who helped popularize Sedona's geography as a high-energy vortex in the 1980s was Page Bryant, a medium and spiritual author. Much of Sedona's subsequent vortical literature and discourses seem to take some direction and inspiration from her writings (Bryant 1983, 1991). Visitors—from the casually curious to the dedicated spiritualistic to the scientistic vortex hunter—cite a wide range of personal, psychic, and epistemological voids that have led them to converge on the area. And yet, for all the differences in their sources of volition (Ivakhiv 2003a, 2003b), their views on the nature of vortexes share the basic components of Bryant's "positive" ontology—a substantialist or materialist explanation based upon the contingent comingling of existent things and processes.[7]

Encircling this "speculative geography" (Woodward 2016)—what Deborah P. Dixon, Harriet Hawkins, and Elizabeth R. Straughan (2013) might call a "wonder-full geomorphology"—are the visitors, the seekers who approach the zone under the sign of absence (the lacuna, the void) and in their search for spiritual or physical healing aim to rediscover lost connections with humanity or with the earth, as inner or outer peace. As Justine Digance (2006) writes of modern secular pilgrims—who themselves may practice religion—they all share the common trait in that they are searching for, and expect also to be rewarded with, a mystical or magico-religious experience—a moment when they experience something out of the ordinary that marks a transition from the mundane secular humdrum world of our everyday existence to a special and sacred state. The moment may be fleeting so that many may not even instantly recognize what has occurred, but perhaps only afterwards when back in their quiet, crowd-free hotel room, and reflecting on their experiences will they realize that they have experienced an encounter with the Other. These experiences can be described in any number of ways, such as transformation, transcendence, life- and/or consciousness-changing event, hierophany, enlightenment and so on, but words seem somewhat inadequate to describe experiences that often are not amenable to reason. (Digance 2006, 38)

There is then something of a break between the various searching narratives converging around, and hailed by, Sedona's vortex sites, and the strangely abundant if undetermined materialisms in vortex ontology. It is in this seeming rupture where the energies get a little unusual. Here we participate in Mitch Rose's (2011) efforts "to illuminate the limits of earthly theory's secular horizon" (119), to test the weird balance that vortexes conjure between personal lack and ontological excess, between the void and the vortex. In following their limits, we trace the distinction between vorticists—spiritualists, scientists, and pilgrims (Terran or Intergalactic) whose voids inspire them to seek out vortexes—and vorticism, the ontology of the vortex. We borrow the term "meta/geophysics" from New Age vorticists to frame an inquiry at their mutual limits.

Vorticists: Subjects of the Void

First-time visitors to Sedona will typically be directed to four well-known vortex sites: Cathedral Rock, Airport Mesa, Bell Rock, and Boynton Canyon (fig. 7). But websites and staff at the local chamber of commerce will also tell you that the area is full of vortexes—we were told there are seventy-five in the area; we were also informed that "vortexes are everywhere, even in Tucson, you just have to be open to them." As sites of concentrated, ampli-

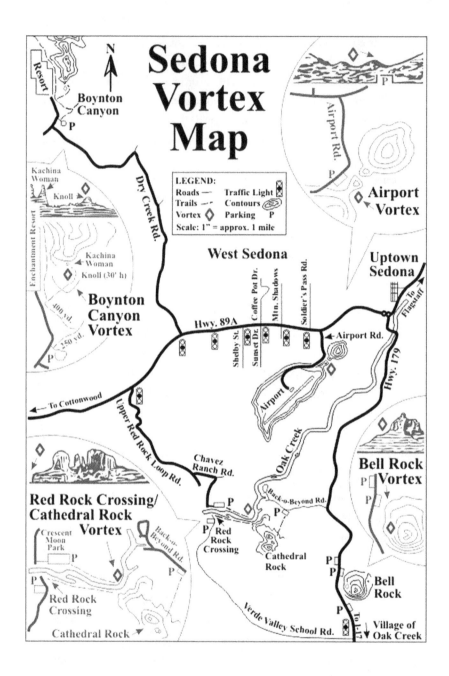

7. Tourist map of Sedona vortexes. 1997–2015. Source: Deva Designs, Sedona, Arizona. Used with kind permission of Micki Baumann.

fied, or magnified earth energy, vortexes are said to have the power to cause twists in tree trunks and, for humans, to heighten physical responses—typically to initiate tingling or to bring on strange sensations and even dizziness and nausea—as well as to enhance one's mental, emotional, and spiritual insights. One's response to these energies reportedly varies—both according to the receptivity of the observer and, for the sensitive, to the type of energy flow at the vortex. Cathedral Rock is a famous "inflow" vortex, meaning that energy arrives from above and goes into the earth. Such sites are typically found in canyons, valleys, and caves, and some vorticists identify these as sites of "negative" vortexes: good for those wanting an introspective, healing experience, such as when you want to recuperate a past-life memory. Bell Rock, by contrast, is said to be an "upflow" vortex, a site of "positive energy" that one tends to associate with "mountains, mesa tops, and pyramidal-type topography" (Sanders 2005, 19). Spiraling upward out of the earth, upflow energy is exhilarating and gives rise to expansive feelings that enable one to tap into universal consciousness.

Theorizing Sedona's vortex experiences is a local industry unto itself. Some vorticists, such as Pete A. Sanders Jr., take a philosophical view, drawing upon the structure of the mind/body problem. Philosophers engage this "hard problem" (Chalmers 1996) of consciousness to account for the emergence of a dynamic, conscious mind from the mechanisms of the material brain. Sanders (2005) amplifies that question with a dramatic structural displacement to explore, through meditation, the relationships between the geophysical energy of vortexes, the higher consciousness of the "soul," and the body: "most of the energy that you are as a Soul actually exists outside of the body, above and slightly behind the head area ... the Soul area that comes into the body, hooks up with the wiring, and helps us run the machine" (29). This wiring includes, according to Sanders, a "voluntary" nervous system of "muscles and physical senses" that remain "dormant" until willed into action and an "involuntary" nervous system that "is always functioning to maintain your homeostatic balances (your temperature, blood pressure, pH balance, and so on). . . . The secret to influencing the involuntary system (the control that contains the psychic/

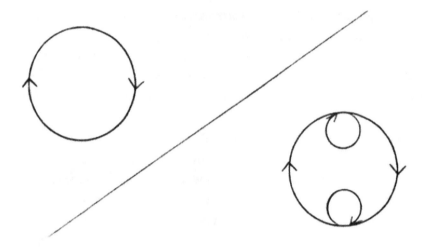

8. Sanders's voluntary nervous system. Source: Pete A. Sanders Jr., 2005. *Scientific Vortex Information: The Free Soul Method.* Sedona AZ: Free Soul, 32. Used with Permission from Pete Sanders; author of *Scientific Vortex Information.*

spiritual interface) is to nudge it into making different loops and following little-used pathways" (Sanders 2005, 33; see fig. 8).

The displaced "psychic/spiritual interface"—a connection of bodily and environmental energies activated via meditation at Sedona vortex sites—constitutes higher consciousness and notably resembles psychoanalysis's non-intentional, topological systems of the unconscious (see Blum and Secor 2011). To be fair, Jacques Lacan's (2006) analysis of the Freudian unconscious, for example, distances itself from experiences that include "the enthusiasm described by Plato, the degrees of the Samadhi in Buddhism, or the experience (*Erlebnis*) one has under the influence of hallucinogens" (673). Following Hegel, Lacan concedes that such phenomena may offer "an object of experience, in the sense of an opportunity to define certain coordinates, but in no way an ascesis that could, so to speak, be 'epistemogenic' or 'noophoric.' . . . Freud prefers the hysteric's discourse to hypnoid states" (673). And yet, the *structure* of Sanders's explanation, its emphasis on the void constituting a subject "elsewhere," however proximate, shares resonances with Lacan. It is a schema that resembles the displacement central

WOODWARD AND JONES

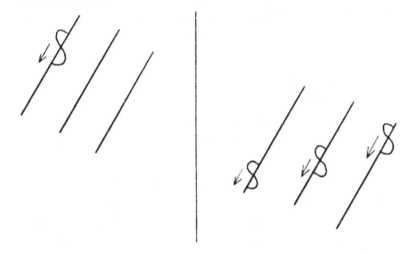

9. Sanders's involuntary nervous system. Source: Pete A. Sanders Jr., 2005. *Scientific Vortex Information: The Free Soul Method.* Sedona az: Free Soul, 33. Used with Permission from Pete Sanders; author of *Scientific Vortex Information.*

to Lacan's "I," one initiated by his fascination with Freud's self-identified "Copernican revolution": "I am thinking where I am not, therefore I am where I am not thinking . . . I think about where I am where I do not think I am thinking" (Lacan 2006, 429–30). Both Lacan and Sanders situate voids at the center of the subject, like two weird reimaginings of Freud: if Lacan famously symbolizes this by way of the "barred S" ($), Sanders seems to capture something oddly similar in the shapes of his voluntary nervous system diagram (fig. 9).

Sanders differs from Lacan where he regrounds his displacements on the energies of localizable physical landforms in Sedona: the sites of upflow and inflow vortexes. If Sanders's void resembles that of Lacan, it is Rose's critique of the "limits of the earthly" that offers a resonant "elsewhere"—one that is localized in geographic materialities. Rose (2011) recognizes that such situated displacements characterize a key signifying dimension of the cultural landscape: "material culture is built in response to a solicitation from that which withdraws: the call to build a physical place (a church, a tomb, a home) where we can hold onto that which always and inevitably eludes us" (119). Here, spatial objects serve as material remainders or sign systems that serve as bridges to the elsewhere constituted by memory or loss. Sanders and other vorticists link this to natural landforms, their energies giving rise to memory and expansiveness.

And yet there is not one, but many vorticists. For example, electrical engineer Ben Lonetree—this is not his real name—has an extensive web presence devoted to explaining vortexes and the mind/body disruptions felt there. He claims, first, to have measured a significant nondipole geomagnetism in Sedona. This is the sort of magnetic force that keeps compasses from working in Red Rock country. Second, he claims to have a scientific explanation for the sensations of spirit felt in Sedona. Specifically the geomagnetism affects our brainwaves, probably by disrupting the atmospheric patterns of extremely low-frequency Schumann Resonances. As a result one can achieve a state of creativity, transcendence, oneness, and presence that "plausibly accounts for reported psychophysical and psychosensory phenomena" (Miller and Lonetree 2017). He backs up his theory by referring to studies undertaken by neuropsychologist Michael A. Persinger (1983), who confirmed that certain stimulations resulting in electrical microseizures of brain activity can bring on "out-of-body experiences, space-time distortions, intense meaningfulness, and dreamy scenes" (1255). This led Persinger to conclude that "God is a result of electro-magnetic stimulation of the temporal lobes . . . [and that] the God Experience is synthesized" (Persinger, quoted in Miller and Lonetree 2017).

But should this sort of scientific overreach into the spiritual world give us pause? Does not the mobilization of mechanical explanation harbor the assumption that, short of such an external explanatory "apparatus" (the system of accepted truths to which such explanation appeals), Lonetree's phenomena are suspect? Writing in the journal *Ecotheology*, environmental scholar Adrian J. Ivakhiv (2003b) says: "It is not difficult to bring in a 'hermeneutic of suspicion' to the study of contemporary Earth spirituality, all the more so since in its popular New Age variant this kind of spirituality is predominantly an activity of middle-class Westerners with the leisure time and wallets that allow them to follow their spiritual desires to some of the more evocative landscapes on the planet" (Ivakhiv 2003b, 16).

He offers a list of valid reasons—each organized around their own void— why we should be suspicious: a commodified spiritualism, the erosion of critical thinking, a nostalgia for nature fueled by environmentalism, skepticism over the promise of scientific rationality, a loss of faith in social institutions (Ivakhiv 2003b, 16–17). But Ivakhiv urges us nevertheless to remain open to what Heidegger called the "unconcealed." Arguing for a middle ground, he writes that "adequately understanding . . . sacred land-scapes . . . requires *both* a hermeneutics of suspicion *and* a hermeneutics of faith" (Ivakhiv 2003b, 25; emphasis in the original). Julian Holloway (2006) urges us along a similar path. In his paper on enchanted spaces, he distinguishes between those who would read séances as a response to secularization of culture and politics and those who would understand their affectivities as conveying some spiritual truth. Between these is a nonreductionist middle ground that "does not deny either the 'reality' of spirits or sensations of the sacred for believers, or the 'reality' of how such sensations inform normative identities, societal discourses, or insti-tutions" (186).

But Lonetree is not a spiritualist. He is an engineer, and he is not giving us a middle ground between science and spirit. Again Lacan—and, by extension, Derrida—helpfully suggests that understanding the circuitry of Lonetree's measurements demands that we remain attuned to the trace of a scientific Other, rather than a spiritual Other. Lacan (2015) builds his lectures on transference—the lectures in which he lays out a description of the subjects of lack—around the notion that "love is giving what you don't have" (34).[8] In another moment of void-frenzied displacement, he explains: "It is insofar as the function of . . . the person who loves, as a lacking subject, comes to take the place of, or is substituted for, the function of . . . the loved object, that the signification of love is produced" (40). The object that Lonetree seeks to explain shares this structure: it is an Other that invades science on its own terms, and with all manner of uncertainty, mystery, and other-dimensionality. It is an Other that resists the category of the scientifically fixed, determined, and possibly damned. It is a science unsettled and unsettling. On this point Lonetree might well be a Sedona version of a Fortean geography (see Dixon 2007). If Ivakhiv and Holloway ask us to negotiate the sacred on its own terms by suspending judgment—by suspending suspicion—perhaps Lonetree's explanation, based as it is on physics and neuroscience, tells us something altogether different: be suspicious of suspicion, for it scrutinizes an abyss of its own.

Vorticism: Excesses of an Energetic Earth

Sedona is the gravitational center around which circle countless vorticists, all subjects of disparate discourses: pilgrims, tour guides, teachers, mystics, capitalists, wanderers, artists, seekers, and visionaries swirl, each with their own histories, encounters and explanations, voids and displacements. Some are visitors keen to settle debates about the nature and discernibility of Sedona's energy flows; others come to amplify an ethics of peace and openness. In any case few shy away from making appeals to broader geological and metaphysical systems, linking material or spiritual components to the space and its purported energy flows, many spilling out to enfold other "paranormal" categories of religious and/or spiritual beliefs, astrology, the occult, ghosts, and UFOs. More generally, these phenomena may be described as "earth mysteries" (Ivakhiv 2005)—that is, as geographical and geophysical phenomena at which, it is speculated, the earth demonstrates more than the usual amount of energy and power over life. In a long arc connecting ancient Mediterranean geomancy and Chinese *feng shui*, Sedona's vortexes are sometimes connected to the more modern concept of "ley lines," attributed to the English amateur archaeologist Alfred Watkins, who wrote in the 1920s. He proposed that ancient commercial trackways were developed by Neolithic peoples as aids to navigating the countryside. These "old straight tracks" connected significant natural features, such as ridgetops, with human-made ones, such as megaliths. Like the paranormal crop circles studied by Paul Kingsbury (2019), earth mysteries often take a broad view on linking multiple geophysical and the metaphysical/spiritual traditions.

Today most New Age sources cite the New Age lecturer, writer, and spiritual *bricoleur* Page Bryant (1943–2017) as an early intellectual/spiritual authority on Sedona vortexes (see Bryant 1983, 1991). Her work first appeared on a famous cassette tape circulated in the early 1980s and then more widely disseminated in *The Earth Changes Survival Handbook* (1983). If the book is typical of its genera with respect to hybrid spiritualism, it also is fascinating for its geographic focus, frequently reading like a *New Age Introduction to Spatial Theory*:

> We wish to discern the difference between a vortex and a grid. A grid is a "pattern" of energy, whereas a vortex is a pattern of energy that has coagulated into a funnel of power. It would be correct to say that the entire Earth is an energy pattern of one form or another. Many people are aware of the grid systems. A grid indicates an area, in our use of the term, that is highly charged, but has not enough energy to actually coagulate into a vortex. As sensitive people pass through such an area, they feel its influence . . .
>
> If you imagine a weather radar screen, you will see the various weather patterns and fronts and formations, as "blotches" of activity. Some of these patterns will be circular in motion, while others will spread out over great distances. Not all will form into actual organized systems (vortex) but will remain to be seen only as concentrated areas of weather activity (grid). Such a grid is the entire Rocky Mountain range. (Bryant 1983, 128)

On the one hand, she offers a geography of energy vortexes, which form a grid of ley lines across the surface of the earth. This form of "energy" seems to read much like the vitalist treatments popular among vorticists such as Sanders, above: an "actual electrical vortex . . . is a powerful vitalizer for life forms. It . . . spews out prana. All life forms can draw energy from its effects" (Bryant 1983, 128). On the other hand, there are magnetic vortices, only one of which, according to Bryant, is located in Sedona—at Red Rock Crossing, with Oak Creek as "its source of magnetism" (Bryant

1991, 13). This system of energy/magnetism (vortexes, lines, grid) is essentially geographical and geological: mapping energetic geometry onto the key landforms (major natural landmarks, but also geophysical forms in the abstract—waterfalls, etc.) plausibly accounts for reported psychophysical and psychosensory phenomena. Bryant (1991) even goes so far as to introduce her own account of geological-metaphysical processes: "part of the Rockies known as the Grand Tetons . . . came very close to forming itself into a full-blown vortex, but did not have enough power" (128). This geological/geographic focus offers a key distinction from the void-centered approaches of the *vorticists*, above. Here, Bryant seems to offer not a system based upon lack, but one that maps the material, energetic fullness of the earth: a *vorticism*.

Vorticism has a genealogy reaching back, at least, to claims by some pre-Socratic thinkers—such as Empedocles (Aristotle 1984, bk. 2, pt. 13–14)—that the movement of celestial bodies was caused by swirling, substantial vortexes (or "whirl") in the heavens. Much later, Descartes, in seeking to describe the totality of the universe as part of one, divine substance, would offer a similar argument, claiming that even the extensive space between bodies was filled with whirling, vortical substance: "Descartes' vortex theory had strived to explain the orbits of the planets by situating them (at rest) in large circling bands of minute material particles, which consist of either the atom-sized, globules (secondary matter) or the 'indefinitely' small debris (primary matter) left over from impact and fracture of the larger elements (with tertiary matter comprising the largest, macroscopic material element . . .)" (Slowik 2005, 1317; see fig. 10). While this movement allowed Descartes to explain planetary rotation, the introduction of swirling substance throughout all space (indeed, *as space*; Descartes 1905, 44) also served to reinforce his equation of God with substance. That is, in Cartesian (and Spinozist) thought, extended substance is theorized as part of an ontological proof for the existence of God and a refutation and rejection of the void.[9] Descartes offers the notion of a vortex of material, substantial forces (much the same is seen in web-based representations of Sedona sites) as an effort to account for movement *against* atomistic views of movement in a void (such as Epicurus's famous "swerve"). Perhaps it is not coincidental that Bryant's vortex-line-grid system so closely resembles the point-line-plane system of Cartesian abstract space, as she aligns herself with a similar vortical substantialism: "If we consider empty space/time as the vehicle for matter, we must realize that it is empty only in the sense that particles have not yet coagulated. Thoughts of Divine Will, along with gravity, brings these atoms through their evolutionary processes to their present state. These are the building blocks of creation. The 'groups' of atoms form every single body of matter, no matter what shape or form it takes, be it a human, a tree, a star or a galaxy" (Bryant 1983, 54–55).

With this, we find ourselves drawn and repulsed by two apparently contrary metaphysical and geological forces, stuck in a weird tension between Sedona's void-riddled vorticists and the cosmically excessive substance of vorticism. How to square the circle—or better, how to render the circle a spiral, or vice versa? One possible solution is indicated by Lacan's analysis of the Freudian unconscious. There one finds that he is obsessed with Freud's claim (in the spirit of Kant's 'critical' turn) that his system offers a "Copernican revolution" for thinking about consciousness (Lacan 2006, 334, 439, 674). Freud seemed to be suggesting a turn to human subjectivity as the center of a psychic universe. But by reframing this in terms of displacement, a Cosmic Lacan throws us back into the heavens. If we follow that path, and with a closer look at Descartes's heavenly vortical map (fig. 11), we discover at its center perhaps not quite what Lacan intended for us to find, but something that shares perverse affinities with the barred S of Lacan's displaced subject. In the place of that $\$$, we discover an encircled S, crossed through (though not entirely!) with dotted lines (rather than a solid bar), suggesting the perpetual vortical movement of substance: S. Rather than being subverted, this S is enrolled. Rather than being displaced, it becomes indiscernible from its own movement. If it is not quite barred, neither is it quite there. In Descartes's accidental signifier, we discover a site that orients metaphysics and geophysics, not as a tension, but as a system of composition: "Meta/geophysics."[10]

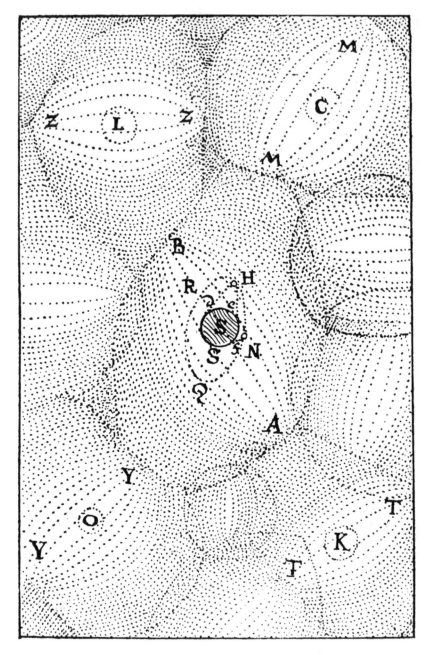

10. Cartesian vortices. Source: René Descartes, 1905. *Principia Philosophiæ.* In *Oeuvres de Descartes, vol. vii, part 1.* Paris: Adam & Tannery, p. 136.

11. Descartes's dotted subject. *Detail*, Descartes's Vortices (center closeup of figure 10). Source: René Descartes. 1905. *Principia Philosophiæ*. In *Oeuvres de Descartes*, vol. 7, part 1. Paris: Adam & Tannery, 136.

Meta/Geophysics

In the popular early 2000s video game *Katamari Damacy* (塊魂: "clump soul"), a diminutive prince is tasked with rebuilding the universe after his father, The King of All Cosmos, destroys all the stars in the universe while on a drunken bender. The prince is equipped with only a tiny, sticky ball (katamari), which he rolls around various spaces, first picking up small items (spiders, thumbtacks), but gradually picking up larger and larger objects (watermelons, park benches, cars, buildings, whales . . .) as the katamari grows. Eventually, this rolling clump of objects grows large enough that it can be gifted to The King of All Cosmos, who in turn sends it to the heavens, where it replaces a lost constellation. Thus, by continuously rolling balls of matter and transforming them into stars, the universe is rebuilt. So, too, it goes for vorticism. Continuously churning matter, rolling, sometimes turning in on itself, sometimes exploding outward, always moving, circulating, building.

Must we distinguish between the vorticist's displaced desire and vorticism's swirling substance? When we think these impossible things together (holding in suspension, for a moment, the principle of noncontradiction), we arrive at a system in which the subject is subject to voids but is *not* barred from the real: Lacan's $ becomes Descartes's S (see fig. 11).[11] Not barred, but dotted—marked, peopled, and constituted by vortical energetic movements. In the end is one substance, meaning that its situatedness makes the difference in what the S signifies; whether it is "Sun" (Descartes), "Substance" (Spinoza), "Subject" (Lacan), or "Sedona" (Bryant), it is always "Site" (Woodward, Jones, and Marston 2012). Can we then go further and propose that Sedona's gravitational power (S) harbors—or simply *is*—an excessive communist force? We want to. For all its posited substantiality, the vortex that is Sedona *qua* site is a specific kind of void, one that *adsorbs* (rather than contains) the always-arriving, contradictory accounts. The surfaces of its moving folds are populated and repopulated by continuous arrivals and departures of pilgrims, visionaries, fraudsters, and feelers. Like Lacan's subject of lack, it is the vortex itself, subject to this endless series of seekers, always incomplete and yet, like the prince's katamari, always turning, always a surface, always gathering.

Notes

We are grateful to Katie Meehan of King's College for her invaluable assistance in this research, and to Deborah Dixon of the University of Glasgow for her comments.

1. Following local custom, we use "vortexes" instead of "vortices."
2. Mann's review of the complicated archaeological record around Sedona rejects this oft-cited claim by locals.
3. See Ward Churchill's (1996) criticisms of New Age and conservative-masculinist appropriations of Indigenous cultural practice in his "Spiritual Hucksterism" and "Indians 'R' Us" essays. The former essay offers a critique of the "plastic medicine men"—including Vincent LaDuke (or, "Sun Bear"), who was a spiritual teacher of Page Bryant, arguably *the* key thinker and earliest writer on the Sedona vortexes.
4. The first "Hollywood film" shot in Sedona was a silent western, *The Call of the Canyon* (1923), based on the book by Zane Grey, who oversaw its artistic production. See McNeill (2010).
5. A male guide professed to be a devotee of QiGong and instructed us in its basics while encouraging us to join the QiGong Revolution.
6. Adrian Ivakhiv has written extensively on Sedona's landscape and its New Age visitors (see Ivakhiv 2001, 2003a, 2003b, 2005, 2007).
7. One guide, for example, offered a fourfold geophysical explanation of Sedona's "sacred sites": (a) a high concentration of mineral ores, and specifically quartz crystals, which magnify energy; (b) the widespread presence of underground lava flows; (c) seismic

activity; and (d) an abundance of subsurface water in the form of underground springs and aquifers.

8. Himself a crypto-vortical thinker, Jacques Lacan continues: "You will . . . see this in one of the essential *spirals* of what we encounter in our commentary" (Lacan 2015, 34; emphasis mine).

9. Spinoza's arguments for God/Nature as a corporeal substance move against the view of substance as composite (known as the "vacuum arguments"). For a substantial discussion of Spinoza's response to the vacuum arguments see Robinson (2009).

10. See the title conference that was the source of Alsgoud Sprinke's 1982 paper on Sedona vortexes (Sprinke 1991).

11. We are moving backward in time at this point. Just as Karatani (2005) does in his reading of Marx and Kant, we need Lacan's analysis to make sense of Descartes's meta/geophysics. Some will complain that this is ahistorical. Perhaps it is just the tachyons talking, but we are fine with this.

References

Andres, Dennis. 2000. *What Is a Vortex? A Practical Guide to Sedona's Vortex Sites.* Sedona AZ: Meta Adventures.

Aristotle. 1984. *On the Heavens.* In *The Complete Works of Aristotle*, vol. 1, edited by Johnathan Barnes, translated by J. L. Stocks, 445–511. Princeton NJ: Princeton University Press.

Blum, Virginia, and Anna Secor. 2011. "Psychotopologies: Closing the Circuit between Psychic and Material Space." *Environment and Planning D: Society and Space* 29, no. 6: 1030–47.

Bryant, Page. 1983. *The Earth Changes Survival Handbook.* Santa Fe NM: Santa Fe Books.

———. 1991. "Sacred Sedona." In *Sedona Vortex Guide Book*, edited by Robert Shapiro and Janet McClure, 3–15. Flagstaff AZ: Light Technology.

Chalmers, David J. 1996. *The Conscious Mind: In Search of a Theory of Conscious Experience.* New York: Oxford University Press.

Churchill, Ward. 1996. *From a Native Son: Selected Essays on Indigenism, 1985–1995.* Boston: South End Press.

Descartes, René. 1905. *Principia Philosophiæ.* In *Oeuvres de Descartes*, vol. 7, part 1. Paris: Adam & Tannery.

Digance, Justine. 2006. "Religions and Secular Pilgrimage: Journeys Redolent with Meaning." In *Tourism, Religion & Spiritual Journeys*, edited by Dallen J. Timothy and Daniel H. Olsen, 36–48. London: Routledge.

Dixon, Deborah P. 2007. "A Benevolent and Sceptical Inquiry: Exploring 'Fortean Geographies' with the Mothman." *cultural geographies* 14, no. 2: 189–210.

Dixon, Deborah P., Harriet Hawkins, and Elizabeth R. Straughan. 2013. "Wonder-full Geomorphology: Sublime Aesthetics and the Place of Art." *Progress in Physical Geography* 37, no. 2: 227–47.

Holloway, Julian. 2006. "Enchanted Spaces: The Séance, Affect, and Geographies of Religion." *Annals of the Association of American Geographers* 96, no. 1: 182–87.

Ivakhiv, Adrian J. 2001. *Claiming Sacred Ground: Pilgrims and Politics at Glastonbury and Sedona.* Bloomington: Indiana University Press.

—— 2003a. "Nature and Self in New Age Pilgrimage." *Culture and Religion* 4, no. 1: 93–118.

——. 2003b. "Orchestrating Sacred Space: Beyond the 'Social Construction' of Nature." *Ecotheology* 8, no. 1: 11–29.

——. 2005. "Earth Mysteries." In *Encyclopedia of Religion and Nature*, edited by Bron Taylor, 525–28. London: Continuum.

——. 2007. "Power Trips: Making Sacred Space through New Age Pilgrimage." In *Handbook of New Age*, edited by James R. Lewis and Daren Kemp, 263–86. Leiden, The Netherlands: Brill.

Karatani, Kojin. 2005. *Transcritique: On Kant and Marx.* Translated by Sabu Kohso. Cambridge MA: MIT Press.

Katamari Damacy. 2004. Namco.

Kingsbury, Paul. 2019. "Go Figural: Crop Circle Research and the Extraordinary Rifts of Landscape." *cultural geographies* 26, no. 1: 3–22.

Lacan, Jacques. 2006. "The Subversion of the Subject and the Dialectic of Desire in the Freudian Unconscious." In *Écrits*, translated by Bruce Fink, 671–702. New York: W. W. Norton.

——. 2015. *The Seminar of Jacques Lacan, Book VIII: Transference.* Edited by Jacques-Alain Miller. Translated by Bruce Fink. Malden MA: Polity Press.

Mann, Nicholas R. 2004. *Sacred Earth: A Guide to the Red Rock Country.* Rev. ed. Flagstaff AZ: Light Technology.

McNeill, Joe. 2010. *Arizona's Little Hollywood: Sedona and Northern Arizona's Forgotten Film History, 1923–1973.* Sedona AZ: Sedona Monthly Books.

Miller, Iona, and Ben Lonetree. 2017. "The Sedona Effect: Earth Energies, Schumann Resonance & Brainwave Resonance." *Sedonanomalies* (Lonetree). https://www.sedonanomalies.com/ (accessed September 17, 2019).

Persinger, Michael A. 1983. "Religious and Mystical Experiences as Artifacts of Temporal Lobe Function: A General Hypothesis." *Perceptual and Motor Skills* 57, no. 3s: 1255–62.

Pynchon, Thomas. 1997. *Mason & Dixon.* New York: Henry Holt.

Robinson, Thaddeus S. 2009. "Spinoza on the Vacuum and the Simplicity of Corporeal Substance." *History of Philosophy Quarterly* 26, no. 1: 63–81.

Rose, Mitch. 2011. "Secular Materialism: A Critique of Earthly Theory." *Journal of Material Culture* 16, no. 2: 107–29.

Sanders, Pete A., Jr. 2005. *Scientific Vortex Information: The Free Soul Method*. Sedona AZ: Free Soul.

Slowik, Edward. 2005. "On the Cartesian Ontology of General Relativity: or, Conventionalism in the History of the Substantival-Relational Debate." *Philosophy of Science* 72, no. 5: 1312–23.

Sprinke, Alsgoud. 1991. "An Overview of the Geophysical Aspects of Vortexes." In *Sedona Vortex Guide Book*, edited by Robert Shapiro and Janet McClure, 195–201. Flagstaff AZ: Light Technology.

Tierra, Cynthia. 2008. *Sedona Vortexes: A Guidebook for the Spiritual Traveler*. Sedona AZ: Healing from the Heart.

Willems-Braun, Bruce. 1997. "Buried Epistemologies: The Politics of Nature in (Post)colonial British Columbia." *Annals of the Association of American Geographers* 87, no. 1: 3–31.

Wolfteich, Claire. 2009. "Animating Questions: Spirituality and Practical Theology." *International Journal of Practical Theology* 13, no. 1: 121–43.

Woodward, Keith. 2016. "The Speculative Geography of Orson Welles." *cultural geographies* 23, no. 2: 337–56.

Woodward, Keith, John Paul Jones III, and Sallie A. Marston. 2012. "The Politics of Autonomous Space." *Progress in Human Geography* 36, no. 2: 204–24.

4   Six Voids

Flora Parrott and Harriet Hawkins

One

The sensor picks up the movement of the bodies in space, and the imposing shatterproof glass doors slide open. The new space pours into the old. We walk out of the first hotel into the soundscape of the shopping center beyond, background music, chattering, announcements over a Tannoy speaker in a blended accent.

The air has the quality of any sealed and regulated space; there is a flow of movement down the arteries between the shops and cafés. We are walking against the main current of people and struggling to keep up with the fast-paced certainty of the rhythm.

The shops have bright and sanitary facades and interiors. Clean and organized with rows of similar products. There are deals, chains, rewards, and loyalty points that could be transferred and picked up in any such mall across the globe.

We stop at a Fedex (*sic*) outlet "Shipping Services Without Borders."
"Hello, where would you like to ship to? Or are you collecting?"
"Oh, sorry, no. I just wanted to buy some fixings. I'm not shipping to anywhere."
We pick up tape, string, and flimsy-looking suction pads and pay.

One incorrect pathway, a no entry sign, an escalator that took us up to an office rather than to a throughway. We cross the road via a glass tube with a slight incline. The glass cuts out any sound from the traffic below.

Back into another hotel lobby. The light from the glass tube is deadened and the shopping center soundscape returns. The same shops but with different staff in the branded polo shirts. The familiarity is disorienting, and the conditioned air left our heads lacking in precision.

Down to the basement of the hotel and into a corridor with light terracotta paint on the walls and plant arrangements that complimented the color; the plants could have been real or plastic. We stopped at the water cooler and drank some water from the thin plastic cups that collapse in the grip of the hand. A bubble rises up in the center of the hard-plastic water container.

Finally, we enter the conference room. There was no natural light and a surface to the walls that meant the flimsy suction pads slid off in seconds. The space was impenetrable. We tried piling the chairs, roll of gaffer tape binding things together, dimming the lights . . . but the smooth slickness of the room rejected our every attempt at interruption.

The conceived idea was to make a void. A void to add to our list of voids. A text would be read out within the gap made in the room in an atmospheric intervention. Can you make a void? Add a void? The endeavor was to use flat surfaces to create a sense of intense and infinite depth. An optical illusion using pictures and the black hole in the smartphones that so many of us carry around. Tipping in and digging out data from a five-inch piece of glass.

The components of the talk were as follows:

A reading outlining three other voids.
An overhead camera link filming and projecting the speaker from above.
A mirror approximately laptop-screen sized.
A four-by-three-meter piece of printed fabric with images of:
    (a) hands reaching into plastic bags over water,
    (b) an entrance way to an artificial cave made from fiberglass and hired
        from the British Caving Association.
Use of the audience's smartphones switched on to camera selfie mode.

The following instructions were given:

(1) Turn on your phone

(2) Switch on the camera and turn it to selfie mode

(3) Place the phone on your lap

(4) A mirror will be passed around the room. Put it on your lap underneath the phone

(5) Keep it for thirty seconds, count it down in your head

(6) Pass it on

The idea was to make a dark and vertiginous space, a space in which the viewer was watching several images at once. A flattening out, a reproduction of the already immaterial, of the once material. A shift away from the authentic until it is hard to remember where the starting point was.

A moment in a mirrored lift or in the seat of a hairdresser when the front and back of your head duplicate and stretch back into infinity.

There is a painting by surrealist artist René Magritte called *The Human Condition*, painted in 1935. A canvas within a cave, painted on a canvas. Magritte said of the painting that he was trying to remove "the difference between a view seen from outside a room from that seen from the inside" (quote from the caption in the Norwich Art Gallery, Parrott's field notes, March 2017).

A thin information panel next to the painting in the Norwich Castle Museum and Art Gallery poses the following: "Our mind is tricked into thinking that Magritte's cave and landscape are real and the painting on the easel is a representation of the landscape behind. In reality, both the actual painting and the painting within it are artistic creations and invite the question, what does 'real' mean?" (Parrott's field notes, Norwich Art Gallery, March 2017).

Audiences are intrigued to know what lies behind the canvas at the center of the painted cave, on the thin painted "real" canvas. Recently it was discovered that the painting has a secret layer. An X-ray revealed another image, a quarter of a canvas with an entirely different composition underneath it. Painted over, painted over.

All this information, all of this depth and time. These bottomless pits of information, lying on a flat piece of fabric less than a millimeter in depth.

So we tried to stretch out the fabric and to generate a void in the thin surfaces sandwiching it together.

But the conference room was already the void. A nonstick, Teflon space.

We could not pull the thing tight, could not get the tension. There was not the air density to pull against.

The door of the conference room opened again; it could have been any time of the day or night. The air rushed out and filled the pale terracotta hallway.

Two

The word *cave* "carries a heavy load"; there is apparently no clear answer to the question "what is a cave?" Scientific response "defines a cave as a natural void beneath the land surface that is large enough to admit humans" (Crane and Fletcher 2015, 5). Subterranean cavities with no way in or out, or vugs, with no opening to the surface, are not caves; "voids hollowed out of the earth by humans are not caves" (5). Perhaps most importantly a hole or fissure too small to admit a human body is not a cave. Caves are, in short, always defined and depicted in relation to humans. Yet caves humble and overwhelm human beings (Devereux 2000). "Suited up against the cold, dripping cave, we rustle as we move, awkward in our 'kit' we apprehensively peer into the dinge ahead. Our guide suddenly turns, 'down here' he says and vanishes feet first through the floor" (Parrott's field notes, May 2016).

Science's equivalence of cave and void is premised on emptiness, yet our encounters with the spatialities of caves, whether our own discomforting wriggles and wrenches or the evocative accounts of others, find caves less as empty spaces awaiting filling (by human bodies or otherwise) than to be positive generative presences.

In both scientific and nonscientific language, the lexicon of cave description is fundamentally dependent on the vocabulary of human life on the surface, and not only because caves are defined by the dimensions of the human body. Cave openings are "gaping mouths" in the dark gullets of the earth or ruptures in the planet's skin that lead to the bowels of the earth (Crane and Fletcher 2015, 6). The vocabulary of caves renders plain the failures of language to grasp the deep, dark places of the earth.

Writing voids, writing into voids, attempting to express spatial emptiness often ends up performing a kind of linguistic generativeness. Robert Macfarlene (2013) experiments in the karst limestone of northern England:

> I was in the crabwalk for perhaps three hours including the retreat. It is a space so extraordinary that common language serves barely even to sketch it.
>
> It is between sixty and a hundred feet high and between three feet and eight inches wide.
>
> Its sides billow out and dip in. It twists and turns.
>
> No, those verbs fall hopelessly short of its tortuousness.
>
> It chicanes, it hairpins, it ogees, it sines, it spindles, it intestines, it volutes. No one could enter it and preserve their sense of orientation.
>
> If you somehow filled it with concrete and then cut away the land that surrounds it, you would be left with a vast umbilicus, or flattened unicorn's horn dipping and coiling its way lower and lower. Each new curve emerges from its predecessor rather as pleat might be shaken from pleat in the unfurling of a cloth, or turn is born always away from turn in the course of a stream.
>
> Navigating the crab walk has aspects of both the rebus and the assault course.
>
> Despite its name it is not something along which you walk. I dipped, squashed, curved, udged (a caver's verb) and poured myself down it, always leading with a shoulder, clothes rasping against the limestone, feet in the rushing stream, head clashing off knoll and billow, body flattened and scraped by the stone's own forms.
>
> . . .
>
> I had expected language to be diminished by the data depleted darkness of the underland and its curtailed cognitive spaces, but instead it flowed and flowered, and I wanted new words for this new world, a liquid language for a liquid landscape and sounds and syllables began to meld into one another, forming ruchey new cocklings and portmanteau meltings-riff-raffs and spealeotrophes or folding out and back onto one another (re-plying, multi-plying) or the rift was a Möbius strip gone mad, and travelling it was like pushing through the voluptuous interior of a theatre curtain. It was a headlong whole body plummet that I did not want to end, but then the vice stopped us dead. (Macfarlane 2013, n.p.)

Three

> Brownie was thoroughly intrigued by the crevasse. As he examined the walls of the grotto, he suddenly came on an opening behind the tapestries of ice crystals. A chasm beyond was hung with immense icicles. Through these he hacked a way, and, shattering more ice curtains, disclosed a long narrow passage, winding its way into darkness. The floor consisted of ice blocks, which must have been wedged many years ago. Every few yards there were tiny gaps; one of these Brownie enlarged and squeezed through to a platform below.
>
> Underneath there was a gloomy hollow which might be depthless; the feeble flicker of his candle caused great shadows to whirl across the walls. Secured by the Alpine Rope he began to climb into the blackness, descending step by step until when about 20 feet below the platform, he suddenly heard a splash of ice chips falling into water below. (Glen 1937, 132)

We take this description and others from the accounts of an Oxford University Arctic expedition in 1936, and we assemble newspaper, foil, plastic bags. Abandoning tables and chairs, we cover the floor in white paper.

"Step into the unknown" we invite, "sit on the floor if you want"; nervous geographers wriggle and sit tentatively on the paper, not yet ready to remove their shoes.

We work this time in a seminar room in a Victorian building in central London. Not such a featureless void as that first conference room, recently refurbished, a contemporary chandelier (on a dimmer switch) hangs from the ceiling. The walls are a tasteful off-white, the desks foldable and stackable. The chilly November air snakes in from the open bay window.

Standing on the paper-covered carpet with socked feet, tentatively at first, eventually gaining momentum, people begin to create, testing the possibilities of newspaper and plastic, exploring the capacities of foil, crafting assemblages of stacking chairs and folded paper. Laughter fills the air, everyone is crawling around on the floor, shoes and suit jackets have been abandoned to the edges.

They work from descriptions; making ice and rock, sculpting voids from the descriptions formed from empirical accounts of an earlier century. Yet, the structures we compose from ordinary bits and bobs cannot be voids, they feel too material, too present, too full. But yet artist Anish Kapoor (1990) noted, "the void is not something which has no utterance. It is a potential space, not a non-space" (45). The void emerges here as hopeful, a shared space full of possibilities, a space in which creativity is born: "A branchless fir-tree had at some time fallen into the pit, and now lay in partial contact with the ruined ladder . . . on the side opposite to the ladder I saw an arch at the foot of the rock, apparently 2 or 3 feet high, leading from the snow into the darkness" (Browne 1865, 6).

Chairs are piled on tables, former heads of department climb precarious furniture assemblages to string paper from light fittings to create the pit, flimsy ladders are constructed from tubes and foil, drifts of tissue accumulate in the tunnels created from boxes and white paper.

Ungrounded by these descriptions and their missing elements, and by the tools we are given to make sense of the world, we narrated how we sculpted these landforms. How we rendered cavernous forms out of the front pages of the *Financial Times* and an upturned table, how drifts of snow emerged from torn up Sunday supplements and the billows of supermarket shopping bags and how curtains of icicles are strung sparkling from plastic wrap and bungee cord, kitchen foil and lattices of cotton.

When we are done making our caves, we instruct our audiences in how to move through these spaces; following written notes and called-out commands we knelt down and crawled in, shimmed on stomachs over the carpet, squeezed around tables and into paper chutes to gaze up at light fittings.

We read our descriptions back, we narrate how we filled in their gaps, how we summoned up katabatic topographies from everyday things, how we tried to make material sense of their linguistic voids.

Four

The artificial cave is available for hire from the British Caving Association; it is necessary to put down a deposit in the form of a check, and to collect the sections in a horse box from the Midlands; you need a four-by-four to tow the box. The artificial cave comes in ten sections, each approximately a four-foot length of tube with an end section of a diameter of one and half feet.

Each of the sections has a hexagonal rim around either end; the rims can be bolted together, meaning that the tube can be combined in a number of sequences. Modular. Infinite. The outside of tube is black fiberglass, painted matte. It is worn in patches that often touch the floor, and in those patches the structural chicken wire has been exposed.

The interior is ice blue in parts and pea green in others. The sorts of colors one might use if painting a glacier for the set of a play. The material is smooth and warm to the touch. The sections are relatively difficult to join together; the twists and turns in the tubing mean that the levels and tension points are uneven. The loads need to be leveled in some areas with bits of wooden plank and scaffolding pipe support structures; all of this is provided in the horse box.

Once a decision has been made about the temporary arrangement of this particular incarnation of the tubes, they are ready for use. The once empty room is now broken up by the tubing; a calm space with nothing in it is now a mess of twists and turns and complexity. A totally new, separate shape carved out in the air with fiberglass edges. More surface area, more hole. The artificial cave has been designed and made for the purpose of encouraging those who are considering trying caving or those training to be a caver. It is often used by youth groups and can encourage users to overcome fears of being underground and of becoming stuck. It looks a lot like a water slide or flume and takes on the heat of the body as the body moves through it. It is likely that it would become extremely hot and sweaty, perhaps even slide-y, if used by a large group of children.

In most ways it is entirely unlike the experience of caving. It is about the squeezing through rather than the being within the rock. Rather than the sense of being immersed in a vast time scape of rock face there is an awareness of the space outside of the fiberglass tube, a sense of the person standing outside with the tube at waist height as the person on the inside contorts their body within.

The artificial cave is an experience in itself. Should a person experience the artificial cave before any other "real" caving, perhaps that person would imagine the earth's internal structure to be like these pale-green-colored fiberglass tubes.

Moving the body through the artificial cave is an authentic experience in itself. It is a copy so far removed from the original that it has its own "aura." Admittedly not the aura or the majesty of deep rock, but the aura of an object that can be conjured up and twist and turn and fill a space, be filled with bodies: "the authenticity of a thing is the essence of all that is transmissible from its beginning, ranging from its substantive duration to its testimony to the history which it has experienced" (Benjamin 1935).

Before the artificial cave is unbolted and packed back into the horse box, the room left empty, it is photographed. The photographs now exist on a laptop and on a number of platforms on the internet, and they can be printed and arranged at a moment's notice.

Five

With the London building known as the Shard framed through a window behind us, we lay out the black painted circles and ovoid forms on the floor. About two feet in diameter, these paper voids provide the backdrop for the creation of caves.

We assemble blocks of wood, clay, drawing materials, more foil. Create a cave, we say; what is a cave? they answer. We talk about snow caves lived in by queens in Narnia; we talk about the caves lived in by bears on the popular television program *Going on a Bear Hunt*. They begin.

The descriptions we gave them to work with might summon up voids, but the work made in the gallery space is very messy and material, very unvoid like.

They traipsed into our space after journeying through a gallery space once compellingly described as "one of the greatest voids in contemporary architecture." Large, cavernous spaces and open stairways sculpted from the abandoned architectures of industry. On their way up to our glass box suspended above the rooftops they would have walked past photographic works that see artists "leap into the void," apparently defying gravity over a Paris street.[1] They would have, perhaps, crossed the now empty site of an installation that asked its audience to enter a large unlit chamber and navigate the space in the dark.[2] They would have passed in front of and maybe mused a while over a series of repeating bowl-shaped fiberglass forms that protrude from the wall into the gallery, their forms describing a recess in space, cupping space, treating, as the artist suggests (in the title for a work of art) "space as an object" (Kapoor 1990).

The art gallery, the Tate Modern, is full of voids, yet the caves that were made in that wood-floored, glass-walled studio space worked with other voids than these abstract, dark black spaces of emptiness, challenges to nothingness. The caves created here had beds, had ice crystal decorations, were cozy spaces for animal friends, were sites of fire and mysticism, and locations for parties. Their creative spaces were sites of connection, new friends were made, cross-generational discussions were had, grandmas were instructed in detail on how to make dinner for the bear or how to cut leaves from newspaper for a bed.

Beginning from descriptions of voids in underground ice, these London caves, these inner-city rocky sanctums, were the site for social relations, for discussions about where it is that we encounter "the wild" in our urban spaces; how it is that we think about subterranean sites, unruly "natural" spaces from such lofty perches.

Six

Below is not anywhere you like, but where heavy and earthy things move.

The myth of the cave is a good place to start or to end.

Read it as a metaphor of the inner space, of the den, the room, or history.

The stage is set. Plato, in the *Republic*, tells us that Socrates tells us that humans, sex unspecified, live underground in a dwelling, a dwelling formed like a cave.

Ground, dwelling, cave, womb—as Luce Irigaray (1985) would have us believe.

The entrance to the cave takes the form of a long passage, corridor, no, a conduit, leading upward, toward the light or the sight of day, and the whole of the cave is oriented in relation to this opening.

Upward. This notation indicates from the very start that the Platonic cave functions as an attempt to give an orientation to that which is there in the cave, a moving upward toward the light, toward enlightenment, toward knowing that is only reached through the abandonment of that cave.

So, humans have lived in this cave since childhood. Since time began. They have never left the cave. They are fixed facing front, which in Plato's telling is the direction toward the back of the cave. And the only thing they can still do is to look at whatever presents itself before their eye. Paralyzed, unable to turn round, they are condemned to look ahead at the wall opposite toward the back wall of the cave. They have been given a light however. It comes from the fire burning at a distance, behind and above them. A light indeed, but artificial and earthly. A weak light, and one that offers the eyes far from ideal conditions to see and be seen.

There is a parade of shapes in front of the light, and this is what these humans know. This is all they know. This is their truth. That is until they are dragged, out of that womb, out of their darkness, up the corridor, conduit, passage, and blinking out into the sun beyond, then they know, then they are brought into the light.

Or so Plato would have us believe of these imaginary caves, caves modeled on the Quarry Grottos of Syracuse or maybe the caves of Mt. Hymettus near Athens, which Plato would have visited (Wright 1906).

Irigaray (1985), in her morphological rereading of this most masculine of cave tales, would have us parse this as a story of privileged knowledge forms, as we are directed to ways of knowing and indeed not knowing associated with these dark, earthy, embodied places and their bodily morphologics, and as these became abandoned for the blinding light of reason.

But others have focused on caves less as sites of ignorance than as locations of gifts. Descent into darkness for a range of cultures is a route to enlightenment, dwelling underground offers the means to acquire knowledge and passage through underground tunnels as a route to divine truth (Ustinova 2009).

Knowing the cave from within or knowing it from without?

To think with caves or within caves is to be required to play with questions of knowing. With a clash of cultures—do you descend to receive knowledge, or do you rather rise to enlightenment?

Caves confound and confuse, are associated with the unsayable, unrepresentable, the insensible. Yet they also demand the making of new knowledge, new ways of experimenting, new ways of saying. Caves are keystone sites of science, loci of knowledge in whose spaces past, present, and possible futures collide and weave.

Knowing, not knowing, the unknowable.

Caves refuse to be fixed; they make us tread these edges, keep us in the space between dark and light, between the unknowable, knowing and not knowing.

Notes

1. *Leap into the Void* is an artist action by Yves Klein in 1960, recorded in photographs and field notes by Parrott (February 2017).
2. Miroslaw Balka's *How It Is* (Unilever Series, 2009); fieldnotes by Parrott, February 2017. This was an art show that took place in the Turbine Hall at the Tate Modern in London.

References

Benjamin, Walter. 1969. *The Work of Art in the Age of Mechanical Reproduction* (1935). In *Illuminations: Essays and Reflections*, edited by Hannah Arendt, translated by Harry Zohn, 217–52. New York: Schocken Books.

Browne, George Forrest. 1865. *Ice Caves of France and Switzerland: A Narrative of Subterranean Exploration*. London: Longmans, Green.

Crane, Ralph, and Lisa Fletcher. 2015. *Cave: Nature and Culture*. London: Reaktion Books.

Devereux, Paul. 2000. *The Sacred Place: The Ancient Origins of Holy and Mystical Sites*. London: Cassell.

Glen, Alexander Richard, with Noel Andrew Cotton Croft. 1937. *Under the Pole Star: The Oxford University Arctic Expedition, 1935–6*. London: Methuen.

Irigaray, Luce. 1985. *Speculum of the Other Woman*. Translated by Gillian C. Gill. Ithaca NY: Cornell University Press.

Kapoor, Anish. 1990. *Anish Kapoor, British Pavilion, XLIV Venice Biennale*. Texts by Thomas McEvilley and Marjorie Allthorpe-Guyton. London: British Council.

Macfarlane, Robert. 2013. *Underland. Granta Magazine*, 123, unpaginated.

Ustinova, Yulia. 2009. *Caves and the Ancient Greek Mind: Descending Underground in the Search for Ultimate Truth*. Oxford: Oxford University Press.

Wright, John. Henry. 1906. "The Origin of Plato's Cave." *Harvard Studies in Classical Philology* 17: 131–42.

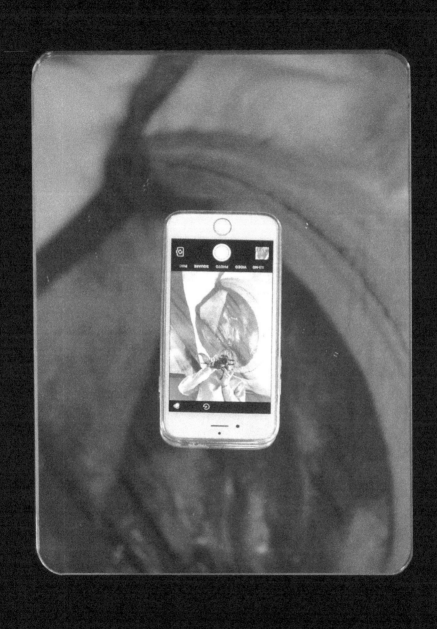

PART 2 Absences

5 Tracking Silence
Place, Embodiment, and Politics

Morgan Meyer

This chapter follows people concerned with sound and silence. Working within fields such as acoustic engineering or soundscape ecology, they use various tools and methods to record sound across the world. While doing so, they are also confronted with silence or, rather, the absence of anthropogenic noise. I examine how silence and quietness are qualified and valued in this process. I mobilize the idea of a "relational ontology of absence" and examine how absence is performed and materialized through relations, processes, and objects.

Quietness is portrayed as rare, as something to be protected and treasured—silent places being increasingly rare across the globe. The recording of sound and silence is thereby closely entangled with discourses about conservation and biodiversity. The chapter shows that tracking quietness is not just a technical but also an ecological and human practice. Quietness is not only something located and recorded; it is also narrated as a valuable entity. The chapter shows how quietness is embodied and "encultured": how it is listened to, experienced, reverenced, and valued.

Kinds of Silence

There are, of course, different places and events where silence is performed and different meanings that silence has in each of these areas. We encounter silence in politics, in music, in religion, in language, in the legal domain, and in art (see Jaworski 1993, 1997). Silence is a polysemic notion, and there are cultural, political, and architectural differences between these different kinds of silence. Some, for example, speak of the "politics of forgetting, silences and erasure" (Grundy-Warr and Sidaway 2006, 479) that is, the practice of remaining silent on certain issues in order to forget them or leave them unspoken (see also Zerubavel 2006). On the other extreme of the political spectrum are commemorative moments of silence in order to remember tragic accidents and the victims of these accidents (the politics of not forgetting). In religious settings, such as cloisters or abbeys, silence is also a common feature (Wichroski 1996). In such spaces, silence is generally seen as a means to establish closer contact with the divine.

In music, the notation used to depict silence is called a rest—a rather active presence in the sense that it constructs rhythm, that it is an instruction not to play any note or that it might even leave room for improvisation. Reggae and dub music, a musical style where silences are particularly common and important, are described as marked by the "embrace of negative sonic space (silence, absence) as a positive musical value" (Veal 2007, 205, 279). Most research on silence stems, however, from within domains such as communication, sociolinguistics, and discourse analysis (Acheson 2008; Jaworski 2005).

One of the most famous silences is without doubt the piece 4'33", composed by John Cage (1912–1992). Cage's piece was first performed in 1952 in Woodstock, New York, by David Tudor. Tudor entered the stage, sat down at a piano but eventually produced no sound at all for 4 minutes and 33 seconds. The reaction of the public ranged from bewilderment and anger to laughter and disappointment. Importantly, the piece was not listened to quietly, but the audience talked and whispered. This was one of Cage's intentions, he himself having declared that "the music I prefer, even to my own or anybody else's, is what we are hearing if we are just quiet." Even more so, "4'33" was . . . a demonstration that the sounds of the environment have a value no less than that of composed music, for in truth there is no silence" (Griffiths 1981, 28). Most interpretations see 4'33" as a piece that does not consist of silence but of ambient sounds that naturally occur within the environment and among the audience (Fetterman 1996; Revill 1992).

Cage's piece is about the impossibility of silence, and it conflicted with what the audience usually expects at concerts: hearing music. I want to stress here that Cage's silent piece can be seen as a silence that is made. Silence is produced deliberately as an art performance with the help of several instruments. It is produced in space and as space. Although, strictly speaking, Cage's piece was not silent, it nonetheless helps us understand silence as an arrangement in space (including its locations, publics, and limits). Such an arrangement is also constitutive of space; that is, it also produces the very particular spatial experience through which silence is made explicit and can be listened to. To put it this way, space and silence coproduce each other.

In this chapter I am interested in "natural" or "outdoor" silence, although, as becomes evident throughout the chapter, these are problematic terms. Helen E. Lees (2012) has argued, "The silence of the outdoors then, in operation, is a space, a place, a feeling, an experience. It is not an absence of sound. . . . It needs the sounds of nature in order to be experienced as what we commonly call aural quietude/ noiselessness. Nature itself is noisy . . . in a way that creates silence" (Lees 2012, n.p.). In other words, silence is something that has a geography, that is connected to our emotions, and that is dependent on—but at the same time that cannot coexist with—sound.

The chapter conceptualizes silence and quietness by following the work of John Law (2010) and Kevin Hetherington (2004) and by drawing upon the idea of a "relational ontology of absence" (Meyer 2012). This means conceiving absence not as an entity in itself but as something that exists through relations that give absence matter. Absences are performed and materialized through processes and material objects. This means, then, that we need to "trace" absence; that is, we need to follow and describe the processes and enactments through which absence becomes matter and absence comes to matter. Absences—be they silences, voids, or holes— are traces: they are residual, incomplete, elusive, ambiguous, yet material entities. By approaching absence through its relationality and conceiving it as a trace, I also want to contribute to the growing literature on absence (see, among others, the recent special issues of *Social Epistemology* [Rappert and Bauchspies 2014] and *cultural geographies* [Meier, Frers, and Sigvards-dotter 2013]; Bille, Hastrup, and Soerensen 2010).

The empirical part of this chapter is based upon an engagement with people who, through their work, have reflected upon silence and quietness. I have chosen to focus in depth on two persons (Bernie Krause and Gordon Hempton) for several reasons: both have been combining technical practices with more cultural endeavors and have disseminated their work across various media (books, CDs, video, documentaries, websites), and they are visible and outspoken persons about the recording of sound. It must be stressed, however, that Bernie Krause and Gordon Hempton are different personalities, that they have different backgrounds, and that this chapter does not aim to compare their practices as such. Krause has been an influential musician, is a respected scientist, and has collaborated with museums, zoos, and aquaria. Gordon Hempton, on the other hand, presents himself more as a lonely adventurer, is less connected to cultural institutions, but relates more with media and private enterprises. Through my focus on these two cases, I aim for a detailed, fine-grained, and in-depth understanding of silence and the way in which silence brings together places, bodies, and people's discourses and concerns about the natural world.

The Soundscape Ecologist

Bernie Krause is a soundscape ecologist and holds a PhD in bioacoustics. While the first part of his career was mostly devoted to music, the second part of his career was—and still is—devoted to the recording of natural sounds (see fig. 14). During his career Krause has been involved in various kinds of activities: recording CDs, writing academic articles and books, doing exhibitions. In most recent years he has been working on the visualization of sound. For instance, he has been a key contributor to an exhibition held at the Fondation Cartier in Paris titled *The Great Animal Orchestra* (July 2016–January 2017). The exhibition contained, among others, a room that was especially designed to make it "extremely quiet" (with padding on the walls, a thick carpet on the floor, and a treated

14. Bernie Krause recording wildlife sounds. Photography by Tim Chapman.

ceiling) and more "intimate" for people to be able to listen to—and see 3D visualizations of—natural sounds that Krause had recorded.

Krause's work crosses the domains of science and art and brings together a concern for the technologies of recording, the representation of sound, and a concern about the environment. He aims to "capture, as best as [he] can, a sense of place and a sense of space, and a sense of that moment" and hopes that, for the listeners, "the sound transports them in a way so that they are getting a sense of what that place might be like" (Krause 2017). In other words, rather than only recording and disseminating sounds as such, he tries to display the spatial and geographical embeddedness of these sounds. When I asked him about his view on silence, he responded, "in the natural world, silence does not exist. There is always some degree of ambient sound." But he added that "tranquil" and "peaceful" places do exist.

During our interview he recalled one instance during which he was confronted with silence:

I've only been in one place ever in the world that had no sound. That was in the Grand Canyon. . . . It was maybe 15 meters across and about 100 meters high, and it was made of sandstone. And it was a small area off the Colorado River. . . . It's what in English is called a box-canyon. It's a very small space. And it was extremely quiet. When I used the measurement device to measure how quiet it was, it went to the very lowest level of that [fifteen or seventeen decibels] and probably was below it. And in order to reorient myself, I had to throw rocks at the side of the canyon to hear noise, because it was so quiet. But I imagine that it was just that time of the day because it was in the mid-afternoon. But in the morning, there would be birds around and birds would make noise as well. . . . I just happened to hit that moment when it was extremely quiet. (Krause 2017)

While Krause avoids the term *silence*, he speaks of "no sound" and extremely "quiet." His experience of this absence of sound is based upon an interplay of several elements: his capacity to hear, the box canyon in which he was located, a technical device that measures the level of sound, and his activity of breaking the silence and seeking orientation through sound. Krause did not just hear "no sound" through a biological process that relates his ear to his brain. "No sound" was a unique, corporal, spatial, and technological encounter with silence. Krause did not passively encounter silence as a preexisting entity that was waiting for him to be discovered, but it was something to be *related with*: he realized and visualized silence, and he made it possible through his body and technological equipment.

Krause (2016) also reflects about sound and silence in his book *Wild Soundscapes: Discovering the Voice of the Natural World*. He quotes a telling passage from *The Third Ear* written by jazz producer and journalist Joachim-Ernst Berendt (1992):

I am lying on a bed of pine needles by the water. . . . Closer at hand, flies flitting past, dragonflies dancing, mosquitoes circling. Not much for the eyes. But I hear: silence. It is the silence which I hear first of all. Like a weight that I can grasp. A heavy, smooth weight. My ears feel it as if they were groping fingers. I observe that the weight feels good. I think: You haven't heard such silence for a long time. I occupy myself with: silence. It is alive. A drop of silence. My ears penetrate it. I am inside it. The drop becomes a universe. A cosmos that begins to resound. (Qtd. in Krause 2016, 64)

In his discussion of this passage (which goes on at length in describing various natural sounds), Krause states that Berendt is concerned with "translating natural sound into spoken language." He notes that not many people have been able to do so and that the vocabulary of humans usually lacks terms to capture the range and variety of natural sounds. Krause's discussion of Berendt focuses, in other words, on the technicality and discursiveness of sound: its recording and the conveying of its richness and complexity into language. There is, however, an additional way to interpret the above quote. Berendt also forcefully describes the corporality and materiality of silence. Silence, in his view, has a "weight" and it is something that envelops its listener—who is "inside."

When Krause records sounds in nature he behaves in specific ways. He carefully selects the places to which he travels in order to make his recordings: he selects remote places "based on their absence of human noise," where the natural habitat is still intact and where there is "a chance for long periods of time where there would be an absence of human noise" (Krause 2017). Equipped with several technical devices and wearing "the kinds of clothes that don't make any noise," he then records sounds. He describes his attitude as follows: "I try to be really quiet, I try to be very reverent, I try to be very aware of what's happening around me at all times. And alert. . . . When I go outside, I try to be as unobtrusive as possible. When I set up my microphones, I usually walk maybe a hundred meters away and so I'm not disturbing anything that's in the area of my microphones" (Krause 2017).

For Krause, recording sound in nature is a "zen experience," very "calming," and he feels "just present" (Krause 2017). Listening is, for Krause, at once an intellectual, corporal, and, in a certain sense, somewhat "submissive" activity. Quietness is a key component in his recordings, and it brings together quiet gestures, quiet clothes, and quiet places.

The Sound Tracker

Gordon Hempton calls himself an acoustic ecologist, although he has "no professional label" (Hempton 2017). His recordings and various activities have been transformed into sound recordings, books, and documentaries. On his business card and in the documentary film *Soundtracker* (Sherman 2010), he presents himself as a "sound tracker."

While recording natural sounds, Hempton has also been concerned with silence, both on a theoretical and a practical level. In his book *One Square Inch of Silence: One Man's Search for Natural Silence in a Noisy World* (Hempton and Grossmann 2009), he reflects in depth about the essence, quality, and values of silence. In the book's prologue he defines silence as follows: "Silence is not the absence of something but the presence of everything. It lives here. . . . It can be felt within the chest. . . . Silence can be carried like embers from a fire. Silence can be found, and silence can find you. Silence can be lost and also recovered" (Hempton and Grossmann 2009, 2; emphasis removed).

He uses various terms to qualify silence in his work, describing it as "rare," "endangered," "relaxing," "quieting," "peaceful," "transformative," "empowering," to be "preserved" or "rescued," and argues that silence has "spiritual cleansing power." To put it differently, people need to do *something with* silence: its ontology needs to be maintained, and its power can be mobilized as a resource. At the same time, he also quantifies silence. In his work he has at various points stated that silence and quietudes are at least fifteen minutes without noise; -16 dBA; 25–35 dBA; less then 45 dBA (dBA stands for A-weighted decibels, a unit to quantify relative loudness as perceived by the human ear).

Hempton's work is also political and ecological in that he has a project called One Square Inch of Silence that was launched in 2005. The idea behind One Square Inch of Silence is "a very simple idea. . . . Instead of noise, we talk about quiet. If we can maintain one point of land, one square inch, in quiet, doesn't that have the same effect of making sure that there aren't noise intrusions . . . for dozens of miles in every direction? Because one square inch affects thousand square miles. . . . You actually end up managing a huge area all around it" (Hempton, qtd. in Sherman 2010).

One Square Inch of Silence is located in the Hoh Rain Forest in Olympic National Park, in the state of Washington. Hempton has physically marked the place by a stone marker: a red stone "resembling living flesh or a piece of sushi-grade tuna" (Hempton and Grossmann 2009, 30). The place originally contained a jar for visitor comments named the Jar of Quiet Thoughts. According to Hempton, the comments that visitors left were "always about love, wonder, and discovery" (Hempton 2017), and he stated that people have become engaged at the site, and others have spread loved ones' ashes there. In his book *One Square Inch of Silence* (Hempton and Grossman 2009), he does not however reveal any specific content, nor quotes, but lists twenty-nine words that visitors have used in their comments, such as *peaceful*, *golden*, *supreme*, and *love*.

The exact location of One Square Inch of Silence can be found on the project's website: in the Hoh Rain Forest at Olympic National Park, 3.2 miles from a visitor center on the Hoh River Trail. The exact coordinates are 47° 51.959N, 123° 52.221W, 678 feet above sea level. Furthermore, visitors can download a map with five pictures and a detailed description of the path leading to *One Square Inch of Silence* (see fig. 15).

The way to One Square Inch of Silence is clearly indicated, and visitor behavior is also "scripted": Hempton asks visitors to act in particular ways and respect certain rules and guidelines. "The publication of the location of One Square Inch increases the likelihood of visitation by hikers. Your visit is encouraged. Please be quiet. . . . the need for quiet and the power of quiet will foster the care needed to preserve this site. At the site is the Jar of Quiet Thoughts, a depository of notes left by visitors. You are welcome to read and add to the Jar. Please respect that these are quiet thoughts from a quiet place—no quotes from the Jar are allowed" (One Square Inch 2019). When Hempton once guided a crew of twelve people to do a shoot of the site for a television news program, he explained: "There is no talking! . . . I'm not going to take you there if you talk" (Hempton 2017).

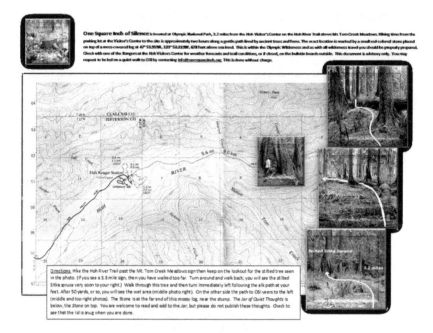

One Square Inch of Silence is located at Olympic National Park, 3.2 miles from the Hoh Visitor's Center on the Hoh River Trail above Mt. Tom Creek Meadows. Hiking time from the parking lot at the Visitor's Center to the site is approximately two hours along a gentle path lined by ancient trees and ferns. The exact location is marked by a small red-colored stone placed on top of a moss-covered log at 47° 51.959N, 123° 52.229W, 678 feet above sea level. This is within the Olympic Wilderness and as with all wilderness travel you should be properly prepared. Check with one of the Rangers at the Hoh Visitors Center for weather forecasts and trail conditions, or if closed, on the bulletin boards outside. This document is advisory only. You may request to be led on a quiet walk to OSI by contacting info@onesquareinch.org. This is done without charge.

Directions. Hike the Hoh River Trail past the Mt. Tom Creek Meadows sign then keep on the lookout for the stilted tree seen in the photo. (If you see a 3.3 mile sign, then you have walked too far. Turn around and walk back; you will see the stilted Sitka spruce very soon to your right.) Walk through this tree and then turn immediately left following the elk path at your feet. After 50 yards, or so, you will see the wet area (middle photo right). On the other side the path to OSI veers to the left (middle and top right photos). The Stone is at the far end of this mossy log, near the stump. The Jar of Quiet Thoughts is below, the Stone on top. You are welcome to read and add to the Jar, but please do not publish these thoughts. Check to see that the lid is snug when you are done.

15. Directions for visitors to find *One Square Inch of Silence.* Source: http://onesquareinch.org.

Hempton has developed the idea of One Square Inch of Silence, chosen a distinct location for it, decided to make it accessible and public, and specified several behavioral norms for visitors. In addition, he has also attempted to get institutional recognition and official protection for the site. Hempton has sent several letters to staff members of Olympic National Park and has traveled to Washington to speak with a senator. In a one-page handout Hempton writes: "It is requested that the Hoh Valley at Olympic National Park be specially designated a *Quiet Place* by NPS Director's Order—a natural place set aside as a sanctuary of silence for present and future generations to enjoy unimpaired by noise pollution. It is asked that this newly designated *Quiet Place* be protected and managed by a simple but effective soundscape management tool called One Square Inch" (One Square Inch. 2019; emphasis in the original).

To date, however, Hempton has been unsuccessful in turning One Square Inch of Silence into an officially recognized site. In fact, One Square Inch of Silence has known various episodes since its establishment in 2005. While in the beginning it was tolerated, it was deemed illegal for a certain period, and the jar with about two hundred visitor comments was removed by the park service. Nowadays the site is being tolerated again, but the jar has not been put back. Several reasons explain this situation and the fact that Hempton has not been able to get institutional endorsement and official support: Hempton's background and the fact that his project is not a scientific one. As Hempton commented, "we do need a research permit and we do need a research scientist. I do not have a PhD and I am not affiliated with a scientific institution" (Hempton 2017). Replying to Hempton's request for a permit, the research coordinator at Olympic National Park wrote: "We do not issue permits for private individuals. . . . And we do not issue permits for 'installations'" (qtd. in Hempton and Grossmann 2009, 319). But there are other reasons as well, including the difficulty of deciding what counts as noise pollution and the complexity of taking concrete measures (such as establishing a no-flight zone). It also seems unlikely that within national parks there is an institutional history and expertise to address "immaterial" entities such as sound and silence, and the latter probably fall outside of the remit of parks and wildlife conservation.

One Square Inch of Silence was vandalized shortly after the book was published. The red stone that indicated its exact location was stolen, and the jar with visitor comments was hidden. Hempton reacted as follows:

When I realized, truly, the stone was missing, I immediately became angry and raged. And immediately embarrassed, because I never felt anything but love, wonder and discovery and natural quiet. And now I was filled with anger. So impulsively, I asked the quiet through my thoughts, through my feeling, just with a blank mind. . . . "What should I do?" And the quiet, it practically laughed at me, said: "What's the problem? It's just a stone. The quiet is still here. Are there not stones at your feet?" And I realized I was really giving too much importance to a symbol, rather than what the symbol truly represents. And so I picked up another stone, put it on the log, and then began our Seeds for Silence program. And now anyone who hikes to One Square Inch of Silence may bring a red stone with them and swop it out for the red stone that's on the log. And now they have a memento. And one of those stones has gone to Italy, and France, and now teaches Chinese children the importance of listening. (Hempton 2017)

Throughout its history, the geography of One Square Inch of Silence has expanded. One Square Inch of Silence now has several topologies: its geographic coordinates, the "thousand square miles" it aims to protect, and its wider reception within media, the public, and private homes. One Square Inch of Silence is, at least for Hempton, an emotional and human experience as well as an ecological endeavor, embedded within biodiversity and conservation discourses.

This case exemplifies well the relationality and spatialities of silence; it shows that silence comes to matter through relations, processes, and objects. People visit and comment upon it, and they are asked to behave in specific ways. Various objects and tools are used to mark its location and measure it. And its preservation and recognition calls for political action—a recognition that is hampered by the lack of scientific and institutional legitimacy. One Square Inch of Silence is a call for stabilizing the ontology of silence, for inscribing it in a territory, and for recognizing it as a valuable resource. However, the silence in the above story proves difficult to be stabilized; it remains ambiguous and elusive both "on the ground" and as a political and ecological object of interest.

It is clear that Krause and Hempton approach silence differently: the former is more scientific and institutionally recognized, while the latter is more spiritual, self-centered, and militant. One could even argue that, more generally, people's experience of silence is necessarily very personal and individual, and that it is not possible to compare them—after all, Krause argues that silence does not exist, and he has only encountered once a moment and a place without any sound, whereas Hempton has chosen a permanent location for silence and calls for its protection. And while we have encountered stones in both their accounts, they were used for very different purposes: Krause used them to break the silence and reorient himself, Hempton uses them to mark silence, to orientate people, and to represent an idea.

Yet, apart from silence being experienced and described in different terms, both Krause and Hempton help us understand that quietness also has a materiality and ontology of its own. The "relational ontology" of quietness has become evident in both stories: it is through socio-technical practices and processes that quietness is enacted and comes to matter. Quietness is not spaceless nothingness, but it is textured. It is an object we find in space. Quietness and silence are specific spatial objects, they *take place*—and they take place differently according to context. Quietness takes place at once as a natural and technological phenomenon. It can be found "out there" in nature, and it is also recorded and measured through technological devices. But quietness is also *distant from*. Quietness, as well as silence, is usually described as the absence of anthropogenic noise, and thus its possibility and occurrence are reliant upon its geographical distance to noise. Quietness and noise/sound need to be separated, asynchronous, and, in a sense, "nonrelational" for quietness to take place (and take time). The materiality and the geography of quietness go hand in hand with its "nonmaterial" aspects: its sensing and the emotions it stimulates. Quietness is thereby embodied and encultured. It is experienced, listened to, cared for, narrated, valued. Another way to put this is to say that space, silence, and sensing are interrelated and that they are coproduced. In order to exist, silence has to be "realized" in the two senses of this word: it has to be *made real* (it has to be made possible by a co-performance of place, sound, and body), and at the same time it has to be *understood* (it has to be recognized and appreciated as a distinct and valuable phenomenon).

I argue that a fruitful way to further think about silence and quietness is therefore to attend to the ways in which they are "tracked." Tracking silence is a technological practice; it is about measuring, recording, and "putting on track" sounds and silences. Tracking also means, in a spatial and geographical sense, locating the places where noise is potentially absent, where there is, in other words, a significant distance between sound and silence, between noise and quietness. As we have seen throughout this chapter, "tracking" quietness is also a sociocultural practice. It is described as something that is followed, often on one's own. The ontological dimension of such a tracking is worth stressing: a person who tracks silence is always, in a sense, "behind" or "below" its object, an object that is rare and slippery, almost impossible to grasp, and that can vanish instantly.

References

Acheson, Kris. 2008. "Silence as Gesture: Rethinking the Nature of Communicative Silences." *Communication Theory* 18, no. 4: 535–55.

Berendt, Joachim-Ernst. 1992. *The Third Ear: On Listening to the World*. Translated by Tim Nevill. New York: Henry Holt.

Bille, Mikkel, Frida Hastrup, and Tim Flohr Soerensen, eds. 2010. *An Anthropology of Absence: Materializations of Transcendence and Loss*. New York: Springer-Verlag.

Fetterman, William. 1996. *John Cage's Theatre Pieces: Notations and Performance*. Amsterdam: Harwood Academic.

Griffiths, Paul. 1981. *Cage*. Oxford Studies on Composers 18. London: Oxford University Press.

Grundy-Warr, Carl, and James D. Sidaway. 2006. "Political Geographies of Silence and Erasure." *Political Geography* 25, no. 5: 479–81.

Hempton, Gordon. 2017. Interview with the author. March 28.

Hempton, Gordon, and John Grossmann. 2009. *One Square Inch of Silence: One Man's Search for Natural Silence in a Noisy World*. New York: Free Press.

Hetherington, Kevin. 2004. "Secondhandedness: Consumption, Disposal, and Absent Presence." *Environment and Planning D: Society and Space* 22, no. 1: 157–73.

Jaworski, Adam. 1993. *The Power of Silence: Social and Pragmatic Perspectives*. Newbury Park CA: Sage.

———, ed. 1997. *Silence: Interdisciplinary Perspectives*. Berlin: Mouton de Gruyter.

———. 2005. "Introduction: Silence in Institutional and Intercultural Contexts." *Multilingua—Journal of Cross-Cultural and Interlanguage Communication* 24, nos. 1/2: 1–6.

Krause, Bernie. 2016. *Wild Soundscapes: Discovering the Voice of the Natural World*. New Haven CT: Yale University Press.

———. 2017. Interview with the author. March 22.

Law, John. 2010. "The Greer-Bush Test: On Politics in STS." In *Débordements: Mélanges offerts à Michel Callon*, edited by Madeleine Akrich et al., 269–81. Paris: Presses des Mines.

Lees, Helen E. 2012. "The Outdoors as the Source of Silence: Access, Curriculum and Something Relational." Presentation at conference, Philosophical Perspectives in Outdoor Education, May 2–4. Moray House, Edinburgh University.

Meier, Lars, Lars Frers, and Erika Sigvardsdotter, eds. 2013. "Absence. Materiality, Embodiment, Resistance." Special issue, *cultural geographies* 20, no. 4.

Meyer, Morgan. 2012. "Placing and Tracing Absence: A Material Culture of the Immaterial." *Journal of Material Culture* 17, no. 1: 103–10.

One Square Inch. 2019. *One Square Inch—A Sanctuary for Silence at Olympic National Park.* http://onesquareinch.org (accessed September 23, 2017).

Rappert, Brian, and Wenda K. Bauchspies. 2014. "Absence." Special issue, *Social Epistemology* 28, no. 1.

Revill, David. 1992. *The Roaring Silence: John Cage, A Life.* New York: Arcade.

Sherman, Nick. 2010. *Soundtracker.* Directed by Nick Sherman. Los Angeles: Fou Films.

Veal, Michael E. 2007. *Dub: Soundscapes and Shattered Songs in Jamaican Reggae.* Middletown CT: Wesleyan University Press.

Wichroski, Mary Anne. 1996. "Breaking Silence: Some Fieldwork Strategies in Cloistered and Non-Cloistered Communities." *Qualitative Sociology* 19, no. 1: 153–70.

Zerubavel, Eviatar. 2006. *The Elephant in the Room: Silence and Denial in Everyday Life.* Oxford: Oxford University Press, 2006.

6 The Void and Its Summons
Subjectivity, Signs, and the Enigmatic

Mitch Rose

L'appel du vide

In 1920 the art historian, travel writer, and self-styled paenist of the American desert, John C. Van Dyke, wrote his final volume on the American West focusing on the Grand Canyon and Colorado River. In one memorable passage, Van Dyke (1927) describes being overwhelmed by the height and immensity of the Grand Canyon and remarks upon his powerful urge to hurl himself over the edge. As Mark Neumann (1999) points out, the impulse to leap to one's death from the canyon is a familiar one and is repeated in travel accounts from the nineteenth century to the present day (92). Often these accounts draw upon Emersonian and Lockean themes, for example, notions of the sublime, the purity of nature, and so on. But for Van Dyke (1927) such accounts falsely imbue the canyon with an immanent spirituality, as if it were a repository of latent energy or dense mystical power. Even as Van Dyke calls the canyon a spiritual and redemptive place, he does not conceptualize those qualities as being defined by its awe, terror, or other metaphysical attributes. Rather, its redemptive nature lies in its silence. The view from the top, Van Dyke suggests, does not overwhelm the observer. On the contrary, what draws the viewer in, what enjoins us to jump, is its emptiness—its vast absence of movement, energy, and noise. It is the quiet of the Grand Canyon that shakes us: not the terror of the abyss but its empty austerity.

L'appel du vide, a phrase that has no direct translation into English but captures a sensibility with which we are instinctively familiar, refers to the urge one gets, when sitting at a great height or commanding position, to jump. The tiny voice that crawls into our heads: How easy would it be? How precarious are our lives? What would it take to walk over the edge, to let ourselves fall into the empty air? The aim of this chapter is to explore this summons. If we understand the void as an absence, an emptiness whose only defining quality is its lack of phenomenality, then how can we talk about this draw, its claim on our senses or inclinations? Why do the blank spaces on the map call us to explore? Why does the awkward silence in a room elicit our speech? Given that so much of our subjective and social lives is currently conceptualized through agencies, affects, and sensibilities that reverberate through the world and do things, it is perhaps timely to ask about the nonpower of emptiness, that is, the acknowledgment of nothing.

In order to make this question more concrete, particularly in relation to debates within contemporary cultural geography, I connect it to the question of signs, a topic that has been resolutely left behind by our contemporary post-representational era. Indeed, while the current conceptual zeitgeist focuses on the corporeal, practical, and broadly noncognitive nature of social life (and eschews an interest in the symbolic), the aim of this chapter is to illustrate (1) how habitual and practical existence is still mediated by signs and (2) how understanding the role of signs allows us to see the elicitive power of the void, that is, how silence and emptiness summon the subject. The chapter is divided into three further sections. The next section (corporeal ontologies) briefly reviews what I crudely refer to as the practice-habit literature; work that draws upon and develops various corporeal ontologies to explain the role of unreflective action in the constitution of subjectivity. In addition, this section concludes by exploring how signs also have a role in the material transaction between body and world. Drawing upon the work of Eduardo Kohn (2013), it explores how signs can be material and play a role in the emergence of consciousness and agency. Section three (an enigmatic dimension) pushes Kohn's discussion of signs further by examining how bodies not only interpret what they sense but also what they do not sense. Specifically, it illuminates what I call the enigmatic dimension of the sign—the emptiness or void at the edge of the sign that withdraws from sensation even as it announces its absence. The aim here is to illustrate that while Kohn and others in the practice-habit literature understand material relations as that which summons subjectivity into being, I would argue that it is the void, the absence at the heart of the sign, that is the catalyst for consciousness, the origin of thought and the engine of subjectivity. The final section (the summoned subject) concludes by developing this understanding of signs into a speculative conception of subjectivity.

Corporeal Ontologies

The literature I have been referring to as the practice-habit literature is an extremely broad one with numerous overlapping interdisciplinary strands. Generally it can be characterized by at least three interests: (1) a focus on the capacities and limits of bodies, (2) valuing of practical sense over cognitive knowing, and (3) an interest in how subjectivity in general (and self-consciousness in particular) emerges through corporeal encounters. In this section I briefly review a selection of this literature to illustrate how it approaches the relationship between body and world and how this relationship leads to a particular configuration of subjectivity.

Tim Ingold's (2000) dwelling perspective is a significant conceptual touchstone in this literature. Drawing upon the phenomenological tradition of Martin Heidegger (1996) and Maurice Merleau-Ponty (2002), Ingold argues against representationalist paradigms that conceptualize subjectivity primarily in terms of mental schemas; ideas, imaginations, and expectations, structured through normalizing routines. In response Ingold (2011) argues that social life is not first and foremost cognitive but practical. Using Heidegger's famous example of the hammer, he reminds us that subjects do not require a mental schema of a hammer to use it. On the contrary the hammer only makes sense as it is picked up and put to task in a world where hammering projects exist. "The forms people build," Ingold (2000) states, "arise within the current of their involved activity, in the specific relational contexts of their practical engagement with their surroundings" (186). Ingold takes from Heidegger the essential idea that subjects are in the world, meaning that their existence inflects a world where certain projects (being a doctor, a shaman, a peasant, or a wife), tools (university, clothes, magic), and capacities (steady hands, spiritual vision, fertility) are always already operative. Our engagement with the world, therefore, is primarily practical; we use the tools we find to pursue the projects we have been bequeathed.

There are two aspects of Ingold's work that have been picked up and developed by geographers. The first is his notion of distributed agency. In the work of Ben Anderson and Colin McFarlane (2011), Steve Hinchliffe (2000, 2008), Kristin Asdal, Tone Druglitrø, and Steve Hinchliffe (2016), and Sarah Whatmore (2002), agency is understood as a system of potentialities that various beings are differentially poised to exploit. Thus, rather than approaching subjects as singular beings with a set of known (or knowable) attributes, subjects are thought of as an assemblage of biological capacities intertwining with the material resources they find to facilitate existence (Ingold 2008). The second aspect is Ingold's emphasis on skill. In an effort to move away from cognitive constructs of experience, the work of Eden and Bear (2011), Hayden Lorimer (2006), John Wylie (2002), and others (Simpson 2013; Pitt 2015) emphasizes the significance of practical intelligence over cognitive reflection. In Eden and Bear's (2011) examination of angling, for example, there is a recognition that the tools used by anglers are always shifting, and the body is in a constant state of adaptation. Thus, there is a dynamism inherent to practical engagement where the skilled practitioner perpetually modifies her comportment to materials in response to their changing conditions.

My interest in this literature, however, specifically concerns its distinctive take on agency and consciousness. In J-D Dewsbury (2011, 2015) for instance, self-awareness is an event that arises in response to the material affordances immanent to a situation and the extent to which those affordances can be appropriated by a body. The archaeologist Lambros Malafouris (2004) makes a similar point when he argues that the origin of thought (not just self-conscious thought but all thought) resides not in the human mind but in the world itself, and specifically in things: "human thinking is, first and above all, thinking through, with, and about things, bodies, and others . . . [it] is not something that happens 'inside' brains, bodies, or things; rather, it emerges from contextualized processes that take place 'between' brains, bodies, and things" (Malafouris 2013, 77–78). In emphasizing the role of materials and objects in the emergence of subjectivity, Malafouris (2004) illustrates the difficulty of attributing agency solely to the human subject. As Malafouris states, "*material culture is consubstantial with mind. The relationship between the world and human cognition is not one of abstract representation or some other form of action at a distance but one of onto-logical inseparability*" (58; emphasis in the original). The form and shape of an axe, for example, has as much to do with what the materials allow and what they deny as it has to do with the skill of its creator. In this sense, every mental resource grows out of a process of engagement, that is, out of a meeting between the material (and what it gives and denies) and the body (and what it senses and seeks). Along similar lines, David Bissell (2012, 2013, 2015) argues that a body's habituation to particular routines can instigate various modes of consciousness and awareness when those routines break down. In his discussion of long-haul air travel, he explores how the breakdown of the body's expectations (to stretch, to sleep, to walk freely) means that long-standing passive propensities are transformed into active desires. It is the body's sense of loss—the fact that it misses certain modalities of moving and comporting—that engenders self-consciousness thought and reflection into being. As Bissell (2009) states, the transformation from passive propensities to active desires engenders "plateaus of consciousness" (435). These plateaus are not incremental stepping stones to self-enlightenment but are thresholds that subjects move across—back and forth—depending on the material affordances that present themselves as well as the subject's capacity to accommodate or resist them. Thus, the movement from unreflective action to self-conscious thought is always in flux, always moving in relation to what is in need of address, that is, in relation to the milieu and the demands that a milieu makes upon a body and its capacities, desires, and dispositions.

In sum, the aim of this discussion is to illustrate how this literature understands the emergence of subjectivity in and through material relations. Rather than understanding self-awareness as an implicit resident attribute or property of a subject, these authors illustrate how subjectivity arises through engagements that are practical, tactile, and sensory. In addition, these engagements are primarily non-representational—i.e., they are not mediated by constructs of meaning and significance residing in the subject's mind but are thought to emerge in degrees vis-à-vis a world that requires it. The point, as Malafouris (2013) suggests, is that materials are consubstantial with mind. The mind emerges through its engagement with materials, that is, through the body's capacity to sense the properties within materials and manipulate them toward its advantage.

Thus far the focus has been on how the practice-habit literature understands subjectivity as something that emerges from immediate corporeal engagements—i.e., engagements that are primarily unthought. To conclude this section I want to draw upon the work of Eduardo Kohn (2013) to illustrate how such engagements are also mediated by signs. To be clear, Kohn (like the authors above) understands thought as something that arises via material engagements with the world. But he also sees signs as playing a significant role. In particular he focuses on the simple indexical relations that humans and nonhumans rely upon in their day-to-day existence—for example, steam coming off water means heat, the heaviness of air means rain. The world, as Kohn effectively illustrates, is full of such signs; it is laden with signifiers that tell the interpreter that something is coming. Through Kohn's exquisite and intimate descriptions of Avila, a network of small villages located in the rain forests of Ecuador, he elucidates how signs introduce moments of prevarication that force beings to become reflective on their situation; intervals that connect a present event to a potential future that requires a decision. Both humans and animals face these intervals, and the decisions they make carry significant consequences. Thus, while Malafouris (2004) emphasizes the immediate manner in which a knapper negotiates a block of stone, Kohn would suggest that the obstacles the knapper finds in the material could be understood as signs—indicators of what is possible and what is not possible and how the body can proceed. The reading of signs, therefore, is a constitutive event in the emergence of subjectivity. Signs, in essence, present beings with problems. They bring them face to face with potential futures—with questions that require an answer—and in doing so elicit whatever thinking capacities are available to respond.

A story Kohn tells to illustrate this takes place during a hunting trip with two informants in the rain forest. When they find a monkey hiding in the canopy, his companion decides to chop down a nearby palm, hoping the noise will scare the animal from its roost. Kohn's interest in the story is how the monkey interprets the noise of the felled palm. She recognizes the falling tree as a sign of danger even as she is unclear about the precise nature of the danger or where it will lead. Thus the sign of the felled palm is an event that initiates a certain anticipation of the future. It leads the monkey to consider her present situation and its potential outcome. "We humans," Kohn (2013) states, "are not the only ones who do things for the sake of a future by re-presenting it in the present. All living selves do this in some way or another. Representation, purpose, and future are in the world— and not just in that part of the world that we delimit as human mind" (41). For Kohn, signs open up a space between the sensibilities our bodies encounter and their potential meaning; a space in which various forms of consciousness, awareness, and judgments are called upon to bridge the gap between the present situation that is sensed and the array of potential futures it could bring. While the precise nature of the consciousness that emerges varies (depending on the cognitive capacities therein), there is a summons situated within the sign itself; an opening that acknowledges— indeed requires—not simply action but thought, reflection, and awareness.

I bring Kohn into the discussion because he represents an interesting advance on the practice-habit literature. While Kohn similarly conceptualizes subjectivity as something that emerges in and through practical engagement, his emphasis on the role of signs provides an effective mechanism for understanding how the world summons, that is, how the world poses questions that require a response. Signs, in Kohn's work, are not human constructs organizing the material world into something knowable and meaningful. They are events: a consolidation of forces that solicit answers.

In this sense, signs mark a threshold through which subjectivity emerges. In illuminating the rift between present and future, signs demand that the opening be filled, that is, that some modality of thinking emerges to fill the gap.

An Enigmatic Dimension

Thus far this essay has made two points: first, that everyday practical engagements are embedded in signs; and second, that these signs open up a space—an interval—through which various subjective capacities (thought, decision, self-awareness, self-reflection) can arise. In this sense, I have argued, along with Kohn, that while social life may be predominantly defined by corporeal practical engagements, those engagements deliver subjects to situations that require various kinds of decisions, that is, decisions that call upon whatever capacities are available to think. The aim of this section is to push this point a bit further. While Kohn understands thought and reflection as emerging from signs, he conceptualizes signs as things that link present situations to future possibilities—that is, possibilities that suggest certain pathways for action. The question at the heart of this section, however, concerns that dimension of the sign that offers no possibilities for action. Specifically, this means illuminating what the psychoanalyst Jean Laplanche (1999) calls the enigmatic dimension of the sign. While every sign by definition has a dimension that signifies, there is also a dimension that does not signify, a dimension that is silent. The remainder of this chapter focuses on explaining this enigmatic dimension and illustrating how it too embeds a summons—a call—that engenders the subject in a different manner.

Perhaps the best way to introduce the enigmatic dimension of the sign is through another story from Kohn's book. During a bus ride to Avila, Kohn relates how his bus gets stranded due to a landslide wiping out the road, trapping the bus by mudslides in front and behind. Kohn's understanding of the terrain and the carnage he has witnessed by past landslides instigates in him a profound anxiety. He is nervous about more landslides falling on the bus and is taken aback by the fact that he seems to be the only one on the bus fretting about their situation—as he states: "as my constant what-ifs became increasingly distant from the carefree chattering tourists, what at first began as a diffuse sense of unease soon morphed into a sense of profound alienation. This discrepancy between my perception of the world and that of those around me sundered me from the world and those living in it. All I was left with were my own thoughts of future dangers spinning themselves out of control" (Kohn 2013, 46–47). For Kohn, the mudslide is a sign that established a relation between his present material situation and a range of potential futures. But while Kohn's anxiety begins as an anxiety about those futures (and the unseen possibilities they hold), he interprets it as an anxiety about his alienation from his material situation. For Kohn the anxiety is an example of thought unanchored—that is, of thought as consciousness spinning away from the conditions that are its origin.

In an attempt to illustrate the enigmatic dimension of the sign, I offer a different reading. The futures Kohn imagined and feared were possible, even as they were mysterious. The landslide opened a sign where the future that was seen by most (we need to turn around, we need to stay the night, our trip will be delayed, these things happen) was haunted by other possibilities: futures that could (perhaps) happen, futures that transcended what could be seen. Indeed, what Kohn's encounter with the mud reveals is not a loss of relation with his situation or his surroundings but rather a recognition that his situation and surroundings offered no basis for relation. The mud and its potential sliding had no relation to Kohn, to the tourists, to his anxieties or their good humor. It stood outside those relations, and those relations had no bearing on whether the mud slid or not. Thus, while I would agree that material problems do give rise to thought, I do not agree that this is always a matter of relation. In this situation I would argue that the mudslide precipitated thought precisely because it eluded relation, that is, because it stood outside relation. Kohn's situation was one where he was at the whim of the world; exposed to agencies of mud and gravity that were utterly unaccountable to him, his anxieties, or his fellow travelers. This is a world over which he had no purchase and no power. It was not something he could lay hold of or touch. On the contrary, it laid hold of him. Thus, I interpret Kohn's anxiety not as an attunement to a broken relation but to his recognition of relation's absence.

The point of this discussion is that signs harbor within them a dual dimension. On the one hand there are the possibilities that Kohn can see—the future possibilities of which he is aware and with which he has some kind of relation. This is the dimension that signifies and thus holds within it the potential to summon Kohn into various modes of thinking and acting; thoughts that can serve to deliver him from what he senses and sees to a future he desires. But there are also the possibilities he cannot see. The landslide points to what we know and to the limit of what is knowable. Thus, while Kohn understands his anxiety as a misplaced relation with what is knowable (the bus is in danger), I would argue it emerges from what is unknowable—that is, that dimension of the sign that lies beyond the material and thus beyond what Kohn could see or relate. A sign that appears to him but only as a silence. This is the void within the sign: a call one senses within the material that simultaneously transcends the material to reveal a dimension that, in its essence, is mysterious and as such defies relation. In every sign we can see both what the sign represents and what it cannot represent. The sign always points to its limits—a dark shadow at the edge of signification—summoning subjectivity into self-consciousness though in a different key than we have seen heretofore.

The Summoned Subject

In conclusion I want to make a few speculative comments about the void at the heart of the sign and how it summons subjectivity. As already suggested, the aim of this essay is not to suggest that subjectivity does not arise out of material engagements with the world, but to suggest that it is not the materiality of these relations that matters. What is revealed through material engagement is both the world's presence and its distance. Its availability and its utter remoteness. While the world may appear to us in gifts and light, we humans (and nonhumans) have no say over—no capacity to touch, hold, or secure—the comings and goings of those offerings. Even as Kohn and others argue that subjectivity emerges from the problems and questions posed by events, I would argue that it is the problems posed at the edge of events (that which we can sense but cannot see) that summon the definitive moment of subjectivity. To see this moment, however, we need to understand the role of signs.

My interest in signs commences from a very different starting point than traditional studies of representation. I am not interested in what signs give—that is, what they mean or how they effect. On the contrary, my question concerns why representation occurs: why do we not simply inflect the world we are thrown into but seek to take ownership of that world—that is, why do we claim it as something that is ours? In this essay I have attempted to illuminate the void at the heart of the sign and how it engenders subjectivity as a claim; an inclination to claim oneself as a self vis-à-vis our inescapable existential precarity. For Kohn, signs present subjects with tangible problems, and thought arises as a means to address them. But I would add that hand in hand with those problems that prompt thought are those that undermine it—that is, problems that make a mockery of any and all solutions that thought can provide. There is, in other words, a whispering underneath the sign, a distant and silent summons that is marked by the void. While the sign asks us to think, the void within the sign reminds us of the limits of thinking; that there is a limit to what thinking can do. Indeed, there is a limit to what any and all of our capacities—to act, to will, to produce—can do. It is only when we understand the summons of the void that we understand why subjectivity is not simply an awareness of the self, but a claiming of the self that one finds. Claiming is an attempt to own that which the void steals away. It marks a desire—an inclination—to lay claim to oneself in the face of the void. The claim is what I have called elsewhere a dream of presence: the dream of being a subject that is self-present and self-possessed (Rose 2006).

The purpose of this preliminary sketch has been to illuminate an under-theorized dimension of the sign. In doing so my aim is to point out a potential avenue (if such an avenue were needed) to move the conversation in cultural geography back to questions of representation and identity.

While I am not suggesting that we become re-enamored with the power of signs, I am suggesting that signification remains an important part of the conversation. If it can be shown that the enigmatic dimension of the sign is what engenders claims to certain forms of subjectivity, then surely it is the signifying dimension that gives those claims a language to do so. In such a framework signification takes on even further significance than it did in its previous epistemological guise. If the void at the heart of the sign summons subjects to signify, then those significations are not simply meaningful but are ontologically necessary. They are the means by which subjects become subjects—not just representational subjects but self-claiming subjects, that is, subjects who claim themselves as subjects vis-à-vis a world that perpetually undermines all such determinations. To understand subjectivity in such terms is to get away from some of the traditional trappings of representational thought while simultaneously allowing us to think about how cultural objects and practices continue to have relevance in our everyday social and political lives. It is to recognize the void at the heart of the sign and adjust our optics in a manner that allows us to consider representation not as something powerful and oppressive but rather as something haunted and desperate. It is to recognize representations of subjectivity as claims—as only ever claims.

References

Anderson, Ben, and Colin McFarlane. 2011. "Assemblage and Geography." *Area* 43, no. 2: 124–27.

Asdal, Kristin, Tone Druglitrø, and Steve Hinchliffe, eds. 2016. *Humans, Animals and Biopolitics: The More-Than-Human Condition.* London: Routledge.

Bissell, David. 2009. "Travelling Vulnerabilities: Mobile Timespaces of Quiescence." *cultural geographies* 16, no. 4: 427–45.

———. 2012. "Agitating the Powers of Habit: Towards a Volatile Politics of Thought." *Theory & Event* 15, no. 1.

———. 2013. "Habit Displaced: The Disruption of Skilful Performance." *Geographical Research* 51, no. 2: 120–29.

———. 2015. "Virtual Infrastructures of Habit: The Changing Intensities of Habit through Gracefulness, Restlessness and Clumsiness." *cultural geographies* 22, no. 1: 127–46.

Dewsbury, J-D. 2011. "The Deleuze-Guattarian Assemblage: Plastic Habits." *Area* 43, no. 2: 148–53.

———. 2015. "Non-Representational Landscapes and the Performative Affective Forces of Habit: From 'Live' to 'Blank.'" *cultural geographies* 22, no. 1: 29–48.

Eden, Sally, and Christopher Bear. 2011. "Reading the River through 'Watercraft': Environmental Engagement through Knowledge and Practice in Freshwater Angling." *cultural geographies* 18, no. 3: 297–314.

Heidegger, Martin. 1996. *Being and Time: A Translation of Sein und Zeit*. Albany: State University of New York Press.

Hinchliffe, Steve. 2000. "Entangled Humans: Specifying Powers and Their Spatialities." In *Entanglements of Power: Geographies of Domination/Resistance*, edited by Joanne Sharp, Paul Routledge, Chris Philo, and Ronan Paddison, 219–37. London: Routledge.

———. 2008. "Reconstituting Nature Conservation: Towards a Careful Political Ecology." *Geoforum* 39, no. 1: 88–97.

Ingold, Tim. 2000. *The Perception of the Environment: Essays on Livelihood, Dwelling and Skill*. London: Routledge.

———. 2008. "When ANT Meets SPIDER: Social Theory for Arthropods." In *Material Agency: Towards a Non-Anthropocentric Approach*, edited by Carl Knappett and Lambros Malafouris, 209–15. Boston: Springer.

———. 2011. *Being Alive: Essays on Movement, Knowledge and Description*. London: Routledge.

Kohn, Eduardo. 2013. *How Forests Think: Toward an Anthropology beyond the Human*. Berkeley: University of California Press.

Laplanche, Jean: 1999. *Essays on Otherness*. Edited by John Fletcher. London: Routledge.

Lorimer, Hayden. 2006. "Herding Memories of Humans and Animals." *Environment and Planning D: Society and Space* 24, no. 4: 497–518.

Malafouris, Lambros. 2004. "Cognitive Basis of Material Engagement: Where Brain, Body and Culture Conflate." In *Rethinking Materiality: The Engagement of Mind with the Material World*, edited by Elizabeth DeMarrais, Chris Gosden, and Colin Renfrew, 53–62. Cambridge: McDonald Institute for Archaeological Research.

———. 2013. *How Things Shape the Mind: A Theory of Material Engagement*. Cambridge MA: MIT Press.

Merleau-Ponty, Maurice. 2002. *Phenomenology of Perception*. London: Routledge.

Neumann, Mark. 1999. *On the Rim: Looking for the Grand Canyon*. Minneapolis: University of Minnesota Press.

Pitt, Hannah. 2015. "On Showing and Being Shown Plants: A Guide to Methods for More-Than-Human Geography." *Area* 47, no. 1: 48–55.

Rose, Mitch. 2006. "Gathering 'Dreams of Presence': A Project for the Cultural Landscape." *Environment and Planning D: Society and Space* 24, no. 4: 537–54.

Simpson, Paul. 2013. "Ecologies of Experience: Materiality, Sociality, and the Embodied Experience of (Street) Performing." *Environment and Planning A* 45, no. 1: 180–96.

Van Dyke, John Charles. 1927. *The Grand Canyon of the Colorado: Recurrent Studies in Impressions and Appearances*. New York: Charles Scribner's Sons.

Whatmore, Sarah. 2002. *Hybrid Geographies: Natures Cultures Spaces*. London: Sage.

Wylie, John. 2002. "Becoming-Icy: Scott and Amundsen's South Polar Voyages, 1910–1913." *cultural geographies* 9, no. 3: 249–65.

7   Derwent's Ghost

The Haunting Silences of Geography at Harvard

Alison Mountz and Kira Williams

In July 2016 in his monthly column to several thousand members of the organization, Glen MacDonald (2016), then president of the American Association of Geographers, made passing reference to the collective knowledge of the end of geography at Harvard University. Geographers know this history sparsely, or more accurately, we collectively misremember, a collective mythology forged through oral history, passed along and canonized in introductory graduate courses in geography. Instructors of these courses often recall and teach geographer Neil Smith's (1987) account of the history published in the *Annals of the Association of American Geographers*. Yet even Smith's account is a partial and speculative one, by necessity due to the lack of empirical evidence available at the time of writing about the institutional erasure of geography at Harvard between the 1940s and 1950s. The collective memory of this closure has always been wrapped in the murk of homophobia operating on university campuses and its specific, insidious incarnations at Harvard at the time (Wright 2006). Such histories are difficult to prove or document with, and certainly without, empirical evidence. Importantly, more empirical knowledge of this history has been made available to the public in the time since Smith's (1987) publication, with the digitalization and release of more faculty and administrative records at Harvard—notably, the archives of geographer and faculty member Derwent Stainthorpe Whittlesey—and the publication of *Harvard's Secret Court: The Savage 1920 Purge of Campus Homosexuals* (Wright 2006). Whittlesey was a well-known political geographer recruited to Harvard in 1928 to build a geography program, which *might* have become a department. Whittlesey was gay, but not out, which would have cost him his job at the time.

Smith's (1987) article, and particularly the more speculative of his observations and the questions his essay left unanswered, served as starting points in our own research. Our visit to Harvard and our cursory casual and then more careful rereading of Smith's article over time provoked curiosity. Rereading prompted us to revisit the archives Smith had consulted and to study the new archives released to the public in the time since. We embarked on this project as visiting scholars at Harvard ourselves, where the memory of geography remains alive, if misremembered, when passed among faculty, students, and staff through oral history. Our year on campus from 2015 to 2016 afforded us easy proximity and access to the Harvard archives, as well as those of Isaiah Bowman in Maryland and city records in Cambridge, Massachusetts. We read additional literature on the topic, including—importantly—Rita Morris's (1962) dissertation on the subject. As we pursued this research, we felt haunted ourselves by Derwent, his absent presence prodding us on, back to the vast archives of this story that he left behind, hidden in plain sight.

How does one assess institutional and personal histories to assemble queer archives (Gieseking 2015)? This chapter maps our pursuit of the ghost of political geographer Whittlesey, mapping his spectral movement through his own and others' historical archives. We are drawn to the sociological concept of haunting, building on Jacques Derrida and Avery F. Gordon, for its ability to situate oppressive forces that are at work, if not entirely visible or known. We begin with a series of inconsistent "empirical facts," and move quickly into the void of haunting—Gordon's (2008, 2011) forms of oppression that appear over and done with yet remain present. In this case the spectral is located alongside material traces of geography's present absence at Harvard University. In this telling of the story, we contend with the unspoken yet written-to-later-be-spoken references and allusions to what geographer, geopolitician, powerful Harvard alum, and member of the board of overseers Bowman called "intimate conditions" in his personal archives. We place these embodied intimacies in the context of their time and place, an effort to establish context.

We studied the broader role of institutions and key figures in the closure of Harvard's geography program. We found our characters haunted by what they could not and cannot write but long to speak or have spoken: geographer Edward A. Ackerman by Harvard president James B. Conant, Whittlesey by his partner geographer Harold Kemp, geographer Smith by geographer Bowman, Bowman by crimes of silence and omission, Alison Mountz and Kira Williams by Whittlesey (see Mountz and Williams 2017a, 2017b, 2017c). Repressed or misremembered in myriad ways, we weave these threads in an effort to restore Whittlesey's humanity to the historical record, and in an effort to heal an open wound that itself continues to haunt the discipline of geography.

Cast of Characters and Their Correspondence

> Haunting raises specters, and it alters the experience of being in linear time, alters the way we normally separate and sequence the past, the present and the future. Haunting and the appearance of specters or ghosts is one way . . . we're notified that what's been suppressed or concealed is very much alive and present, messing or interfering precisely with those always incomplete forms of containment and repression ceaselessly directed towards us. (Gordon 2011, 2)

And so, we found ourselves sweating on a humid day in June 2016 in the city of Cambridge's court records, lost in a bureaucratic maze with bewildering, disordered shelves upon shelves of records of obituaries, hand-recorded in monochrome gray binders that had been damaged over the years by flood and fire. We were, in that precise moment, ensnarled in our pursuit to better understand the entanglements of two deaths: the study of geography at Harvard and Whittlesey himself. We knew that these two were entwined, and that we needed to learn more about the intimacies of both. Throughout our research we had sought empirical evidence to lay to rest certain elements of this story that remained open, including, for example, details and confirmation of the romantic relationship between Whittlesey and Kemp. The archives left open no question that the two had been together for decades, from their correspondence to travel records and shared residence. We went in search of their obituaries to learn more about their deaths and, specifically, the guarantor of their wills. This guarantor turned out to be geographer, housemate, and confidant Edward A. Ackerman in both cases. These wills and their recording registered by Ackerman in the city of Cambridge adds to the material traces of geography and geographers at Harvard.

This chapter offers glimpses of a straight telling of this story, and the mere beginning of a queer recovery and retelling (the subject of additional writing in progress). Both involve ghosts and their haunting of the main characters of this history, including those of us who have taken on its retelling. During the 2017 annual meeting of the AAG in Boston, we presented *our* "straight" rendition of the history at the political geography preconference, which was held on Harvard's campus, two blocks from the apartment that Whittlesey, Kemp, and Ackerman once shared during their time together on faculty—known affectionately as The Loft—at 20-A Prescott Street. We returned to this same location a few days later, this time leading approximately twenty-five geographers on a walking tour of campus to recount and reconstruct these intimate and institutional histories. Our tour started at Harvard Square, went quickly to The Loft on the edge of campus, passing the former building of the Geographical Institute, and ending at the Geological Museum, where the program in geography was once housed and was slated for expansion. Our third presentation that week engendered this particular essay: a queer retelling in the sessions "Into the Void," organized by Anna Secor and Paul Kingsbury.

Geography at Harvard: A Straight History

Let us begin with a brief summary of our straight history, recounted more fully in our monograph. As Smith (1987) surmised, any history of the untimely decline of geography at Harvard must be interwoven with the life of its foremost human geographer: Dr. Whittlesey. Using newly available evidence from archives, interviews, and secondary literature, our "straight" institutional history describes Harvard's geography program from 1642 to 1959 to identify how, why, and when the program ended. This "straight history" follows the rise and fall of geography at Harvard based on empirical evidence, especially regarding its human geography program. In the late 1940s university politics, homophobia, and the Cold War culminated in President Conant's decision to effectively end that program. Although this was not the only cause of geography's decline, we explain the decision's wider consequences until the formal end of the program in 1959. We then briefly explore geography's afterlife at Harvard.

Available evidence suggested that geography existed at Harvard University since 1642 (Davis 1924; Morris 1962, 17). The university reestablished and created a more permanent instruction in geography beginning in the 1860s. Through its rapid growth and the presence of notable scholars, the Department of Geology and Geography became a leading center of physical geography in North America by the early 1900s (Davis 1924; Morris 1962, 106–7). Physical geography peaked in the first decade of the 1900s and declined until the rise of human geography.

Human geography began at Harvard in the late 1920s, including and emerging from instruction in regional and topical geography in the early 1900s. President Lowell's administration sought to begin a human geography program as early as 1926 and succeeded in 1928 with the recruitment of Whittlesey, who had worked at the University of Chicago as an assistant professor for the program (Whittlesey correspondence to Dean Moore, April 20, 1928, Whittlesey's Papers). Geography at Harvard reached its zenith under Whittlesey's leadership following the end of the Second World War. The program grew from 102 students enrolled in seven courses taught by five staff members in 1927 to 634 students enrolled in twenty-four courses taught by twelve staff members in 1947 (Harvard University Archives 1928, 1947).

The program experienced important achievements and setbacks during the 1930s. At least four conditions limited geography's growth during this time: the Great Depression, newly elected president Conant, the political

MOUNTZ AND WILLIAMS

position of Harvard's Institute of Geographical Exploration, and competition for limited resources with geology. The Geography Program expanded throughout the 1930s, despite these setbacks. Whittlesey and instructor Kemp expanded training in topical geography, making Harvard the leading institution in study of political geography in the United States (Morris 1962, 166, 241). While the foundation of the Institute of Geographical Exploration damaged relations between the Geography Program and university administration, it provided a beautiful building (which still stands) with a library and state-of-the-art facilities originally designed solely for geography.

When classes and research in geography peaked at Harvard in the 1940s, the program was on course in its progression to become a department, attracting more students, personnel, and resources in the process. The problems of the 1930s persisted, however, and the administration quietly began to unravel geography, culminating in President Conant's explicit declaration of a policy to "let geography die" in 1948: "It seems to me that with all the demands on our funds we might as well make the policy decision of saying, 'This is one of the things like meteorology that Harvard is not going to have'. . . . I have never been able to see that there was a real need for a University Department of Geography or that the subject was a science in any proper use of the word. . . . It is now time to make a policy decision by saying that geography is one of the things we will not develop at Harvard" (Conant 1948).

The importance, independence, and success of geography expanded rapidly in the 1940s. The department intentionally took on new staff, graduate students, and courses "because of their direct application to defense and war training" and as "knowledge necessary to win the War" (Harvard University Archives 1941, 1942). During the Second World War, the program trained military officers and students in geographical knowledge and state ideologies. What would become of the prospective Department of Geography with new hires and expanded course offerings? Perhaps most importantly, the department and administration confirmed Whittlesey's position and accomplishments by giving him tenure in 1943 (Harvard University Archives 1943). The Division of Geological Sciences (1944), which included the Department of Geology and Geography, explicitly asked for the creation of a Department of Geography in a detailed report to the dean of the Faculty of Arts and Sciences on July 1, 1944.

The problems of the 1930s, however, persisted into the 1940s, as the administration began to quietly reduce geography's resources as the war ended. Instead of falling, though, geography's total enrollment would increase from 317 to 634 students from 1945 to 1947 (Harvard University Archives 1946, 1948). Despite this rapid growth, the administration further reduced the program's resources by withdrawing tutorials by 1947 (Correspondence from the President's office via David Bailey to Whittlesey, May 5, 1947, Whittlesey's Papers). It also removed geography as a field of concentration and actively challenged the promotions of Ackerman and Edward Ullman and the hiring of teaching fellow Richard Logan in 1947 (Whittlesey, March 28, 1947, Whittlesey's Papers; Harvard University Archives 1948). By endangering the instructors just as Whittlesey was retiring, Harvard threatened the existence of the entire program.

President Conant perpetuated geography's inability to receive adequate funding. While the Great Depression had ended and the university was richer than ever, he opposed what he saw as the government intrusion into higher-level education (Hershberg 1993, 391). Conant likely opposed geography on additional grounds: the institute's political position, its continual integration with the social sciences, and the operation of institutional and personalized forms of homophobia. While finding archival evidence of individual homophobia was difficult, available records implicated multiple instances of challenging Whittlesey and Kemp due to their sexuality via their "character" (Bowman 1948b; Stamp 1952). William Wright (2006) showed that these types of character attacks were commonly used to defame allegedly queer people, and he demonstrated institutional mechanisms Harvard University used in its marginalization of queer people.

The administration's policy to "let the department die" in 1948 eventually led to the decline of geography at Harvard (Conant 1948). President Conant actively perpetuated this policy in response to the promotions of instructional assistant Logan and assistant professors Ullman and Ackerman in 1947. By the end of that year, he had effectively terminated Logan and Ackerman while relieving Ullman of all duties in geography. This outcome dealt a severe blow to Whittlesey's program and permanently put all plans for a department on hold. As Whittlesey himself wrote: "It turns out that if Ackerman leaves now geography at Harvard will wind up and come to a stop. If we cannot retain him, we cannot get anybody else now whom we could get past the administration" (Whittlesey 1947).

We believe that Ackerman's termination was a homophobic response to allegations of relationships with Kemp or Whittlesey, that fears of homosexuality drove Conant into his decisions about geography at Harvard, in spite of positive votes on Ackerman's case by multiple actors and committees within and beyond the university, and amid widespread opposition to the decision from faculty, students, and scholars well beyond Harvard (as documented in Whittlesey's archives).

President Conant's policy to let geography die at Harvard ultimately led to its complete decline by 1959. This decline, moreover, was only ultimately possible due to its continued implementation by the Conant and Nathan Marsh Pusey administrations. This continual decline had three necessary, joint conditions:

1 The administration's refusal to consider or accept review of its policy with respect to geography;
2 Harvard University's refusal to allocate new resources to geography; and
3 Geography's total loss and reallocation of its existing resources.

These conditions slowly diminished the Geography Department's resources until the program no longer had any personnel, infrastructure, or funding to continue research or instruction. Whittlesey died an untimely— and, we believe, sudden—death in November 1956, mere months after his retirement. His death ended permanent geographical instruction at Harvard, which the university filled with visiting professors until cutting all instruction in 1959.

Geography lived on at Harvard after the program's decline, though its times and places of instruction and research were few and far between each other. The Graduate School of Design (GSD) brought in Associate Professor George Lewis as a visiting scholar for regional planning and geography in 1960 (Harvard University Archives 1961). The GSD was a center for spatial analysis and "theoretical geography" throughout the 1970s (Wilson 2017). Harvard University established the Center for Geographical Analysis, housed in the Weatherhead Center for International Affairs (WCFIA), in 2005 (Center for Geographical Analysis 2017). WCFIA additionally hosted Mountz as a visiting scholar in 2008 and 2015, who taught political geography in the Department of Government, and Williams as a visiting fellow in 2015.

INCONSISTENT "EMPIRICAL FACTS"

Empirical inconsistencies mounted as we conducted our archival research into the queer history of geography at Harvard University, seven of which we explore here. First, the university's administrations, especially as led by President Conant, claimed that geography was in decline at Harvard during the 1930s and 1940s. The statistical records we reconstructed from Harvard's archives, however, showed that the geography program reached its zenith by the Second World War. Between 1927 and 1940, for example, the program increased from 102 to 418 enrolled students, from seven to twenty-nine courses, and from five to fourteen lecturing personnel (Harvard University Archives 1928, 1941). Second, the Conant and Pusey administrations claimed that there was little or no funding available for geography. By the end of the Great Depression, however, and during the Second World War, the university was richer than it had ever been thanks to generous endowments and public funding, such as the GI Bill (Harvard University Archives 1946).

Third, President Conant contested the positionality of geography as a science. This challenge came both to the validity of the discipline as a whole and its increasing association with the burgeoning social sciences (Harvard University Archives 1940). Geography, however, was rapidly growing as a discipline throughout the United States, as recorded by historians such as Morris (1962).

MOUNTZ AND WILLIAMS

Fourth, the Conant and Pusey administrations questioned the use of the human-focused, topical geography that was emerging at Harvard; they claimed that if the university did something, then it must be the best at it or not do it at all. Archival records demonstrated, though, that the geography program had become the leading center for the study of political geography in the United States, with esteemed researchers and advanced infrastructure (Morris 1962).

Fifth, the Conant and Pusey administrations abhorred the existence and operation of Alexander Hamilton's Institute of Geographical Exploration, claiming that it marked geography's decadence (Bowman 1937; Hershberg 1993, 76). While not without its problems, the institute provided uniquely advanced and technical equipment and a library in a building dedicated purely to geography, which was unprecedented in contemporary American geography.

Sixth, President Conant criticized Whittlesey's character as problematic for the program—annotated in Bowman's notes in the margins of his meeting notes with Conant and the Board of Overseers (Bowman 1948b). In contrast, Whittlesey's archives, particularly his correspondence from colleagues, students, and friends, as well as obituaries written after his death, all indicated that he was a widely beloved, kind, and thoughtful person, who worked diligently to protect and expand the program into a prospective department. Whittlesey showed care and dedication to his colleagues and students, evident in his correspondence and his obituary (Ackerman 1957).

Lastly, and perhaps most importantly, popular mythologies as well as Smith (1987) identified the end of the "department" occurring in 1948. Our research revealed, however, that although 1948 was when a policy of explicitly ending geography began, the program itself slowly petered out until its final demise in 1958–1959, shortly after Whittlesey died. Geography's decline was thus slow. The Conant and Pusey administrations brought it about through their refusal to consider or accept a review of its policy, refusal to allocate new resources, and geography's total loss and reallocation of existing resources.

Haunting Harvard: The Void of Geography

It was hard not to fall in love with Whittlesey when reading his corre-spondence. First, because he was charming and thoughtful, taking time and care in his extensive correspondence to colleagues, students, family, and friends around the globe. He meticulously filed these letters, and we meticulously and perhaps unfairly devoured them. Second, because he seems to have always tried to do the right thing. Third, because his own mundane work life was shockingly like our own. We held in common with him a surprising number of things, working some seventy-five years later as queer political geographers at Harvard. We read and write today about how universities have changed, but Derwent's quotidian life was much like our own. The archives showed squabbles over reimbursement, apologies for late manuscripts, and letters of recommendation for students.

Derwent Whittlesey's correspondence also demonstrates what happened to geography over time, including the loss of Ackerman, and forecasts the subsequent haunting of this void across the country:

August 1, 1947, Letter to Lt. Colonel Hubert Schenck, who wrote to Dean Buck in support of Ed:

> Geography barely got started at Harvard 20 years ago when the long finan-cial depression precluded all further expansion. When the war and postwar demand struck, we found ourselves seriously understaffed. Unlike many universities, Harvard has no[t] increased its faculty because the adminis-tration expects to reestablish a limitation on the student body. It so happens that Ackerman is the only young man in the country for whom we can obtain a permanent post at this time, partly because he is favorably known here, but chiefly because he is the top-ranking geograph[er] of his age-group. If he comes back to us in February, we shall be able to go forward. If he does not, the subject will disappear from the Harvard curriculum. That would be a body blow to an important earth science throughout the country, because other universities look to see what Harvard does.

Conant's administrative records also reveal the demise of geography in formal reports and informal correspondence. For example, Harvard's administration contracted a UK-based academic named Dudley Stamp to conduct research and write a report on geography. There is correspondence to Stamp from Conant about his (Conant's) inability to meet with Stamp in person, but his provision of notes on the report nonetheless. Here Conant's views on Derwent emerge: "I believe he has allowed himself to be unduly influenced by his friend Kemp—a dilettante whose interests in art and music—admirable in themselves—have led him right away from any serious contribution to his subject for many years" (Stamp 1952).

Bowman, in his role as new member of the Board of Overseers when Conant shared this decision, also left handwritten notes in the margins for future historians. Whereas Bowman invested heavily in curation and conditions of access to his archives (restricted to men of a certain age and of international repute); Whittlesey, we believe due to his sudden and untimely death, had little intervention in the organization of his archives; only meticulous organization of files likely moved directly from his office when he died. Bowman wrote: "Of course, I am surprised at the thoroughgoing way in which geography will be practically eliminated . . . The declaration that geography is not a university subject I shall attempt to counter on broad lines . . . Some time when we meet, I would like to talk about some of the more intimate conditions in the geographical field at Harvard . . . The forces in a university are complex and I suppose there is much on the other side that you and I do not know but which will come out in the course of time" (Bowman 1948a).

Also indicative of homophobia's quiet haunting of this entire affair are Bowman's meticulous notes in the margins, left behind in his archives after this meeting: "The night before C. had spoken to us new overseers of 'budgetary control' of policy + here was an example of it preceded by a personal judgement on a subject of which he knows nothing—the—reasons for his objections—Whittlesey's character + Rice's Institute—never appearing on the surface" (Bowman 1948a).

Reading letters from Ohio-based scholar Emmeline McSweeney to Whittlesey painted a reflection back on the personalization of these institutional events and how they affected Whittlesey and Kemp, mapped through close friendship and intimate correspondence over many years. When news of the closure arrived, Kemp and McSweeney discussed Whittlesey's distress, his lack of sleep, and his decision to leave Cambridge for a while to recover. Kemp wrote, "Everything Whit says [about Harvard geography] is true. We are in a mess, just when it seemed that we had found our place in the sun. . . . What effect it will have on other universities to learn that Harvard has abandoned geography, I hate to think. I think it may be a serious setback all along the line" (Whittlesey 1947). Derwent's partner Kemp wrote this on the back of his letter to Colby.

McSweeney wrote the following in one such letter: "I can hardly believe that Harvard would adopt such a short-sighted policy as to eliminate a science so increasingly important as geography. It just doesn't make sense . . . I can understand how you seem to stand in the ruins of your world . . . But the feeling that your work of 20 years has gone into the ashcan is nonsense . . . I am just terribly distressed and disturbed. It is hard to know that you are so unhappy" (Emmeline McSweeney to Derwent Whittlesey, March 17, 1948, Whittlesey's Papers).

When Whittlesey died suddenly in November 1956, shortly after a clean bill of health from his doctor (also recorded in the archives), we believe that Kemp and Ackerman were struck with grief. Rather than cull Whittlesey's archives, they moved them in their entirety into the Harvard University Archives. These documents included extensive personal correspondence, including letters between Kemp and Whittlesey and long, loving, mischievous letters to McSweeney. She knew everything, including how to cheer up Whittlesey after Kemp's termination and exit from Harvard in 1948.

In Gordon's (2011) analysis haunting is about oppression that may appear to be over and done with but never actually disappears—it is always present and making itself known, if not seen.

> Something is being freed and there's a reach for it. The reach is key. The something-to-be done is not ever given in advance, but it can be cultivated towards more just and peaceful ends. This emergent rather than fatalistic

conception of haunting often (to the extent that it is or is becoming an explicitly subversive or rebellious consciousness) lends the something-to-be-done a certain retrospective urgency: the something-to-be-done feels as if it has already been needed or wanted before, perhaps forever, certainly for a long time, and we cannot wait for it any longer. We're haunted, as Herbert Marcuse wrote, by the "historic alternatives" that could have been. (Gordon 2011, 5)

This chapter signals our first contribution to this collective "reach" to restore all that has not been spoken from geographers' collective memory of this history. In our archival research and discussions, we found ourselves early on joking about Derwent's ghost. But as time went on it became more appropriate to draw on haunting as a framing. Everything in this history comes back to Derwent's ghost and his hauntings of the present. Geography remains unfinished business. We continue to try to make sense of what *Derwent* left behind *for us*, and how we (geographers, Harvard students) are all part of—haunted by—the story we have only begun here. What can we learn from the history and politics of geography, and from Whittlesey's history?

And which audiences are ready to hear this history? During both of Mountz's years as a visiting faculty at Harvard, students were hungry to learn political geography and eager to learn this history as well. In February 2016 Mountz organized a panel of geographers to speak on this institutional history and on why geography matters. Panelists included Peter Bol (vice provost of Harvard), Mona Domosh and Richard Wright (Dartmouth College), Tim Cresswell (then at Northeastern University), and Williams, introduced and moderated by Mountz. The event had standing room only (Williams and Mountz 2016). Not long after, a journalist for the student paper, *The Crimson*, wrote an extensive investigative story on the history, twice interviewing the authors of this chapter. Her essay was never published.

We have to accept some uncertainty in our interpretive analysis, drawing on what Jen Jack Gieseking (2015) calls "useful in/stability" in the unpacking of the social and spatial dialectic and thinking through queer archives. By useful in/stability Gieseking (2015) refers to the archive as "both stable in its physical form and unstable in its sociality" (2). For us, useful in/stability proves helpful in embracing the uncertainty of silences in the archive and in placing correspondence in the context of its time, as we read and imagine what it would have been like to have been Whittlesey, Kemp, and other queer faculty and students at Harvard during the Cold War.

Of course, geography is still practiced in some ways at Harvard, our own presence, visits, and teaching of political geography there notwithstanding. Although Whittlesey died in 1956, visiting scholars taught courses until 1958. In the 1960s, the lab for spatial analysis was founded, its history documented by geographer Matthew W. Wilson (2017). In the 1970s this work took place in the Graduate School of Design. The 2000s saw the founding of the Center for Geographic Analysis and its expansion in the time since. We believe that 2010 and 2016 were likely the first years that political geography courses were again taught following Whittlesey's retirement in 1956. In these ways and others Whittlesey's history is our own. How has this past (institutional, homophobia, secret court, geography's insecurities, Harvard's void, oral history on campus) never gone away?

Some things go willingly into the void; others are thrown in. So it was with the queer history of geography at Harvard University, as manifested through the lives of geographers Whittlesey, Kemp, and Ackerman. Queerness was a void. Geography was a void. And Harvard University voided these voids. Yet Harvard could not make itself devoid of these things, as much as it tried, and so they kept leaking out—through its secret garden where we met to discuss the archives and secret trials that transpired long before our time on campus.

> For better or worse, the emphasis on the something-to-be-done was a way of focusing on the cultural requirements or dimensions of individual, social, or political movement and change. And one of those requirements was that the ghost him or herself be treated respectfully (its desires broached) and not ghosted or abandoned or disappeared again in the act of dealing

MOUNTZ AND WILLIAMS

with the haunting, even if the ghost cannot be permitted to take everything over, a complicated requirement that's especially pertinent with the living who haunt as if they were dead. To repeat, for me haunting is not about invisibility or unknowability per se, it refers us to what's living and breathing in the place hidden from view: people, places, histories, knowledge, memories, ways of life, ideas. To show what's there in the blind field, to bring it to life on its own terms (and not merely to light) is perhaps the radicalization of enlightenments with which I've been most engaged. This particular approach to or definition of haunt. (Gordon 2011)

We have focused on Derwent Whittlesey because he has not been amply positioned in this institutional history in the slim public record to date. With the opening of his archives, a fuller accounting was both possible and necessary. Ever since the duress caused to Whit and his colleagues, a persistent "something-to-be-done" has haunted U.S.-based geographers and Harvard-educated students denied the opportunity to learn geography since 1959. "I thought at that meeting point—in the gracious but careful reckoning with the ghost—we could locate some elements of a practice for moving towards eliminating the conditions that produce the haunting in the first place. For me, this is as much a personal as an intellectual question, and as an intellectual approach it reflects my desire to try to learn how to end the suffering, not merely how to diagnose or diagram or justify or witness" (Gordon 2011, 5).

This story matters not only for Harvard's faculty and students, past, present, and future, and their inability to learn geography, but for the discipline of geography—and particularly geography in the United States. The outcome, secrecy, and political fight surrounding Ackerman's tenure and promotion file continues to haunt geography. The absence of geography at Harvard represents a void within the discipline that seems to tap into geographers' relentless anxieties about their place in the academy. It is worth a collective dwelling in and deepening of our understanding the past where this void takes root with the hope of a different future. We wonder, what closures and new openings might be forged through a fuller empirical accounting of and reckoning with the past?

References

ARCHIVES

Bowman, Isaiah. 1937. Letter to no one, released after death. Johns Hopkins University, July 27. Baltimore: Johns Hopkins University Archives.

———.1948a. Letter to Kirk Bryan. John Hopkins University, March 22. Baltimore: Johns Hopkins University Archives.

———. 1948b. Notes from Harvard University Overseers' Meeting. Harvard University, October 11. Baltimore: Johns Hopkins University Archives

Conant, James. 1948. Letter to Provost of Faculty of Arts and Sciences Dean Paul Buck. Harvard University, January 13. Cambridge MA: Harvard University Archives.

Harvard University Archives, Harvard University Library

 1928. "Reports of the President and the Treasurer of Harvard College 1927–1928." http://nrs.harvard.edu/urn-3:hul.arch:15004 (accessed October 26, 2017).

 1940. Issue Containing the Report of the President of Harvard College and Reports of Departments for 1938–1939.

 1941. "Reports of the President and the Treasurer of Harvard College 1940–1941." http://nrs.harvard.edu/urn-3:hul.arch:15003 (accessed October 26, 2017).

 1942. "Reports of the President and the Treasurer of Harvard College 1941–1942." http://nrs.harvard.edu/urn-3:hul.arch:15003 (accessed October 26, 2017).

 1943. "Reports of the President and the Treasurer of Harvard College 1942–1943." http://nrs.harvard.edu/urn-3:hul.arch:15003 (accessed October 26, 2017).

 1946. "Reports of the President and the Treasurer of Harvard College 1945–1946." http://nrs.harvard.edu/urn-3:hul.arch:15003 (accessed October 26, 2017).

 1947. "Reports of the President and the Treasurer of Harvard College 1946–1947." http://nrs.harvard.edu/urn-3:hul.arch:15003 (accessed October 26, 2017).

 1948. "Reports of the President and the Treasurer of Harvard College 1947–1948." http://nrs.harvard.edu/urn-3:hul.arch:15003 (accessed October 26, 2017).

 1961. "Reports of the President and the Treasurer of Harvard College 1960–1961." http://nrs.harvard.edu/urn-3:hul.arch:15008 (accessed October 26, 2017).

Whittlesey, Derwent Stainthorpe. 1947. Letter to Charles Colby. Harvard University, April 25. Cambridge MA: Harvard University Archives.

———. 1908–1956. *Papers of Derwent Stainthorpe Whittlesey*. Cambridge MA: Harvard University Archives.

OTHER SOURCES

Ackerman, Edward A. 1957. "Derwent Stainthorpe Whittlesey." *Geographical Review* 47, no. 3: 443–45.

Center for Geographical Analysis. 2017. "About: Center for Geographical Analysis." *Harvard University*. https://gis.harvard.edu/about (accessed October 26, 2017).

Davis, W. M. 1924. "The Progress of Geography in the United States." *Annals of the Association of American Geographers* 14, no. 4: 159–215.

Division of Geological Sciences. 1944. "Post-War Plans for Geology: Report to the Dean of the Faculty of Arts and Sciences." Division of Geological Sciences, Harvard University, July 1.

Gieseking, Jen Jack. 2015. "Useful In/stability: The Dialectical Production of the Social and Spatial Lesbian Herstory Archives." *Radical History Review* 122: 25–37.

Gordon, Avery F. 2008. *Ghostly Matters: Haunting and the Sociological Imagination.* 2nd ed. Minneapolis: University of Minnesota Press.

———. 2011. "Some Thoughts on Haunting and Futurity." *Borderlands* 10, no. 2: 1–21.

Hershberg, James G. 1993. *James B. Conant: Harvard to Hiroshima and the Making of the Nuclear Age.* Stanford CA: Stanford University Press.

MacDonald, Glen M. 2016. "The End(s) of Geography?" Featured News, President's Column. *Newsletter of the American Association of Geographers.* July 1. http://news .aag.org/2016/07/the-ends-of-geography/ (accessed September 22, 2019).

Morris, Rita. 1962. "An Examination of Some Factors Related to the Rise and Decline of Geography as a Field of Study at Harvard, 1638–1948." PhD diss. Harvard University.

Mountz, Alison, and Kira Williams. 2017a. "Derwent's Ghost: A History of Geography at Harvard University, 1929–1956." Political Geography Preconference, American Association of Geographers, Harvard University, Cambridge MA, April.

———. 2017b. "Derwent's Ghost: A History of Geography at Harvard University, 1929–1956." Annual Meeting of the American Association of Geographers, Boston, April 5–7.

———. 2017c. "Derwent's Queer Cambridge." Annual Meeting of the American Association of Geographers, Boson, April 5–7.

Smith, Neil. 1987. "'Academic War over the Field of Geography': The Elimination of Geography at Harvard, 1947–1951." *Annals of the Association of American Geographers* 77, no. 2: 155–72.

Stamp, Dudley. 1952. "Report on Geography at Harvard, October 12, 1952." *Harvard University.*

Williams, Kira, and Alison Mountz. 2016. "A History of Geography at Harvard." Panel: Why Geography Matters, Harvard University, Cambridge MA, February 11.

Wilson, Matthew W. 2017. *New Lines: Location-Aware Futures and the Map.* Minneapolis: University of Minnesota Press.

Wright, William. 2006. *Harvard's Secret Court: The Savage 1920 Purge of Campus Homosexuals.* New York: St. Martin's Griffin.

8 "It Watches You Vanish"
On Landscape and W. G. Sebald

John Wylie

In this chapter I pursue a particular argument regarding landscape. This is something of a stark argument; one that contends that landscape is always a matter of vanishing and disappearing. But I take the sign of the void, the animating concern of this book, as granting a kind of permission to pursue this contention, however unforgiving or singular it may at first seem. My specific inspiration and preoccupation here is the work of the German writer W. G. Sebald, born in southwest Germany in 1944 but resident in England as a tenured professor of European literature at the University of East Anglia from the early 1970s until his death in a car accident in 2001. In particular I am guided by one short poem of his—the very first poem, in fact, in the English language translated collection of his work *Across the Land and the Water* (2012). Here it is in full:

> For how hard it is
> to understand the landscape
> as you pass in a train
> from here to there
> and mutely it
> watches you vanish. (Sebald 2012, 3)

The poem is untitled, as many others in the collection also are; the contents page simply lists it by its first line, "For how hard it is." Brief and compressed, it has a Haiku-style resonance, without perhaps achieving the oneiric and crystalline qualities of a classic Haiku. It already announces and explains itself too much for that. But a startling fact for me, and maybe also for any reader who knows Sebald's writing, is that this short poem was written in 1964, when he was but a twenty-year-old student at Freiburg in Germany, and was published, along with several other pieces similar in tone and length, in a student magazine, the *Freiburger Studentenzeitung*. It is almost, in other words, a piece of juvenilia. And yet it uncannily anticipates and encapsulates the themes that dominate the major prose works of the 1990s for which Sebald will undoubtedly be remembered: themes of landscape, travel, exile, incomprehension, forgetting, and disappearance.

My concern in this chapter is not just with an exegesis or analysis of this particular brief poem—and this would be a challenge to sustain, given its brevity. Instead, I adopt the poem as a structuring device and take its lines as both headings and prompts, thus establishing a route for wider reflection on the issue of how and why landscape might be understood as a kind of vanishing. Along the way, though, I comment and draw further on Sebald's wider work, given I believe it offers not simply an illuminating literary example but also a key ethical and aesthetic intervention in terms of our understandings of landscape. Sebald's body of work is widely acknowledged today as one of the signature achievements of late twentieth-century German and European prose writing and has already generated a notably large secondary academic literature.

While Sebald's writing ranges widely across many topics and venues, it is deeply shadowed by the Second World War and by the crimes of the Holocaust in particular. It would not perhaps be accurate to call Sebald a "Holocaust writer" in any very direct or prescriptive way—and if indeed there *is* any such writer. But the war and the events of the Holocaust are undoubtedly germinal to his sustained, circuitous, and labyrinthine reflections upon, and investigations into, themes of landscape, memory, identity, and belonging. This means there is on one level an undeniable specificity of address and reception in relation to his work, as a postwar German-born author. In this chapter, though, my aim is not only to offer a contextual analysis of Sebald. Instead, in what follows, I use his work as a touchstone and point of salient contrast in relation to notable current understandings of landscape and perception in cultural geography and phenomenology in particular.

One final comment by way of introduction is to note that Sebald's poem is distinguished by a late twist. As you will have already seen, its last two lines enact an abrupt reversal of perspective, wherein it is the landscape that "watches you vanish." Following the poem as I go here, I seek to diagnose and understand this reversal in more detail in the penultimate section of the chapter. But I know that it catches the eye from the outset, and that much of the intrigue of the poem lies herein. So I flag here at the start this specific entwining of *watching* and *vanishing*, which I have come to feel is integral to the concept of landscape, as the key message of the chapter.

For How Hard It Is / to Understand the Landscape . . .

If I talk of vanishing, I must risk falling into a sense of difficulty, and sometimes even of mystery, that often seems to accompany thinking and writing about landscape. More than many geographical motifs and tropes, landscape appears to invite a kind of reifying veneration that renders it resistant to final technical description or definition (though maybe something similar could be said about *place* or even *region*). Some find *landscape* as a concept obscure, precious, and even tiresome in consequence. Others (myself included) succumb to the appeal of attempting over and again to reckon with this grail, to arrive once more at landscape. But perhaps *arrival* is an apposite term here? Because the difficulty, and the allure, is that this is exactly what you *cannot* do with landscape; you cannot *arrive*. Instead its phenomenology is ghostly. It remains perpetually at least to some degree out of reach, at a distance, on the cusp of a vanishing point of disappearance. We could say that this is one way in which, as a point of principle, any landscape must involve an element of vanishing and disappearing.

One set of responses to this kind of thinking, which arguably risks mystifying landscape all over again, is to insist instead upon the *material presences* of landscape and thence upon a set of techniques, approaches, and dispositions—more traditionally empirical or phenomenological— that will help determine the nature and range of these presences. Hard-won understanding of landscape can thus be gained by observational diligence, descriptive endeavor, and conceptual clarity. Whether through analysis of the varied objects, deposits, rhythms, and patterns that furnish the land, or *via* encounters among the lived, embodied presencings of its inhabitants, human and nonhuman, the landscape materially shows itself. It *appears*, it shows up, in layers of meaning and habits of living, in footpaths, fairy tales, and field systems, and so in this way it can be narrated and understood.

The absences of landscape, all that which is invisible, lost, or elsewhere, can in fact be readily appeased and accommodated within these kinds of analyses—at least to some extent. The passing of time, for example, can be taken as less a process of irretrievable loss and fracture and more as one of rhythmic unfurling, recycling, rotting away and blossoming afresh. Therefore, footfalls by those now gone and forgotten may still appear and endure as pathways affording lifeworlds anew, and their memories may yet rematerialize objectively and visibly in the evident present. An abyssal sense of absence and disappearance is in this way transformed, and maybe even tamed, into the more poignant affectivities of "absent presences."

Critical-historical analyses of landscape perhaps offer a sharper acknowledgment of the constitutive role of absence in landscape. Their insight is that any landscape, and in particular any story of landscape, must necessarily be created through acts of exclusion and silencing. This calls attention to aspects of landscape that are irreconcilable, in particular to ghosts that can at best only aspire to a doubtful, unsettling kind of presence, but that, in doing so, can at least call into question the status of all objects and patterns that seem to be apparently and indisputably present.

Here again, however, absence remains in a sense subservient to presence, or at least to a process of revealing and of revelation—of "bringing to presence." Instead of the landscape's materiality constituting a kind of ontic and ontological plenitude, for critical analysis this apparently solid and meaningful presence is a kind of masquerade, facade, or veil. Behind its smiling face in the sunlight the landscape has something to hide and conceal, something that's not right, something that needs to be uncovered by vigilant watching and reading. In this way the workings of the landscape that were previously hidden and invisible are lifted into view.

For Sebald, however, the landscape is hard to understand chiefly because of its "numbed" and amnesiac character. In the final pages of *Vertigo*, the first and perhaps most fraught of his book-length prose works, the narrator is once again journeying by train and still watching the landscape of Germany in which "everything appeared to be appeased and numbed in some sinister way" (Sebald 1990, 253). The insight that the landscape is a facade composed of willful erasure and semi-deliberate forgetting does not, though, become a passageway to revelation. We confront instead a blinding, incomprehensible field of vision. The landscape remains insusceptible to any ideological critique; instead it is as if this idea of landscape as a veil or a shroud, hiding things away, is carried to a kind of delirious fever pitch. For Sebald it seems that the way that a landscape makes things vanish and disappear is both historical and hauntological. In other words a landscape is both a narratable process of remembering and forgetting, *and also* an ineluctable kind of testimony to a never-present, never-accessible, and always-haunted sense of the world.

In her highly perspicacious reading of Sebald and questions of representing the past, Jessica Dubow (2011) pinpoints this sense of landscape: "Sebald's characters are not travellers who see sites, but those who can no longer make sense of the seen, and try to make visible this loss. . . . Here, time and space, deprived of their usual imaginary consistency, open onto a certain void or invisibility. No longer capable of securing the foundations for reflection and recollection, they become passages to a kind of depthless forgetting, to a ground in which experience cannot take root" (Dubow 2011, 189).

Quite often, then, in Sebald's accountings a landscape is a bland but on reflection bewildering surface that prompts not a determined investigative critique or expose, but rather a terror-stricken response involving a loss of sight and sense. Early in Sebald's (2001) *Austerlitz*, in the dungeons of the Breendonk Second World War prison camp, the narrator is overcome such that "black striations began to quiver before my eyes" (33). A few pages but many years later, this sudden blindness recurs in the narrator's home and garden, with "figures and landscapes familiar to me in every detail [resolving] indiscriminately into a black and menacing cross-hatching" (47).

Elsewhere, the experience of landscape-as-void in Sebald's writing prompts other anguished bodily responses. The narrator feels nauseous, reels dizzily, or falls into a fugue-like state. In extremis we see a body rendered wholly prostate, or even one that simply turns and flees. If self and landscape in their classically understood form are codependent—that is, if a landscape demands the organizing perspective of a self, and if a composed self equally requires an assured and reliably present landscape— then for Sebald the price of landscape's amnesiac dislocation from itself is a self in disarray. The landscape is hard to understand, not because it is ineffable or sublime, but because it opens up to the onlooker's gaze as an incomprehensible absence—because what it offers, to quote from Dubow (2011) once more, is "a ground in which experience cannot take root" (189).

As You Pass in a Train . . .

For all that he is perhaps best known as a compulsive landscape wanderer, Sebald is also one of the greatest train writers. Few others make as much use as he does of the imaginative possibilities and affective atmospheres of trains, carriages, stations, waiting rooms, and rail networks. Across the whole body of his work, railways and trains are a recurrent feature, whether as a device to move the narrative onward to a new locale, or more forbiddingly as an often-unspecified symbol of threat and danger. Or, if this sounds too vague and ominous, the train is more simply sometimes an opportunity for an observational interlude. The landscape is not always a mute blankness, as it is in the poem I am following here; it is often described in arresting detail. And fellow travelers—striking women and grotesque men—sometimes also catch Sebald's eye. Yet, just as a Sebaldian sense of landscape is shaded by horror, destruction, and loss, and by the event of the Holocaust especially, so repeatedly railways also figure as a premonition, or a memory, of flight, exile, fear, and oblivion. The elegiac tone of Sebald's poem acquires a jagged edge if we suppose, hopefully without too much presumption, that the "you" of its address is a captive *en route* to vanishing.

But this could also be a regular carriage, of course, with seats, windows, and light, and time allowed for watching. And maybe like me you have sometimes wondered about the specific qualities of landscape as viewed from a moving train. It is simple mechanics in some ways, perhaps—a quality to do with a certain sense of velocity and sustained above all by the generally flat and even course of the voyage. But this might only become apparent when disrupted. Some years ago I was in Japan; while there I caught the bullet train, the Shinkansen, from Tokyo to Kyoto. The train glided out from the teeming, flashing station as smoothly as a snake over sand. Then it accelerated, or lunged as I thought, and our velocity and momentum steadily increased until we were hurtling headlong through the infinite Tetris jumble of the Tokyo suburbs, and I was clutching the armrests of my seat as I do on a plane at takeoff. Now the train was simply going *too fast* for watching and reflecting. Looking out of the window was very quickly nauseating. Even when we reached the countryside, and the view expanded onto rice fields, golf driving ranges, and distant hills, the foreground still whipped by in an uncannily rapid way, and little steady sense of landscape and perspective could be maintained—at least by me.

Of course, what was disrupted here was a quite particular understanding of landscape, in terms of a normative framing of the scale and depth of spaces; one that has only a partial resonance within Japanese culture, for example. But at least this experience clarified for me, by way of contrast, the complex *milieu* of modernity, reverie, and melancholy in which much European long-distance literary and philosophical train travel seems to take place, and to which Sebald's poem certainly seems to belong.

This *milieu* is exemplified by the unmatchable final lines of Philip Larkin's (2001) *The Whitsun Weddings*, where, as the train journey in this case nears its end, "there swelled / A sense of falling, like an arrow-shower / Sent out of sight, somewhere becoming rain" (13). In a state of incessant recession and continual disappearance before the gaze of the traveler, the landscape comes to be saturated with melancholy and wistfulness. Reciprocally the traveler is left to feel departed and gone. Perhaps this is why, sometimes, and especially at the end of longer journeys, as you gather your things, and even if you have spent the whole time *not* watching out of the window, but absorbed instead by other types of screens, there is a sense arising not just of ending and beginning over again—there is a sense as well of something that has been irretrievably lost.

But most of all there is distance and separation—this is what is distilled most potently in the situation of landscape envisioned through a moving train's window. Sometimes this is thought of as "cinematic" in nature; in Wolfgang Schivelbusch's (2014) influential work on the advent of the railways, for instance, the world becomes a dissociated landscape-panorama, reeling by a newly modernized perceptual consciousness. A precise rendition of this is offered by Michel de Certeau's (1984) in *The Practice of Everyday Life*, one that perhaps overdoes a sense of train travel as "incarceration," (111) but that distinctively captures how the window and the train's irresistibly linear motion configure together "two complementary modes of separation" (112):

> The first creates the spectator's distance: You shall not touch; the more you see, the less you hold—a dispossession of the hand in favour of a greater trajectory for the eye. The second inscribes, indefinitely, the injunction to pass on; it is its order written in a single but endless line: go, leave, this is not your country, and neither is that—an imperative of separation which obliges one to pay for an abstract ocular domination of space by leaving behind any proper place, by losing one's footing. (de Certeau 1984, 112)

It cannot be a coincidence, I think, or exclusively a historical gesture that Sebald's reverie on vanishing is train-bound. No other mode of moving and being chimes better with both a sense of landscape as incessant distancing—and a sense of self gone awry, in "leaving behind any proper place."

From Here to There . . .

"From here to there," the poem travels. From a to b, from nowhere in particular to somewhere equally unmemorable. Nothing could be more alien to Sebald's sensibility than any local "sense of place" or a feeling of "place attachment." But, of course, this is not a simple rejection of locatedness in favor of some free, unfettered mobility. Sebald's characteristic form of mobility is instead fugitive and exiled, occurrent as an ongoing displacement of self and landscape. In this way, place is, as it were, always already being undone by displacement. And displacement "from here to there" is figured as the ongoing condition of any perception or apparition of landscape.

It seems odd in hindsight that *landscape* and *mobility* could ever have been understood by cultural geographers in particular as opposing, as terms in need of dialogue and reworking (see Merriman et al. 2008). It is straightforward to argue that far from connoting some idealized, motionless spatial view, myriad qualities of movement are absolutely integral to any wholehearted or holistic sense of landscape. The walk to the ridge or hilltop to set the land in perspective. The movements of the others accompanying you, present or absent. The course of the sun across the skies above. The wind in the trees, and through the clothes on the line. The rhythms of the road traffic, your heartbeat, your breathing. The eye focusing in upon, and following its way through, the structured depths of the picture-space. The aching tread from picture to picture in the gallery. The familiar pathways and itineraries of a weekday. The flickering of distant lights and stars.

I write the sentences above with the work of Tim Ingold on landscape, dwelling, and movement particularly in mind. He consistently stresses the aliveness of landscape—the inherently flowing and moving qualities of land and life. In Ingold's (2007) *Lines: A Brief History*, though, he rails in particular against the reduction of such a holistic sense of environmental movement—what he terms "wayfaring"—to mere "transportation" in modern cultures. Frequently today, in cars, trains, and planes, Ingold argues that existence is at best a kind of suspended animation—suspended in the course of passive transport from "from a to b." This is not simply a question of technology or mechanism, however. Ingold's issue is rather with an entire approach to life in which movement is reductively conceived as transportation between fixed points. This state, he argues, is characterized by "the dissolution of the intimate bond that, in wayfaring, couples locomotion and perception" (Ingold 2007, 78). The engaged walker (or weaver, hunter, kayaker) participates in the world's ongoing unfolding as one integrated element of it. A place is itself a pathway here, a whorl of itineraries clustering and branching out again. In contrast the self-subjected to transport perceives places as but fixed points or destinations and sees between them only an interval of enforced stasis. The experience of transport is thus far removed from any perception of time's passing in terms of growth, change, and possibility. Instead the experience focuses upon a sense of time being "lost," of impatience and endurance. The train or plane passenger is haunted by an impossible ideal: instantaneous transportation from place to place. Harried by this specter, and "unlike the wayfarer, who moves *with* time, the transported traveller races *against* it" (Ingold 2007, 102; emphasis in the original). In contrast Ingold's (2007) wayfarer experiences a synergy of time, movement, perception, and landscape. They are in sync with their world, moving assuredly along "the line of wayfaring, accomplished through the practices of dwelling and the circuitous movements they entail" (167). Indeed for Ingold "the inhabited world is a reticulated meshwork of such trails . . . continually being woven as life goes on along them" (83–84).

It is tempting to view Sebald's geographies as a kind of extreme or hysterical version of the baleful world of transport invoked by Tim Ingold. These geographies seem forever caught between "here and there" and so are bereft of even the functional satisfactions of departure and arrival. Narrators and events are instead seemingly perpetually marooned within a sense of time's loss and of opportunities for connection and affirmation continually being misplaced.

But it is also possible to sense in Sebald something beyond a simple binary of alienated transport and engaged wayfaring. As many commentators have noted (for example, Catling 2003; Leone 2007), his approach sometimes calls to mind the image of Walter Benjamin's *flaneur*, a compound of modernity, motion, and anomie, drifting rootless through landscapes both ruinous and beguiling. The heavy gravity, even solemnity, of Sebald's style, which persists even through recurrent episodes of dream and hallucination, is quite removed, however, from the dilettante and lyrical landscape aesthetics sometimes associated with the *flaneur*. The contrast with Ingold's wayfarer is more telling, I think, when considered in terms of tone and in particular *trajectory*. The wayfarer, as I understand it, is self-assured and usually successful. His or her landscape mobility feels fluent and forever oriented *onward*. Even as every step recapitulates the memories of other pathfinders, it is also fresh and new in its quality. In contrast, for Sebald it is as though every step is a *sidestep*. In his book-length prose work as in this early poem, *en route* "from here to there" (and, in doing so, vanishing), to be mobile in a landscape is to be fugitive, potentially assailed, and always ready to move quickly out of the way, to *step aside* and withdraw from view. The mobile body, often understood as an environing locus of sense, is refigured as wraith-like and as a continual process of withdrawal. Movement becomes as much a means of *hiding away* as of being disclosed and assuredly evident as a landscape-figure.

And Mutely / It Watches You . . .

Having established its situation—a conventional one; a traveler watching a landscape from a moving train—Sebald's poem reaches its crux and twists, with an abrupt reversal of perspective: "and mutely / it watches you." The theme of watching, and being watched, is one that recurs in the work of many of the most prominent mid-twentieth-century French writers on questions of perception and selfhood. It is a preoccupation, perhaps even an obsession, for Maurice Merleau-Ponty, particularly in his later work. In his final essay, "Eye and Mind," he turns, as is his wont, to painting as a vehicle for expressing his insight: "Inevitably the roles between the painter and the visible switch. That is why so many painters have said that things look at them . . . We speak of 'inspiration,' and the word should be taken literally. There really is inspiration and expiration of Being, respiration in Being, action and passion so slightly discernible that it becomes impossible to distinguish between who sees and who is seen, who paints and what is painted" (Merleau-Ponty 2003, 129).

For Merleau-Ponty, the fact that I both see *and* am seen is a revelation that never loses its glamour. It means that I am part of the world that I see, both perceiver and perceived, actor and object—and this reversibility is both a guarantee of my place in the world, *and* something that lifts me beyond myself, allowing for "a participation in the being of space beyond every particular point of view" (Merleau-Ponty 2003, 134).

I can still recall quite clearly the shock that went through me when I first read Sebald's essay on the painter Jan Peter Tripp, published as part of their collaborative work, *Unrecounted* (Sebald and Tripp 2004), and read him quote, in relation to Tripp's hyperrealist close-up drawings of staring human eyes, the very same lines from Merleau-Ponty's (2003) "Eye and Mind" that I have just cited above: "it becomes impossible to distinguish between who sees and who is seen." It should have been a serendipitous moment; two writers coinciding unexpectedly on the page. It was actually jarring and disturbing, one of those moments when you feel as if all you say and do is somehow preordained and already known elsewhere.

Ten years on, though, it still seems difficult to think of Sebald and Merleau-Ponty together. The latter's accounts of seeing and being seen have very little, almost nothing, of the sense of paranoia and trepidation that characterize Sebald's accounts of a watchful world. A better match, at least in mood, would seem to be Jean-Paul Sartre's ([1957] 2003) well-known account of "the look" in *Being and Nothingness*. Not the situation of the peeping Tom caught watching through the keyhole, but the first account of the solitary watcher in the park disturbed by the encroaching presence of another seer. At this point, Sartre ([1957] 2003) claims, the first-person perspective, and the sense of assurance that accompanies it, is dismantled: "there unfolds a spatiality which is not my spatiality; for instead of a grouping towards me of the objects, there is now an orientation which flees from me" (254). The other watcher "has stolen the world from me," Sartre says (255), and this further suggests that no steady co-presence of self and landscape can be maintained. "It appears that the world has a kind of drain hole in the middle of its being," Sartre goes on, "and that it is perpetually flowing off through this hole" (256).

Whatever issues we might have with Sartre's first-person-centered existentialism, in which others seem to be always only objects or voids, it does serve to highlight a particular affective situation germane to questions of landscape experience. As Norman Bryson (1999) notes, when many perspectives are in play across a scene, almost like duelists, then "the watcher self is now a tangent, not a centre, a vanishing point not a viewing point, an opacity on the other's distant horizon" (89). The lesson he goes on to draw takes us back straight to the conundrum of Sebald's poem: "The viewpoint and the vanishing point are inseparable: there is no viewpoint without vanishing point, and no vanishing point without viewing point. The self-possession of the viewing subject has built into it, therefore, the principle of its own abolition: annihilation of the subject as centre is a condition of the very moment of the look" (Bryson 1999, 91).

It is certainly true that a question mark hovers perpetually over perception in Sebald's accounts of self and landscape. The sense that the narrator's perception might be not just mistaken, but caught in a crisis state of dissolution and draining away, becomes itself an animating feature. But what of the "it" that watches us here? This landscape that *watches* is not—I think—like an active, singular other with whom we might readily correspond, and nor is this merely the indifferent stare of a nonhuman nature. It watches *mutely*, Sebald says—its silence could be taken as a kind of reproach. Or as the silence of an apparition, a reminder, returning without ever becoming fully visible or intelligible. A watching that persists whether *we* see it or not, "a spectral asymmetry" of vision as Derrida (1993, 6) puts it, in which "*the ghost, always, is looking at me*" (134; emphasis in the original).

Vanish . . .

> For how hard it is
> to understand the landscape
> as you pass in a train
> from here to there
> and mutely it
> watches you vanish. (Sebald 2012, 3)

Sebald's poem is like a kind of motif, I think, encapsulating a particular way of thinking about self-landscape relations. It clarifies something different from other classic incarnations of self and landscape. It is clearly different from the regard of the viewing subject who commands the scene from on high. While still marked by elegy and reverie, it stands at one remove also from the romantic epiphanies of the nature lover. It seems distinct too from any thought of self and landscape as mutual immersion in perceptual harmony. It is almost like a needling question repeatedly put to all these incarnations—how to account for phenomenologies of distance, absence, and disappearance in landscape?

What is *gained* by emphasizing that a landscape is always a kind of vanishing? Firstly some nuance, perhaps. A means of attending to absences as otherwise than latent presences, for example. An insight into the specific spatialities of perspectival landscape, organized around one or more vanishing points. And access to a skein of phenomenological and spatial thinking that weaves through and sometimes counter to a mainstream narrative of capable perception, conducted within a context of positive and dynamic worldiness.

More widely, we leave home behind here; we enter an unhomely landscape—a phrase that might even summarize the experience of reading Sebald. For the art critic Robin Kelsey (2008), the landscape way of seeing is a "fantasy of not-belonging" to the world (204). It is ultimately only a fantasy for Kelsey, whose argument is premised upon an idea of humanity's inextricable ecological codependence with the earth. But what if this were not just some passing train-bound daydream? What if landscape named *not-belonging* is a lived, existential condition? Sebald's landscape is a world without original inhabitants, a world where no one seems to belong. This is where ontological questions around absence and vanishing become more sharply ethical and political. Is it possible to escape nationalist or nativist framings of landscape as homeland (see Wylie 2016), where subjects and land seem locked together in mutually regarding presence? I believe so. Because, to say that landscape must always entwine watching and vanishing, is to confirm that landscape can never be a homeland for us.

References

Bryson, Norman. 1999. "The Gaze in the Expanded Field." In *Vision and Visuality*, edited by Hal Foster, 86–108. New York: New Press.

Catling, Jo. 2003. "Gratwanderungen bis an den Rand der Natur: W. G. Sebald's Landscapes of Memory." In *The Anatomist of Melancholy: Essays in Memory of W. G. Sebald*, edited by Rüdiger Görner, 19–50. Munich: Iudicium.

de Certeau, Michel. 1984. *The Practice of Everyday Life*. Translated by Steven Rendall. Berkeley: University of California Press.

Derrida, Jacques. 1993. *Spectres of Marx: The State of the Debt, the Work of Mourning and the New International*. London: Routledge.

Dubow, Jessica. 2011. "Still-Life, After-Life, *Nature Morte*: W. G. Sebald and the Demands of Landscape." In *Envisioning Landscapes, Making Worlds: Geography and the Humanities*, edited by Stephen Daniels, Dydia DeLyser, J. Nicholas Entrikin, and Douglas Richardson, 188–97. London: Routledge.

Ingold, Tim. 2007. *Lines: A Brief History*. New ed. London: Routledge.

Kelsey, Robin. 2008. "Landscape as Not-Belonging." In *Landscape Theory*, edited by Rachael Ziady DeLue and James Elkins, 203–12. London: Routledge.

Larkin, Philip. 2001. *The Whitsun Weddings*. London: Faber & Faber.

Leone, Massimo. 2007. "Textual Wanderings: A Vertiginous Reading of W. G. Sebald." In *W. G. Sebald: A Critical Companion*, edited by J. J. Long and Anne Whitehead, 89–101. Seattle: University of Washington Press.

Merleau-Ponty, Maurice. 2003. "Eye and Mind." In *The Merleau-Ponty Aesthetics Reader: Philosophy and Painting*, edited by Galen A. Johnson, translated by Michael B. Smith, 121–63. Chicago: Northwestern University Press.

Merriman, Peter, George Revill, Tim Cresswell, Hayden Lorimer, David Matless, Gillian Rose, and John Wylie. 2008. "Landscape, Mobility, Practice." *Social & Cultural Geography* 9, no. 2: 191–212.

Sartre, Jean-Paul. (1957) 2003. *Being and Nothingness: A Phenomenological Essay on Ontology*. Translated by Hazel E. Barnes. London: Routledge.

Schivelbusch, Wolfgang. 2014. *The Railway Journey: The Industrialization of Time and Space in the Nineteenth Century*. Berkeley: University of California Press.

Sebald, Winfried Georg. 1990. *Vertigo*. Translated by Michael Hulse. London: Harvill Press.

———. 2001. *Austerlitz*. Translated by Anthea Bell. London: Hamish Hamilton.

———. 2012. *Across the Land and the Water: Selected Poems, 1964–2001*. Translated by Iain Galbraith. London: Hamish Hamilton.

Sebald, Winfried Georg, and Jan Peter Tripp. 2004. *Unrecounted*. Translated by Michael Hamburger. London: Hamish Hamilton.

Wylie, John. 2016. "A Landscape Cannot Be a Homeland." *Landscape Research* 41, no. 4: 408–16.

PART 3 Edges

9   *enfolding*

An Experimental geographical imagination system (gis)

Nick Lally and Luke Bergmann

The transcontinental railroad carves a narrow corridor through the land-scape, linking together tiny stations in small towns between major metrop-olises, giving passengers glimpses into otherwise inaccessible landscapes as the train slowly makes its way through canyons and deserts and mountain passes. Today the anachronistic experience of train travel might seem impossibly slow, especially when compared to the jets that crisscross the sky above, but the previously unimaginable speed of train travel not only funda-mentally changed the space of the American continent by bringing distant places much closer together; it also profoundly shifted a passenger's situated experience of space. As the changing landscape whisks by the window, the passenger experiences a slice of the geography, sometimes as dream, other times as exhibition, as the narrow viewing corridor of the train's path pro-gresses along the tracks. Far above, another space is being produced and experienced, as jets connect major cities together. For these passengers the spaces between airports are hazy and distant, viewed through a tiny portal from thirty-five thousand feet, interpenetrated with dreams, interrupted by clouds, and usually only at the edge of a distracted consciousness. So too do cars, buses, fiber optic cables, satellite relays, cellular signals, books, newspapers, aromas, sounds, hate, and love produce rifts in space-time, carve wormholes between distant places, fold space in surprising ways, and leave the unconnected, in-between spaces ever more distant.

Human geographers have produced rich and complex ways of describ-ing and understanding how space is produced in and through various relations, technologies, and infrastructures, but what happens when we attempt to map these phenomena? Using commonly available geographic information systems (GIS) software, we might plot the paths of railways or flights by precisely locating those trajectories using Cartesian coordinates and dropping them onto a projected and flattened representation of Euclidean space rendered on a plane. What results is an all-seeing view from nowhere (Haraway 1988) with various paths and connections, probably in different colors or using different symbolization, overlaid onto a base map. Representations such as this are useful, of course, giving important insights into geographic understandings of phenomena, but when compared to the rich descriptions of space produced in human geographic theory, these representations and the software functions that make them possible seem quite limited in their ability to account for differentially situated spatialities.

It is for an expanded sense of space that we call for a shift from currently existing geographic information systems (GIS) to a broader realm of *geographical imagination systems* (gis).[1] Our conceptualization of gis is marked by expanded computational and conceptual grammars that move from representing things in a taken-for-granted space to also having gis engage space as such. Holey spaces, relational spaces, blank spots on the map, the unknown and the uncertain, the unmappable (and that which should not be mapped), the dreamscape, and other spatial concepts that are unworkable in GIS as we know them become starting points for dealing with space in gis. Instead of space solely acting as a backdrop for individuated things and phenomena, gis is predicated on the understanding of space as being produced in and through relations and phenomena. This means that the relations produced in and through the transcontinental railroad result in a different space than that of the network of air travel. These geometries differ too from the situated and differential experiences of those who are passengers on these modes of travel. How, then, can gis produce meaningful visualizations of these complex spatialities that resist space becoming a taken-for-granted container in which stuff happens? How can space become a matter of concern, as it has for so many human geographers, posed as a problem, always in motion, worthy of attention, and always unfinished?

LALLY AND BERGMANN

To these ends we have suggested the need for an expanded understanding of gis and have begun iteratively creating a prototype example we call *enfolding* (Bergmann and Lally 2020). This software platform is one possible beginning of a more experimental approach to visualizing space and geographic phenomena, where users are not confined to the limitations of software rooted in Euclidean understandings of space, but where space is coproduced with phenomena (Sieber 2004; Sheppard 2005). By freeing spatial representations from the confines of a particular sedimented mathematical understanding of space, we believe this tool, and the broader concepts of which it is a part, help free geographical imaginations. Space, understood as relational or absolute, static or always in motion, becomes a medium to be sculpted, collaged, torn apart, and reconnected in creative ways, while being grounded in spatial concepts developed throughout the history of geography.

enfolding

Planar maps, spherical globes, and other spatializations of the enlightenment geodetic project are but the simplest surfaces capable of offering us geographic imaginations of human (or more-than-human) experience. *enfolding* offers an expanded visual practice of mapping that unfolds in conversation with complex, even contradictory notions of spatiality the interlocutor inputs through a web platform. In *enfolding*, the user does not directly fold, crumple, cut, or montage space in the manner that a map artist working with existing planar map materials might. Instead, the user expresses notions of distance, proximity, connection, rupture, and ambiguity; *enfolding* then tries to reconcile these with each other, with the resulting algorithmic reading-as-deformation (cf. Ramsay 2011) rendered in a two- or three-dimensional image.

enfolding's design reflects the principle that *enfolding* does not facilitate *directly* manipulating 2D images through collaging and crumpling. Were it to be a platform where actions were taken on the objects directly, *enfolding* could have a single window in which the user would work. Instead, *enfolding* differentiates between activities in two interconnected views—one view for

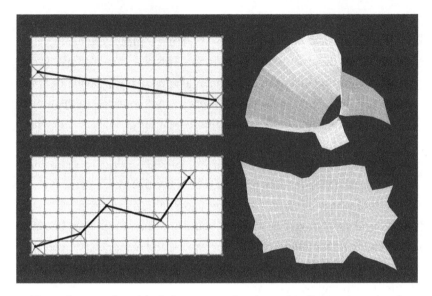

16. Two archetypes of spatial relations: connections bypassing distance (*upper*) and paths of smoother travel (*bottom*). Source: Lally and Bergmann.

intervening in a "plane of relations" (see left half of figure 16 for a simplified representation) and one for rendering and exploring spaces that result (see right half of figure 16). Moving back and forth between these two views, engaging each, is the core practice of the *enfolding* platform.

In the plane of relations, one brings in images (often maps) and proceeds to define the proximities among points within or between such images. Are distances within a map consistent and comparable across the map? We may often assume so when we look at a new map, but *enfolding* does not make this assumption when a new image is imported into the plane of relations. Instead, *enfolding* asks the geographer to explicitly define distances along connections among different points in the image. When one imports a new image, *enfolding* defaults to assuming that the four edges of the rectangular image connect the four corners of the image. Those edges connect corners with distances by default proportional to the conventional dimensions of the image encoded in its file. As a practical matter the next step is usually to employ a "grid" tool on the image, a feature *enfolding*

LALLY AND BERGMANN

provides to create a further mesh of points whose distances among them are similarly initially set to Euclidean defaults. This reinscription of the image into a Euclidean spatiality is fleeting, however. It serves to render legible the subsequent departures from the Euclidean space usually assumed for the map. From the starting point of such a rectangle or grid, geographers are free to edit any of the distances that compose the grid. Most importantly geographers are free to add new connections among new (or existing) points within (or between) the images and specify the distances those connections should have.

It is in a separate view, of "resultant" space, that these competing claims about affinities and alienation within and across images are worked through and renderings of other spaces produced. The set of connections specified in the plane of relations among points within the images defines a network. The software fills in the distances among all points, not just those distances directly specified by the geographer in the plane of relations. Distances among points are assumed to be the shortest-path summation of distances among intermediate points; the Floyd-Warshall algorithm calculates these. Once *enfolding* has the distances among all defined points within the images (in a matrix), it reconciles these distances the best that it can into a configuration that is capable of being rendered on a 2D screen or within 3D virtual reality. This is a problem of dimensionality reduction. Especially given that geographers have a long history of using multidimensional scaling (MDS) techniques to approximate higher-dimensional spaces in lower-dimensional coordinate systems (Kruskal and Wish 1978; Gatrell 1983), we too have used MDS in *enfolding*, though this is only one class of a larger set of possibilities. The result of applying MDS to the matrix of interpoint distances is a new set of coordinates for those points in 2D or 3D (the geographer's choice) whose Euclidean distances attempt to approximate the distances among points specified in the original matrix. Finally, in a concession to spatial continuity, we drape the original images over and between their corresponding points in the new space, stretching, curving, crumpling, intersecting, and overlapping. As we only really know with any definitiveness where the anchor points in the original images translate into the new space, we must have a method of estimating how the rest of the original images map to the new space. To do so, we calculate separate Delaunay triangulations for each set of points within the original images; each facet of this triangular mesh then is linearly interpolated into a corresponding triangular mesh in the transformed space. In that resulting space there are a variety of options to vary the rendering (and thus the interpretation), including panning, zooming, rotating, and changing translucency. There are also options to export the results for post-processing. We thus complete one iteration in the journey from the specification of anchor points and distances within the images of the plane of relations to the folded images in the resultant space.

Abstract examples of how the plane of relations and resulting spaces interrelate, shown in figure 16, are helpful in understanding the practices and possibilities of *enfolding*. In each row a blank image with a white grid is enfolded. The planes of relations on the left side are shown with their corresponding resulting spaces on the right side. Within the planes of relations, anchor points between the image and the network of connections between said points are small grey circles. Connections themselves are medium grey or black; medium grey connections have the default Euclidean distances associated with them, while black connections are shorter than Euclidean distances would have them. The upper resulting space is rendered in 3D; the bottom, in 2D, to show both options.

Figure 16 illustrates two archetypes of spatial relations—among what is an undetermined larger number of possibilities—whose interpretation *enfolding* facilitates. The upper row illustrates how affect, war, dreams, or finance might bypass what would have appeared, by other means, to have been great distance. The bottom row, by comparison and contrast, also shows connections over distance but has its faster or shorter connections intersecting with the rest of the landscape at many points along the way, drawing many intermediate areas into its channel.

We have drawn these examples with the abstract underlying imagery of the light grid because we wish to invite you to fill them in with your own geographical imagining. It is also informative to examine how spatial rela-

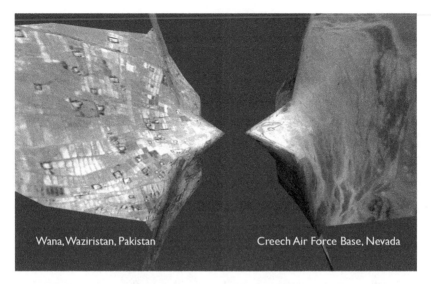

Wana, Waziristan, Pakistan   Creech Air Force Base, Nevada

17. Interpretation of drone strike as sociospatial wormhole using *enfolding*. Source: Lally and Bergmann.

tions find expression in concrete illustrations. The preceding examples were of relations within a single image. Yet *enfolding* foregrounds the multiplicity, montaging, and discontinuities of spaces by allowing for more than one image to be loaded into the plane of relation and subsequently interrelated. In figure 17 we offer an interpretation of a drone strike as having reconfigured understandings of distance and proximity between two places—a military base and a town (see Gregory 2011). Each has an associated image that was loaded into the plane of relations and separately overlain by grids of Euclidean distances. The two images were then placed into relationships with each other through adding connections between them in the plane of relations. *enfolding* thus allows the interpretation of wormholes—here, spatial relationships produced by globalization (Sheppard 2002).

Distance and proximity, as *enfolding* constructs and renders them editable in the plane of relations, are worth reflecting on here. Distances in *enfolding* are all positive numbers with an arbitrary unit of measurement. This concept is inherited from the ideals embedded in the Euclidean map (even if distance is one of the measures that is hardest to render consistently across a classical cartographic projection). The meanings of these numbers used for distances within *enfolding* need not be those of the cartographic map—as implied above, these distance numbers may stand in for any of a whole range of notions of proximity, affinity, awareness, correspondence, displacement, or disjuncture. But distances remain as numbers, at least within the current conceptual frame and available algorithms of *enfolding*.

Further, distances within *enfolding* are all symmetric and equidistant between pairs of points. This is potentially limiting for the expressiveness of the resulting spaces. Sociospatial relationships are often not symmetric, interwoven as such relationships are with power, position, and meaning (Wood 1978; Massey 1991). An example is found in figure 17, where the relations between the parts of the space interconnected by the wormhole are hardly ones of equality or equivalence. Although the present approach of *enfolding* cannot directly reflect such relationships within single geometries, it does support other avenues toward expressing unequal relationships. One is the making of multiple maps, each expressive of the view from a different positionality or with a different understanding of distance and proximity. A different set of approaches is being developed by enabling the alteration of the rendered spaces of *enfolding*. A tool provided within the view of the resulting space within *enfolding* affords the ability to adjust the transparency or opacity with which images render. When the terrain of the military base in figure 17 is rendered somewhat transparent, it might be signifying the haunting of the town landscape by the wormhole of the surveillance and strike. In other, rather different ways, landscapes expressing dreams or other temporalities might likewise be rendered translucent, allowing them to engage and decenter the unitary reality otherwise suggested by many maps.

In another consequence of *enfolding* having emerged as a creative critique of the traditions of cartography and GIS that themselves have largely chosen the world of surfaces as their geometric ontology, *enfolding* likewise focuses on the creation and manipulation of flat surfaces and images. Geographical imagination systems should not all be limited in such a

LALLY AND BERGMANN

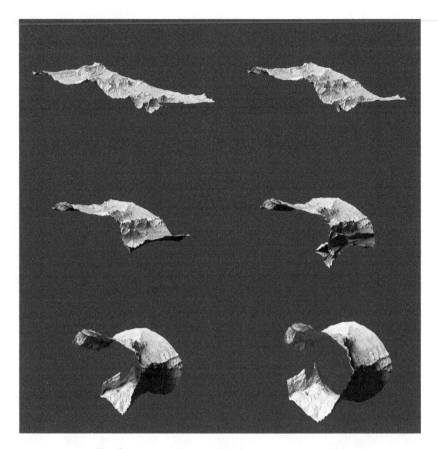

18. Animation stills of a map morphing under changing measures of distance. Source: Lally and Bergmann.

manner. Mathematically it is relatively straightforward to imagine ways in which the present *enfolding* "plane" of relations could be extended to higher dimensions and to time, such that animations, cinema, and even virtual realities could be interrelated and then resulting spaces explored. The current *enfolding* already supports the use of virtual reality to engage its results. It remains a challenge shared with virtual and mixed realities more generally as to how *enfolding* might conceptualize and actualize a user interface facilitating such manipulations of spaces beyond the surfaces of maps and images.

Space as a Process

With its focus on building networks of relations and playing with measurements of distance, *enfolding* offers entryways into topological theories of space as they have been taken up within geography. Topology, as a socio-theoretical concept (in conversation with, but not reducible to, discourses of mathematics), is concerned with identifying connections between a set of points, to understand how figures can undergo "bending, stretching, and squeezing" while maintaining the same set of connections (Secor 2013, 431). For spatial theorists, topology can then be deployed "to conceptualize the dialectic between continual change and enduring relations" and to undermine static, metaphysical, and ontological notions of space, which is one reason it has been attractive to many poststructural theories of space (Martin and Secor 2014, 422). One way of using *enfolding* to explore socio-theoretical topology is to define a set of point and nodes, change distances from their default Euclidean values to user-defined measures, and explore how the resultant map changes.

Maps can then be saved and morphed into other maps with equal numbers of points and connections, but with different measures of distance (see fig. 18). In mathematical topology, figures that can undergo such a transformation are considered to be homotopic. Transformations like these afford the ability for space to be conceptualized as dynamic or processual while retaining enduring connections that maintain legibility across figures (Allen 2011). Within *enfolding*, animations become a means to explore and speculate on the plasticity and dynamism of spaces (Forer 1978) understood topologically. Animations further serve to undermine the map's seemingly objective claims to knowledge, instead foregrounding the subjective, partial, and fragmented nature of knowledge, further suggesting the need for interpretive and speculative readings (Drucker 2009).

Another contribution of topology to social theory is its ability to break down distinctions between inside and outside. Topological figures such as the Möbius strip, the torus, and cross-cap all "interiorize their exteriors and exteriorize their interiors" in different ways (Secor 2013, 437). This affords theorists the possibility to give a formal language to certain relational claims, such as "the global as part of what constitutes the local, the outside as part of the inside" (Massey 1994, 5), or Gillian Rose's (2007) description of paradoxical space, which resists representation in Euclidean space. Rose writes, "This space is multidimensional, shifting and contingent. It is also paradoxical, by which I mean that spaces that would be mutually exclusive if charted on a two-dimensional map—centre and margin, inside and outside—are occupied simultaneously" (140). The breakdown of binaries that typifies many poststructuralist accounts of space, like those of Massey and Rose, makes topological language appealing as a theoretical tool. In his examination of the complex geopolitics of the colonial present, for example, Derek Gregory (2004) uses topology as a way to explicate the complex, twisting and turning of borders, thresholds, and states of exception that bring together interiors and exteriors, and the "us" and "them" of colonialist legacies (255).

Jacques Lacan deployed topological figures, like the ones described above, to understand the subject as both interior and exterior, offering a corrective to Freud's inability to make Euclidean space "work" as more than a metaphor (Blum and Secor 2011, 1032). Lacan (2006) insists that his use of a torus to represent the subject is "more than a metaphor—it manifests a structure," one whose "peripheral exteriority and central exteriority constitute but one single region" (264). This allows for a reconceptualization of the subject as co-constitutive with the site (Secor 2013, 429), breaking down the separation between material and psychic space (Blum and Secor 2011, 1045). Or, for example, through the figure of the Möbius strip, we can better understand "on the one hand, the transference of people's intimate feelings, thoughts and beliefs on to an external object, and, on the other hand, the stirring and blooming of people's inner feelings, thoughts and beliefs by an external object" (Kingsbury 2007, 245).

enfolding offers possibilities for creating, exploring, and playing with some of these topological figures. None are given in advance but must be created by defining relations in the 2D editing interface, which are then algorithmically translated into 3D figures. To map in a way that blurs inside and outside, then, requires an understanding of the underlying relations that make such a space possible. Rather than complex topological forms existing as pregiven figures to inform theorizing, such figures are only produced through the mapping process, giving the geographer a deeper understanding of their characteristics while also opening the possibility for new figures that are immanent to the relations and spaces being mapped.

From GIS Out into Wider gis

"Can *enfolding* do X?" has been the starting point for experiments and extensions as the possibilities for GIS open up once freed from the imaginative confines of Euclidean space. Just as it has been argued and shown that GIS need not be a positivist practice (Schuurman 2002), we see gis as a realm for further epistemological and ontological experimentation in geographic computation and spatial theorization alike. If gis can aspire to be other than a "mirror of nature" (Rorty 1979), what other metaphors might we use to organize practices of gis? One possibility is that gis can be coded to reflect the reading and writing of texts, interpretation, and inscription (Drucker 2009; Bergmann 2016). What would a gis be if it were avowedly hermeneutic and, further, made less distinction between different types of texts—whether they be code, visuals, mathematical formulae, or writing—helping us think of them all as complementary approaches to theorizing space and geography?

enfolding is indeed just one of many possible geographical imagination systems. In some cases to relax or change the assumptions that constrain and enable *enfolding* may be possible within *enfolding*'s general framework. *enfolding*, as it is today, may be run in a web browser at https://foldingspace .github.io/enfolding. Its code may be found (and extensions suggested) at https://www.github.com/foldingspace/enfolding. We hope others will join us in building and using *enfolding* and other experimental platforms that help us move out of GIS into the broader realms of gis.

Notes

The authors are grateful to the Simpson Center for the Humanities at the University of Washington for supporting this work, especially through its Society of Scholars and Digital Humanities Summer Fellowship.

LALLY AND BERGMANN

1. Our thanks go to Jamie Peck for suggesting that we change what we had been styling Geographical Imagination Systems (GIS) to geographical imagination systems (gis).

References

Allen, John. 2011. "Topological Twists: Power's Shifting Geographies." *Dialogues in Human Geography* 1, no. 3: 283–98.

Bergmann, Luke. 2016. "Toward Speculative Data: 'Geographic Information' for Situated Knowledges, Vibrant Matter, and Relational Spaces." *Environment and Planning D: Society and Space* 34, no. 6: 971–89.

Bergmann, Luke, and Nick Lally. 2020. "for geographical imagination systems (gis)." *Annals of the American Association of Geographers.*

Blum, Virginia, and Anna Secor. 2011. "Psychotopologies: Closing the Circuit between Psychic and Material Space." *Environment and Planning D: Society and Space* 29, no. 6: 1030–47.

Drucker, Johanna. 2009. *SpecLab: Digital Aesthetics and Projects in Speculative Computing.* Chicago: University of Chicago Press.

Forer, Pip. 1978. "A Place for Plastic Space?" *Progress in Geography* 2, no. 2: 230–67.

Gatrell, Anthony C. 1983. *Distance and Space: A Geographical Perspective.* Oxford: Oxford University Press.

Gregory, Derek. 2004. *The Colonial Present: Afghanistan, Palestine, Iraq.* Malden MA: Blackwell.

———. 2011. "From a View to a Kill: Drones and Late Modern War." *Theory, Culture & Society* 28, nos. 7–8: 188–215.

Haraway, Donna. 1988. "Situated Knowledges: The Science Question in Feminism and the Privilege of Partial Perspective." *Feminist Studies* 14, no. 3: 575–99.

Kingsbury, Paul. 2007. "The Extimacy of Space." *Social & Cultural Geography* 8, no. 2: 235–58.

Kruskal, Joseph B., and Myron Wish. 1978. *Multidimensional Scaling.* Beverly Hills: Sage.

Lacan, Jacques. 2006. *Écrits: The First Complete Edition in English.* Translated by Bruce Fink, with Héloïse Fink and Russell Grigg. New York: W. W. Norton.

Martin, Lauren, and Anna J. Secor. 2014. "Towards a Post-Mathematical Topology." *Progress in Human Geography* 38, no. 3: 420–38.

Massey, Doreen B. 1991. "A Global Sense of Place." *Marxism Today* (June): 24–29.

———. 1994. *Space, Place, and Gender.* Minneapolis: University of Minnesota Press.

Ramsay, Stephen. 2011. *Reading Machines: Toward an Algorithmic Criticism.* Urbana: University of Illinois Press.

Rorty, Richard. 1979. *Philosophy and the Mirror of Nature.* Princeton NJ: Princeton University Press.

Rose, Gillian. 2007. *Feminism and Geography: The Limits of Geographical Knowledge.* Repr. Cambridge: Polity Press.

Schuurman, Nadine. 2002. "Reconciling Social Constructivism and Realism in GIS." *ACME: An International Journal for Critical Geographies* 1, no. 1: 73–90.

Secor, Anna. 2013. "2012 Urban Geography Plenary Lecture Topological City." *Urban Geography* 34, no. 4: 430–44.

Sheppard, Eric. 2002. "The Spaces and Times of Globalization: Place, Scale, Networks, and Positionality." *Economic Geography* 78, no. 3: 307–30.

———. 2005. "Knowledge Production through Critical GIS: Genealogy and Prospects." *Cartographica: The International Journal for Geographic Information and Geovisualization* 40, no. 4: 5–21.

Sieber, Renee. 2004. "Rewiring for a GIS/2." *Cartographica: The International Journal for Geographic Information and Geovisualization* 39, no. 1: 25–39.

Wood, Denis. 1978. "Introducing the Cartography of Reality." In *Humanistic Geography: Prospects and Problems*, edited by David Ley and Marwyn S. Samuels, 207–19. Chicago: Maaroufa Press.

10 Beyond the Feminine Void

Rethinking Sexuation through an Ettingerial Lens

Carmen Antreasian

Freudian and Lacanian psychoanalytic tradition has historically treated the female sex as unknowable. For Jacques Lacan ([1973] 1998a, 1998b), the vaginal is symbolized through language but represents an inherent lack. That which is beyond the vaginal, however, is not acknowledged because this space exists in the real and therefore evades symbolization. This uniquely feminine space beyond the vaginal—the womb—has remained a mystery in psychoanalysis, both Freud and Lacan resolving to place the female, or woman, in a position of lack, a void. Although the subject demands primordial love beyond the female subject's symbolic vaginal veil, Lacan's phallic logic does not attempt to express through language the kind of primordial, intrauterine intimacies to which the subject demands to return (Lacan 1998b, 2002). Feminist psychoanalytic theorist Bracha Ettinger (2006), however, argues that Lacan's phallic logic is not adequate for analyzing the feminine and proposes a new theory that expresses the primordial love the subject and archaic m(O)ther share while the subject, or presubject, forms within the womb. Ettinger (2006) argues for an alternative logic born from the female sex. This logic is not constructed around the phallus but rather identifies with the nature of the feminine, characterized by the depth and flexibility of the vaginal cavity and the growing and becoming of the presubject in the womb.

Prominent feminist theorists before Ettinger have called for a new understanding of the feminine through a feminist psychoanalytic lens, notably Luce Irigaray (1997), Judith Butler (1990, 1993) and Simone De Beauvoir

(2010). Irigaray (1997) in her essay "This Sex Which Is Not One" speaks of the vagina's inherent autoeroticism, beautifully stating: "A woman 'touches herself' constantly without anyone being able to forbid her to do so, for her sex is composed of two lips which embrace continuously" (249). This feminine autoeroticism does not fit into patriarchal views of sex because it does not require the male role; however, in relation to the phallus, Irigaray (1997) clearly situates this autoeroticism within the virgin/whore complex: the virgin dearly defending her autoeroticism, warding off penetration, and the whore giving up on her vagina's autoerotic potential completely, keeping her legs spread. Irigaray (1997) reinforces the dichotomy put forth by phallic logic that considers the space within and beyond the vagina as void, hole, and home for the phallus (Lacan 2002).

This chapter explores the ways in which the space beyond the symbolic vaginal acts as void in traditional, phallocentric psychoanalysis and presents an alternative, feminist way of understanding psychoanalysis that goes beyond phallic logic's limitations of the feminine. Throughout this chapter I refer to Ettinger's (2006) alternative theory of sexuation as *matrixial sexuation* and the meaning making produced through the view of matrixial sexuation as *matrixial logic*. The word *matrix* in *matrixial* comes from the word *matrice*, meaning "womb," and is a reference to Freud's (1955) "The 'Uncanny,'" in which Freud discusses *Muttersleib-phantasie*, or womb-fantasies, which relate to the subject's initial connection to the m(O)ther. Although the theory of sexuation is based in the functions and relations of male and female sex organs, it is used to describe the subject's role in the search for fulfillment of the subject's desire in the symbolic through the Other, whatever that evasive desire may be. Ettinger (2006) posits that traces of matrixial sexuation in the real can influence the subject in the symbolic. As an artist, Ettinger describes the process of artmaking as an example of the feminine at work in the symbolic. To exemplify the effect matrixial sexuation produces in the symbolic, I discuss different artists and instances of both creating and experiencing art that further demonstrate the importance of matrixial logic and matrixial sexuation.

Phallic Sexuation versus Matrixial Sexuation

Lacan's theory of sexuation presents a dichotomous view of the desiring subject's role in relation to the Other's desire through binary male and female roles. Though the functions and imagery of sexuation are rooted in biological sex and heterosexual relationships, Lacan (2002) is clear that a subject's biological sex does not necessarily determine its role as a sexuated male or female subject. According to Lacan (1998b), the female subject, regardless of her literal biology, possesses two specific attributes: the vaginal, the dialectic of the phallus, and a desire, defined in relation to the phallus. In his theory of sexuation, Lacan (1998b, 2002) expresses male and female sexuation as a dichotomy, where male has one distinct form of sexuation in seeking the phallus and female has two dialectic forms in either seeking to be the phallus for a male subject or seeking the phallus in contestation with the male subject. Regardless of her role in relation to desire in the phallic function, however, the female subject is to parade as the phallus for the male through masquerade. He sees her as his object cause of his desire, as the embodiment of the phallus, but through his pursuit of the Other's desire (*l'objet petit a*), the male subject will never experience the satisfaction of *jouissance* in obtaining the phallus. This phallic jouissance "lends itself to thinking in terms of pluses and minuses," where the female subject is seen as 'minus' or void because in phallic sexuation she is in a position of lack (Soler 2006, 39).

According to Lacan's (1998b) theory of sexuation, the female role is to veil the lack of the phallus through masquerade, but the female subject's masquerade is not a mask, per se, because nothing is concealed. The female subject is "not-all" and inherently beyond phallic symbolization, unknowable and unobtainable, an entity beyond symbolism, situated in the real, which is always a position of void in the symbolic (Soler 2006). Slavoj Žižek (1995) states that "every singular woman is split from within, part of her is submitted to the phallic function and part of her exempted from it." In relation to phallic sexuation, then, the female subject is a split subject, a part of which is always constituted as a void beyond the symbolic. Lacanian

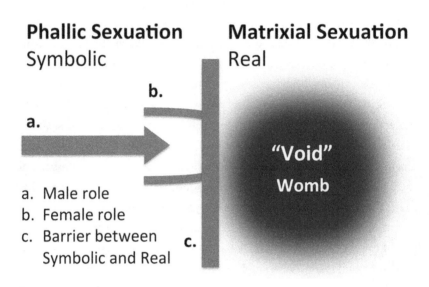

Phallic Sexuation
Symbolic

Matrixial Sexuation
Real

b.

a.

"Void"
Womb

a. Male role
b. Female role
c. Barrier between
   Symbolic and Real

c.

19. Phallic sexuation in relation to matrixial sexuation. Source: Antreasian.

sexuation ultimately positions the female subject as wholly unknowable. Žižek (1995) insists that the inability to fully signify the female subject in phallic sexuation brings her in relation with the primordial father because of their similar evasions to castration and subsequent inhabitance within the realm of the real. However, for Žižek (1995) this "Woman" who evades phallic castration and phallic signification is similar to the primordial father in that she is also "the figure of an extremely cruel Master not bound by any Law." Perhaps this Woman, Žižek's "Lady in courtly love," or even Colette Soler's (2006) Woman as the real of jouissance is a cruel master thinking in terms of phallic sexuation, but there is the possibility of another sexuation, a matrixial sexuation, which positions this Woman in the real as an(O)ther kind of nurturing m(O)ther and which uses symbolism born of the feminine space beyond the vaginal rather than relying on the dominance of the phallic signifier.

The image presented in figure 19 is a symbolic representation of matrixial sexuation in the real in relation to phallic sexuation in the symbolic. This diagram represents the theoretical male and female roles in phallic sexuation and the extent of these roles in the symbolic. Because the key functions of the female reproductive organs are pregnancy and childbirth, the maternal connection to the prebirth subject is key to understanding the relationship between the womb, or matrixial, and subjectivity. The space beyond the vaginal must elicit psychosexual meaning, for the womb is not simply a dark, foreboding chasm but the pathway to life. Ettinger (2006) proposes that the intrauterine connection between the presubject and m(O)ther is the basis of understanding nonphallic subjectivity, for it is prebirth and, therefore, subsymbolic—not fully symbolic but in the process of becoming so. Placing the womb as another site of a subject's realized sexual identity defies Lacanian sexuation in that it is fluid and transitory in nature rather than defined by sexed male and female subjects' relation to phallic jouissance. Ettinger (2006) suggests a nonphallic, matrixial sexuation at the site of the unborn presubject in the m(O)ther's womb, where the distinction between subjects is classified as presubject and m(O)ther rather than male and female. Matrixial sexuation does not solicit the bounded symbolic rules of the father-figure role, The-Name-of-the-Father, but rather concerns itself with the role of m(O)ther, the maternal figure placed in the role of the Other.

Desire in matrixial sexuation calls for a nonphallic matrixial *objet a* used not in place of, but in conjunction with, Lacan's phallic *objet a* (Ettinger 2006; Fink 1995). According to Lacan, *objet a*, or *l'objet petit a*, is the castrated subject's cause of desire, the Other's desire, that which the subject learns during its phase of childhood development wherein it realizes that its desire, m(O)ther, desires something other than the subject (Fink 1995). Lacan's *objet a*, along with all absent or lacking objects, has traditionally followed phallic logic, but because *l'objet petit a* holds traces of the m(O)ther, it actually has a *"beyond-the-phallus* dimension" that cannot be reduced to the phallus (Ettinger 2006, 42; emphasis in the original). The lacking *objet a* emerges during the subject's primal separation from the archaic m(O)ther; therefore the formation of *objet a* originates at the site of the womb with the subject's prebirth connection with the m(O)ther. Following this phase, the child, subject, develops the Oedipus complex in its solidified desire that the m(O)ther desire the subject in return, but the subject then resolves the Oedipus complex through castration, resulting in the subject's inevitable inability to acquire its desire and leaving the subject's desire, which is to be the desire of the m(O)ther, inherently unattainable (Fink 1995; Lacan [1973] 1998a, 1998b, 2002).

Fulfilling the subject's desire to be the desire of the m(O)ther is an incestuous desire prohibited by the Name-of-the-Father, or the law, so the subject's cause of desire, the m(O)ther's desire for the subject, must not exist (Fink 1995; Lacan [1973] 1998a; Soler 2006). Thus, the subject's object cause of desire, *objet a*, must necessarily be a lacking object, and those things or pursuits that stand in as the subject's desire merely act as facades that cover the true absence of *objet a*. During matrixial sexuation, however, the presubject must necessarily interact with the m(O)ther from within the m(O)ther's sex organ, creating a scenario that mimics an incestuous relationship between subject and m(O)ther.

This relational process between the presubject and m(O)ther in the womb is termed intrauterine incest, in which the presubject is the object of the m(O)ther's desire and is simultaneously in the process of becoming a subject who will view the m(O)ther as object in the symbolic (Ettinger 2006). The m(O)ther, in turn, is a fading subject who is becoming object to her fading object of desire, the presubject. Thus, the emerging subject and m(O)ther are trading roles without ever fully occupying one role or the other. They exist in the matrixial borderspace, or matrix, wherein subjects and objects are both emerging and fading simultaneously in relation to other emerging and fading subjects and objects. The emerging subject, fading object is classified as *I*, and the emerging object, fading subject is classified as *non-I* in the matrixial borderspace.

This is how the matrix, existing on a subsymbolic level, influences the symbolic within the m(O)ther: these relationships between subjects on the borderspace influence how subjects link or relate to one another—not as subject versus object but as subject/object + object/subject (*I*/*non-I* + *non-I*/*I*).

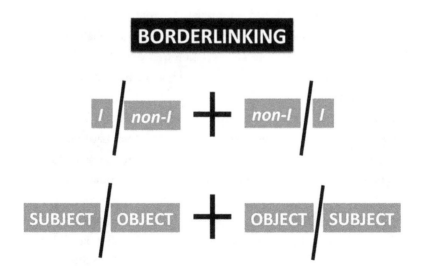

20. Borderspace diagram. Source: Antreasian.

21. Borderlinking diagram. Source: Antreasian.

The matrix, therefore, is not antisymbolic, but rather subsymbolic (Ettinger 2006). As the symbolic is the site of castration and the Oedipus complex, the subsymbolic is the site of intrauterine incest, or the matrixial complex. The subsymbolic is where interconnectivity happens between the presubject and m(O)ther (see fig. 20), where links occur between subjects (*Is*) and objects (*non-Is*) (see fig. 21). In this subsymbolic space, the m(O)ther and presubject are not fully subjects or objects but a bit of both in relation to each other. Once the subject is separated from the m(O)ther and enters into the symbolic, the borderlinks shared with the m(O)ther are repressed into the subject's unconscious.

Ettinger's theory of intrauterine incest and the matrixial recognizes the vast importance of the vaginal in the subject's transition from the subsymbolic into the symbolic, for the vagina is the subject's final passageway into the symbolic; the subject's final moments of connection to the m(O)ther occur during its journey through the vagina. The passing of the becoming subject through the vagina from the subsymbolic matrix into the symbolic realm is coined *matrixial metramorphosis*, traces of which come forth through creative or affective experiences in the symbolic (Ettinger 2006). Matrixial metramorphosis adds meaning to the role of the feminine in providing a vaginal passage to the symbolic realm alongside phallic sexuation. Thus, two types of logics emerge in relation to the symbolic: phallic logic (widely accepted, Freudian, Lacanian) and matrixial logic, which derives meaning from the feminine.

Through the process of sexuation, phallic logic and matrixial logic demonstrate a working relationship with one another. Lacanian psychosexual development operates dichotomously, separating male and female roles in a strict binary. In Lacanian sexuation the boundary that divides the sexes is immovable, unchanging, static, and uncompromising. Lacan proposes that there are two sexual options, both defined in relation to the phallus, and within those sexual categories there are two sexual identities for the female subject and one for the male subject. When Ettinger's theory of the matrixial borderspace is added to Lacan's theory of sexuation, however, the line dividing the sexes becomes blurred, allowing for fluid movement between male and female, between subject and object. This is the freedom matrixial logic allows psychoanalysis.

The Matrixial in Art

Matrixial logic can be used to describe situations in the symbolic that fall outside the realm of phallic logic, such as creative experiences with art. In the process of artmaking, the more an artist makes art, the more the art influences the artist, who then continues to create art based on their connection to their art, and the cycle continues throughout the process. Although the artist as subject and the art as object exist in the symbolic, once the process of artmaking begins, the boundary between art and artist in the symbolic begins to fade. That boundary emerges instead as the matrixial borderspace, where no subject or object is absolute but always partial. This mutual transformative relationship between the artist and their art acts as a process of borderlinking that transforms both the artist and their art into partial subjects and partial objects. In this relationship of cocreation the artist becomes *I* and the art becomes *non-I* in a matrixial relationship that results in metramorphosis, as both *I* and *non-I*, artist and art, transform each other through shared affect (see fig. 20; fig. 21).

However, the artist is not the only subject to experience metramorphosis in relation to art. Ettinger (2006) proposes that the viewer also experiences metramorphosis, for when a viewer gazes at an artwork, the boundary between subject (viewer) and object (artwork) blurs as the viewer becomes transformed by their perceived meaning of the artwork, and the meaning of the artwork is transformed by the viewer's interpretation. This transformative exchange of meaning between viewer and art demonstrates a matrixial relationship in the symbolic that reveals traces of intrauterine cocreativity in the matrixial borderspace and results in a kind of metramorphosis of both viewer and art, demonstrating the importance of the matrixial logic in the process of not only artmaking but of viewing art through a matrixial gaze.

Ettinger, herself an artist, reveals the potential of the matrixial borderspace in her paintings. Her renditions of classical allegorical motifs rethink the portrayal of female characters, specifically Greek mythology's

Eurydice and Shakespeare's Ophelia (Ettinger 2001–2009; 2002–2009), as well as Christianity's pietà (Ettinger 2013–2015)—an artistic representation of the Virgin Mary holding Christ's body postcrucifixion ("Pietà" 2014). All Ettinger's paintings of these female characters involve movement, technically referencing Marcel Duchamp's (1912) *Nude Descending*, or *Nu Descendant*, evidenced explicitly by the titles of Ettinger's (2006–2012; 2006–2013) works such as *Eurydice nu descendrait no. 1* and *Eurydice nu descendrait no. 2*. Not only are Ettinger's works similar to Duchamp's in intent, but they also share a similar aesthetic of abstract, yet recognizable, bodies progressing in space. As opposed to Duchamp's (1912) work, however, Ettinger's (2006–2012; 2006–2013) painted figures are not bound by solid black lines but rather seem to emerge and fade into the background, representing her theory of the matrixial gaze as producing an unbound, fluid identity.

Other representations of the matrixial gaze can be seen in both creating and viewing art. In this next section I discuss the differences between the phallic gaze and the matrixial gaze in the process of artmaking as well as in viewing an artwork, as demonstrated in Leo Tolstoy's (1997) famous novel *Anna Karenina*. I then discuss John Singer Sargent's (1883–1884) classic painting *Madame X* as a further example of how an artwork transforms the viewer's perception of the artwork's subject, which contributes to the meaning of the artwork. Finally, I discuss Anna Von Mertens's (2009) modern work *Madame X's Aura, after John Singer Sargent* as an example of an artwork produced in response to a matrixial viewing of a classic piece of art that demonstrates, as do Ettinger's paintings, the matrixial's complex and transitory nature through a representation of the vaginal.

Phallic Gaze versus Matrixial Gaze

The idea of cocreative experiences between art and artist in the process of artmaking is not a new concept but one that had yet to be explored in psychoanalytic terms before Ettinger's work. In his classic novel *Anna Karenina* esteemed writer and philosopher Tolstoy (1997) demonstrates the difference between a painter who is emotionally estranged from his art and one who is engaged in a cotransformative relationship with his art.

Tolstoy's descriptions of these two painters show the difference between phallic logic and matrixial logic. An analysis of these two painters' separate processes provides a clearer understanding of how the phallic gaze and the matrixial gaze provide differing influences in creative endeavors.

The two kinds of painters Tolstoy (1997) describes in *Anna Karenina* are the one who imitates and the one who transforms, the former using the phallic gaze and the latter using the matrixial gaze. These two different painters play out in two characters: Vronsky, who imitates other paintings, and Mihailov, who constantly transforms his paintings throughout the art-making process. Vronsky's process of painting imitations of classic artworks is mechanical and emotionless; he is educated in art and only concerned with the technique he has learned in his upper-class education. There is a barrier between Vronsky and his paintings. Vronsky treats his paintings as objects without further meaning or the possibility of his art producing in him an affect that would emotionally connect him to his paintings.

Mihailov, on the other hand, is not concerned with technique and is described by Vronsky and his upper-class companions as a "savage" of the lower class (Tolstoy 1997, 426). Tolstoy, however, describes Mihailov as one who paints from the heart, one who stores bits of visible information in his unconscious for later use. Thus, the subjects Mihailov paints are remnants of the unconscious in the imaginary, and he paints best when he's in an emotional state. Tolstoy (1997) states that Mihailov's paintings are alive: "the figure from a lifeless imagined thing had become living" (427). Mihailov has a matrixial relationship with his paintings, as he is transformed by, and in response also transforms, his paintings. When Mihailov paints, he is not changing his subject based on technical inaccuracy but rather "getting rid of what concealed the figure . . . stripping off wrappings which hindered it from being distinctly seen" (Tolstoy 1997, 428). Mihailov paints with Ettinger's (2006) matrixial gaze, unearthing his paintings organically by allowing meaning to pass between him and his paintings, bringing forth the imaginary into the symbolic, transforming and being transformed by his paintings through the inspiration of this passage of meaning.

The barrier between Vronsky and his objectifying, phallic gaze during artmaking is broken between Mihailov and his art because Mihailov allows his art to gaze back at him and evolve based on its influence. Tolstoy (1997) notes that technique is "understood as a mechanical faculty . . . entirely apart from its subject," revealing that the more one is focused on the technical aspects of painting, that which only exists in the symbolic, the more of a barrier is put between the artist's gaze and their art (431). In other words the more engrained the artist is in the symbolic, the less ability the artist has to achieve a matrixial gaze, or cotransformative relationship with their art. Vronsky paints in the symbolic, only allowing the symbolic to influence his work, while Mihailov paints with the matrixial gaze, allowing him to link traces of the matrixial from his unconscious in the symbolic. Where Vronsky acts as a subject who treats his paintings only as object, Mihailov becomes a partial subject while painting, which allows his painting to also become a partial subject in its transformative relationship with him.

Tolstoy's (1997) *Anna Karenina* also exemplifies the role of the viewer's gaze. To revisit Vronsky and Mihailov's artmaking processes, Vronsky's art is not only conceived through the phallic gaze but also is received through the phallic gaze, the viewers of his art appreciating it for its technical precision, retaining the barrier between viewer as subject and art as object. Mihailov's art, created through the matrixial gaze, transforms the viewer. Notably, Mihailov paints a portrait of Anna Karenina, and despite her social standing as a fallen woman who has left her husband for her lover, Mihailov's portrait captures Anna's essence in such a way that influences the opinion of those who gaze at the portrait. For example, Levin, a character who had previously despised Anna because of her blatant infidelity, is transformed by Mihailov's portrait. The portrait creates a cycle of meaning between Levin and the portrait, altering Levin's opinion of Anna from that of a debased woman to that of a woman with intelligence, character, and an intense, piercing soul (Tolstoy 1997). Thus, the matrixial gaze produces a kind of metramorphosis in the viewer if the viewer allows themself to also gaze at art from a matrixial mindset, which exists beyond the symbolic and requires an openness to the possibility of a cotransformative experience.

Vaginal Art in Response: Madame X

Displayed in the Boston Museum of Fine Art's collection of modern art is a large, thin, rectangular quilt, hung vertically and dyed shades of red, pink, orange, and yellow. The outside edges of the quilt are a deep, dark wine color, which fade into a dark magenta oval. This magenta oval encapsulates nearly the entirety of the quilt, yet within it, shades of dark and bright magentas merge with shades of hot pink and bright peach, establishing the oval as a dynamic, multidimensional space, within which a bright yellow globe emerges just above center. Artist Anna Von Mertens (2009) has not only dyed the cotton fabric in such a way as to create the illusion of dynamism among the colors within the oval, but she has also stitched the fabric in hardly noticeable curved lines across the entirety of the fabric, successfully allowing the viewer to witness the expansion of the yellow space. This incredible work of art is a meticulously crafted representation of Von Mertens's (2009) muse, and the title of her piece, *Madame X's Aura, after John Singer Sargent*. But who was Madame X, and how does Von Mertens's (2009) piece reflect her "aura" after late nineteenth-century artist Sargent?

In 1884 American painter Sargent (1883–1884), in an effort to make a name for himself among the elite Parisian artists, debuted his full-length oil portrait of Madame Pierre Gautreau in Paris, and much to his dismay and embarrassment, received scathing reviews. The portrait depicts the American-born, white-Creole socialite in a full-length black gown, her waist tightly cinched, her low-cut sweetheart neckline exposing the entirety of the pale, nearly translucent, white skin of her chest above the breasts, arms, shoulders, and neck, sans jewelry, save for two thin straps—one having seductively fallen from her right shoulder (Sargent 1883–1884). The daring way in which Sargent positions Mme Gautreau's body to face straight front, shoulders back and head turned to her left side, exposing the sensual line of skin from jawline to right shoulder and breast—unobstructed by fabric, jewelry, or even strap, as it is fallen off her shoulder—speaks volumes of Mme Gautreau's confident sexuality. However, the portrait, according to the Parisian elite, was scandalous and improper for displaying the overt sex appeal of a young, married woman. The object of the portrait, Mme Gautreau, also trying to become part of the Parisian elite, was disgraced, and throughout the rest of her life, she never quite recovered her social standing in Paris society. In response, Sargent (1883–1884) painted over the fallen strap—repainting the right strap over her shoulder—and eventually renamed the portrait *Madame X* upon selling it to the Metropolitan Museum of Art in 1916.

Understanding the context behind Sargent's (1883–1884) *Madame X* helps explain Von Mertens's (2009) *Madame X's Aura, after John Singer Sargent*. Examining Von Mertens' (2009) work from afar, noting both its shape, depth and color arrangement, one recognizes that the object of the piece is none other than the vagina—another clue being a light pink bean-shaped dot of color surrounded by dark magenta toward the top of the oval, a bit above the yellow circle, clearly representing the clitoris. Yet rather than this artistic depiction of the vagina being light around the edges and becoming darker toward the center, Von Mertens (2009) depicts the opposite: the yellow circle above the center being the focal point from which the oval expands, as the yellow circle seems to visually grow outward, widening in all directions, opening and infringing upon the pink within the oval, as the vagina expands during intercourse and childbirth. Von Mertens's (2009) representation of the vagina does not recede into a void or chasm but allows for that space beyond to emerge as light. If this increasing illumination of the vagina is a depiction of Mme Gautreau's "aura, after John Singer Sargent," then Sargent's (1883–1884) painting of Mme Gautreau's exposed female sexuality is the catalyst to Mme Gautreau's ensuing reputation as an overtly sexualized female—her sexuality portrayed by the increasingly illuminating yellow light, emitting from within the vagina in Von Mertens's (2009) piece.

Von Mertens's (2009) artwork depicts the space beyond the vagina as a pathway to light in response to the reception of Sargent's (1883–1884) painting of Mme Gautreau, who is forever marked by her overwhelmingly feminine sexuality. However, rather than reifying the negative connotation placed on Mme Gautreau's blatant femininity, Von Mertens's (2009) artwork portrays the possibility of meaning and power in Mme Gautreau's exposed sexuality. As both Tolstoy (1997) and Von Mertens (2009) demonstrate, a matrixial gaze in viewing and creating artworks, specifically of overtly sexual women, transforms viewer and artist and results in an exchange of meaning making that would otherwise be prohibited by phallic logic's imposed barriers.

"Although they are repulsed by the symbolic, although they are a stain in the imaginary and a hole in the real, the matrix and the woman are not simply sentenced to the fatal choice between phallic sublimation of the feminine and its psychotic foreclosure" (Ettinger 2006, 88). Ettinger's quote exposes the traditional limits placed upon the feminine subject, "woman," and the subject's role and relationship with the m(O)ther. As Ettinger (2006) expresses, there are unfortunate outcomes of those limits within the parameters of phallic logic. Because Lacanian sexuation within phallic logic does not attempt to symbolize that which lies beyond the vaginal veil, an alternative theory of sexuation is necessary—one that does not pertain to phallic logic but instead fits within matrixial logic, stemming from the m(O)ther and the process of reproduction from a feminine perspective.

Although Lacan (2002) is correct in saying that we as subjects can never fulfill our demand for primordial love, for we can never again be presubjects inside the womb, Ettinger (2006) proposes that we can, in fact, experience traces of the kind of love the subject seeks, intrauterine connectivity with the m(O)ther, through creative experiences in the symbolic. This chapter explores the possibility of symbolizing the subject's evolution within the womb through matrixial sexuation, in which the presubject and m(O)ther relate with one another in stages of becoming and fading as both subjects and objects. The coconstructed, emerging identities within Ettinger's matrixial borderspace, where m(O)ther and presubject relate, can be used to supplement Lacan's binary model of phallic sexuation, as it explores the role of the feminine in experiences that cannot adequately be expressed with phallic logic.

The affective, cotransformative relationship produced through both creating and viewing art clearly demonstrates the power of matrixial sexuation. While experiences in artmaking and the meanings art produces are seen and expressed in the symbolic, the processes of meaning making in creative experiences are not adequately defined through a phallic gaze, which places a barrier between the artist or viewer as subject and the artwork as object. A matrixial gaze, born of the presubject's intrauterine relationship with the m(O)ther, opens the possibility of an unbounded relationship with creation, where subject and object are not fixed but evolving with and in response to each other.

Matrixial logic allows for the feminine to be treated as a site of meaning in psychoanalysis, beyond phallic limitations. Matrixial logic has proven its ability to work with phallic logic through the process of sexuation—a subject's psychosexual development, which establishes a subject's sexual role in relation to desire in the symbolic. Matrixial logic establishes the matrixial borderspace, opening up new possibilities within Lacanian sexuation's framework. The emerging identities within Ettinger's matrixial borderspace, the subject and m(O)ther relating with each other in stages of becoming and fading as subjects and objects, can be used in conjunction with Lacan's model of binary phallic sexuation, as it predates phallic sexuation in a subject's development. The symbolic importance of matrixial sexuation lies in its ability to describe the psychoanalytic nature of a subject's affective, creative, or transformative experiences that evade phallic logic. Experiences with art demonstrate the necessity of matrixial sexuation for understanding how a subject's relationship with an object, or artwork, can result in mutual transformation and meaning making. Thus, matrixial sexuation does not dismantle traditional phallic sexuation, but rather posits meaning in the space beyond the extent of the symbolic, beyond the vaginal veil, shining light in a space that has been classified as void.

References

Butler, Judith. 1990. *Gender Trouble: Feminism and the Subversion of Identity*. New York: Routledge.

———. 1993. *Bodies That Matter: On the Discursive Limits of "Sex."* New York: Routledge.

De Beauvoir, Simone. 2010. "The Second Sex: Introduction." In *Feminist Theory Reader: Local and Global Perspectives*, 2nd ed., edited by Carole R. McCann and Seung-kyung Kim, 34–42. New York: Routledge.

Duchamp, Marcel. 1912. *Nude Descending a Staircase (No. 2)*. Oil on canvas, 57 7/8 by 35 1/8 in. (147 by 89.2 cm). Philadelphia Museum of Art. http://www.philamuseum.org /collections/permanent/51449.html (accessed August 2017).

Ettinger, Bracha. 2001–2009. *Ophelia and Eurydice no. 1*. Oil on canvas, 20 1/4 by 8 in. (51.5 by 20 cm). New York, Callicoon Fine Arts. http://www.callicoonfinearts.com /artists/bracha-l-ettinger/images (accessed August 2017).

———. 2002–2009. *Ophelia and Eurydice no. 3*. Oil on paper on canvas, 10 by 14 3/16 in. (25.4 by 36 cm). New York, Callicoon Fine Arts. http://www.callicoonfinearts.com /artists/bracha-l-ettinger/images (accessed August 2017).

———. 2006. *The Matrixial Borderspace*. Minneapolis: University of Minnesota Press.

———. 2006–2012 *Eurydice nu descendrait no. 1*. Oil on paper mounted on canvas, 9 1/4 by 9 1/4 in. (23.5 by 23.5 cm). New York, Callicoon Fine Arts. http://www.callicoonfinearts .com/artists/bracha-l-ettinger/images (accessed August 2017).

———. 2006–2013. *Eurydice nu descendrait no. 2*. Oil on paper mounted on canvas, 10 3/5 by 10 3/5 in. (27 by 27 cm). New York, Callicoon Fine Arts. http://www.callicoonfinearts .com/artists/bracha-l-ettinger/images (accessed August 2017).

———. 2013–2015. *Pieta no. 1*. Oil on canvas, 11 5/8 by 9 5/8 in. (29.5 by 24.4 cm). New York, Callicoon Fine Arts. http://www.callicoonfinearts.com/artists/bracha-l-ettinger /images (accessed August 2017).

Fink, Bruce. 1995. *The Lacanian Subject: Between Language and Jouissance*. Princeton NJ: Princeton University Press.

Freud, Sigmund. 1955. "The 'Uncanny.'" In *The Standard Edition of the Complete Psychological Works of Sigmund Freud*, vol. 17 (1917–1919): *An Infantile Neurosis and Other Works*, edited and translated by James Strachey, with Anna Freud, assisted by Alix Strachey and Alan Tyson, 217–56. London: Hogarth Press.

Irigaray, Luce. 1997. "This Sex Which Is Not One." In *Writing on the Body: Female Embodiment and Feminist Theory*, edited by Katie Conboy, Nadia Medina, and Sarah Stanbury, 248–56. New York: Columbia University Press.

Lacan, Jacques. (1973) 1998a. *The Seminar of Jacques Lacan, Book XI: The Four Fundamental Concepts of Psychoanalysis*. Edited by Jacques-Alain Miller. Translated by Alan Sheridan. New York: W. W. Norton.

———. 1998b. *The Seminar of Jacques Lacan, Book XX: On Feminine Sexuality, The Limits of Love and Knowledge, 1972–1973 (Encore)*. Edited by Jacques-Alain Miller. Translated by Bruce Fink. New York: W. W. Norton.

———. 2002. "The Signification of the Phallus." In *Écrits: A Selection*, translated by Bruce Fink, with Héloïse Fink and Russell Gregg. New York: W. W. Norton.

"Pietà." 2014. In *Encyclopædia Britannica*. https://www.britannica.com/topic/Pieta -iconography. Last updated September 10, 2019. (accessed August 2017).

Sargent, John Singer. 1883–1884. *Madame X (Madame Pierre Gautreau)*. Oil on canvas, 82 1/8 by 43 1/4 in. (208.6 by 109.9 cm). New York, Metropolitan Museum of Art. http://www.metmuseum.org/art/collection/search/12127 (accessed August 2017).

Soler, Colette. 2006. *What Lacan Said about Women: A Psychoanalytic Study*. Translated by John Holland. New York: Other Press.

Tolstoy, Leo. 1997. *Anna Karenina*. Translated by Constance Garnett. New York: Barnes & Noble Books.

Von Mertens, Anna. 2009. *Madame X's Aura, after John Singer Sargent*. Hand-dyed and hand-stitched cotton, 83 by 44 in. (210.8 by 111.8 cm). Boston, Museum of Fine Arts. https://www.newamericanpaintings.com/blog/power-presence-anna-von-mertens-elizabeth-leach (accessed October 2019).

Žižek, Slavoj. 1995. "Woman Is One of the Names-of-the-Father, or How Not to Misread Lacan's Formulas of Sexuation." *Lacanian Ink* 10: 24–39. http://www.lacan.com/zizwoman.htm (accessed September 2018).

11 Politics for the Impasse

Jess Linz and Anna J. Secor

We are all used to having our dreams crushed, our
hopes smashed, our illusions shattered, but what
comes after hope?

—J. JACK HALBERSTAM, *The Queer Art of Failure*

There are impasses, and there are impasses. There is the ontological impasse
that is always there, like a parallel dimension where our everyday certainties
dissolve within a field of potentiality. Then there is the impasse that emerges
as a legible present crisis. The crisis impasse is provoked by the collapse of
the assurances of futurity, the dissolution of our hopes and fantasies. We
find ourselves in such a crisis when we have exhausted our repetitions,
and the object to which we are attached (upward mobility, democracy,
freedom, humanitarianism, etc.) no longer sustains us but instead causes
us harm and holds us immobile (Berlant 2011).

   In 2016 and 2017, when the precarity of American institutions and ideals—
and our attachment (however qualified) to their continuity—jutted into
view, an impasse of this sort yawned open. In a remarkably short interval
Donald Trump and those empowered by his election shredded the paper-
thin overcoding of American society by the liberal-democratic genre and
its principles of equality, refuge, and freedom. For many of us whose bodies,
communities, and mobilities were threatened by the coming to power of
white supremacy, the ordinary showed itself to be an impending crisis,
and questions of adjustment and survival consumed us. Yet despite the

immediate crisis provoked by this forced awakening to the failure of the liberal-democratic genre, the situation was neither new nor unique. For the majority of those living within American borders, the failure of genre had already made itself apparent in the ongoing colonization, domination, and oppression of black, brown, Muslim, female, queer, disabled, poor, noncisgendered, and foreign-born bodies. And for the majority of those living beyond U.S. borders, having been incessantly undermined by U.S. imperialism and the forces of totalitarianism, democracy and its associated goods (such as freedom of the press, or free and fair elections) had already collapsed again and again. Some enter this impasse of a reinvigorated U.S. imperialism with fear of a new future, while others bring an ongoing trauma from the past and present. Meeting each other and ourselves in this impasse, entering through these different portals, demands action that not only blocks the emergence of fascist futures but also avoids any return to the catastrophe of the status quo.

This chapter offers some tools for holding the impasse open, for enacting a politics in this savage place that defies the closures of history and futurity. This is not a list of practical actions (call your representatives, disseminate information, protest, donate money, etc.) that contribute to resistance. Our tools are orientations and affects, experiments and molecular becomings. Strange bedfellows abound: Walter Benjamin and queer theory, quantum field theory and psychoanalysis. We picked up what we found lying about and put it to work without regard for genealogy, without an attachment to a final coherence. We want to "write to the nth power, the n-1 power," to "write with slogans" without planting the seed of a manifesto; we are only growing offshoots (Deleuze and Guattari 1987, 24). This is a method for becoming-minor: an attempt to subtract a minor space from the dominant order, to connect ourselves to an immanent politics, and to engage with the tools we find in that upside-down space (Deleuze and Guattari 1986; Katz 1996). Impasse politics as a minor practice upends the functioning of the major, of politics as "the fantasy . . . of an order, an organization, that assures the stability of our identities as subjects and the coherence of the Imaginary totalizations through which those identities appear to us in recognizable form" (Edelman 2004, 7). Impasse politics works against identity, closure, and totalization; it is molecular antifascism. It is what Gilles Deleuze and Félix Guattari (1986) call a "creative line of escape" that "vacuums up in its movement all politics, all economy, all bureaucracy, all judiciary" in order to render audible "still unknown sounds that come from the near future" (41). We hear the "*diabolical powers that are knocking at the door*" (Deleuze and Guattari 1986, 41; emphasis in the original)—powers not only of "Fascism, Stalinism, Americanism" but also of the unbearable status quo that allow our current moment to appear as though it is the telos of our barbaric history. A politics of and for the impasse holds open the portal to the ontological impasse—to the void as a fluctuating field of emergence in all its potentiality and danger—that the crisis impasse makes visible. This impasse or void is dangerous, uncertain, and prone to closure. Yet it offers much: the decomposition of structures, new configurations, new connections. It is a generative, creative space that offers us tools and politics for our slow plummet down the White Rabbit's hole. It is an affective politics beyond hope; one of apathetic solidarities and no future.

In the Impasse

The impasse is a funny kind of space: it is a void. It has no walls, no ground, no fixed dimensions. It is subterranean: we enter its tunnels of under-ground intensities "like a dog digging its hole, like a rat digging its burrows" (Deleuze and Guattari 1986, 18). The hole we dig out is "a space of internal displacement" that "shatters the normal hierarchies, clarities, tyrannies, and confusions of compliance with autonomous individuality" (Berlant 2011, 48). The impasse is a wormhole, the crux of a paradoxical circuit of difference and sameness. To be in the impasse is to be suspended in the cut, to inhabit the unlocalizable twist of the Möbius, to arrest oneself right where one encounters the impossible. Inhabiting the impasse means subsisting in uncomfortable dissonance, in the paradoxical copresence of irreconcilable affirmations. The impasse is the gap where the antinomy closes/opens/becomes—"dialectics at a standstill" (Benjamin 1999, 463 [AP N3,1]). By entering an impasse and holding it open, by guarding "against every new closure, every new reconstitution" (Deleuze and Guattari 1986, 14), we blast open the potentiality of the now and create the conditions for a different way of being in the world, a becoming-minor that resists the dream of being major.

The problem is, it is not easy to stay there, in the space of the impasse. You don't get welcomed at the door of an impasse. In fact, there's not even a door. It's more like a trapdoor you fall through to find yourself crumpled on the ground. The impasse-space appears like a parallel universe inhering within the space you were passing through. Unadorned, it does not cater to its guests with predictability or decorum. It is more savage. It is dark in the impasse; it is a space that requires heightened senses, because it makes no promises. In the impasse adjustment style prevails over history and genealogy. This is an unholy space of flux, reconfiguring, and recoding of meaning. In the impasse you can't move forward with any rapid clip. This does not mean that nothing is happening, though. In an impasse an active passivity overtakes you, reconfiguring molecules and changing operations. As Lauren Berlant (2011) puts it, "An impasse is decompositional—in the unbound temporality of the stretch of time, it marks a delay that demands activity. The activity can produce impacts and events, but one does not know where they are leading" (199).

It is the gap. It is the shift in gears. It is the time-out. But this does not mean it is nowhere or that it is merely a holding station or a space-time of hibernation. It is the opposite. This is the site of gestation that allows something very different to emerge from the other side. The impasse is a disjunct, an aporia, but it is also a cornucopia, teeming with virtual multiplicities. We can learn from quantum mechanics: "the vacuum is not a boring place; it's alive with virtual particles" (S. Carroll 2010, 59). This is because uncertainty—the inability "to pin down the observable features of any system into one unique state with perfect precision" (S. Carroll 2010, 59)—means that there is plenty of potential for finding something in nothing. Physicist James Owen Weatherall (2016) explains "the nonzero probability of finding 'something' when we make a measurement in the vacuum state in some small region of space and time" as "reflecting the possibility that we will catch the field 'fluctuating' away from the zero state" (185). He describes the vacuum like this:

> The intuitive picture is that the vacuum is a roiling sea of activity—or better, of possibility, since the fluctuations concern what could happen on measurement, and not actual events in the classical sense. You might think of static on an old TV or on a radio between stations: there is no signal to speak of—no persistent particles—and yet there isn't silence, either. There's just white noise: random, incoherent background. Fluctuations. In fact, in some experimental scenarios in physics, vacuum fluctuations look exactly like white noise. (Weatherall 2016, 185)

The impasse is just such a roiling sea of activity, churning with virtual events. Ghostly fragments of music and half-emergent images seethe in the field of static. We don't change the channel to search for programming. The fluctuating absence of the signal *is* the transmission. In the impasse "something" and "nothing" are not mutually exclusive.

To work in the impasse you need to pick up what you find there. Stuff tends to show up when you try to detect it. So, we lowered our scintillator (particle detector) into the chaosmos, found some things, and picked up what we found. The tools themselves are shards of nothingness, bits of broken impasse, crumbs of nonbeing, fragments of failure. So they are not just things that work *in* an impasse such as this one; they *make* the impasse. More accurately, they make a multitude of tiny and gigantic impasses. They give us something to do as we plummet slowly down the White Rabbit's hole. In this essay we offer eight tools for holding open the impasse. They are only eight of an infinite and expanding number, yet they are more than enough to get started. We will begin with snacks.

HAVE A SNACK

No man's land. Here in the place where the water runs off, here where our tire went flat, let's settle into this unexpected circumstance. We won't resist an accidental stopping by the side of the road, where no one stops. The tire explodes and destroys the continuity of the journey, arrests us where we never meant to pause, in an unhopeful place where it seems nothing could happen. The rupture defers our arrival at the expected destination. But rather than resisting, we are just going to sit down right here in the space of elision, right here where the apostrophe holds open a gap. And when you take out the snacks, you know you are not going anywhere fast. We need to resist the urge to give up, get angry, go home, to judge definitively about this pit stop. Sharing a snack is a feminist practice for staying here in this abysmal place (Smyth, Linz, and Hudson, 2019). We may never make it where we were headed anyway, so we abandon the desire to get there.

STAY IN BED

When we wake up, we tend to throw down an anchor. The anchor catches, and we have hooked ourselves to a past, an identity, a familiar, major cartography (an orientation to the door, the window, the dresser, the world). Wake up differently! "A dream wakes you up just when it might let the truth drop, so that the only reason one wakes up is so as to continue dreaming—dreaming in the real, or to be more exact, in reality" (Lacan 2007, 57). Arrest yourself between the sleeping and waking dreams, in the moment between, when you do not yet grasp where you are, why you are there, or how long you have been asleep. Hover in that moment before you reassemble the narrative continuity that places you—as though inevitably—as the telos of a foregone history. Leap in the open air: let the facts become something that has just now happened to you. To be struck anew—to unleash "the flash of awakened consciousness" (Benjamin 1999, 388–89 [AP K1,2])—to become the blur between waking and sleeping. Let the anchor plummet infinitely through the dark waters of that subterranean sea, the endless drift where representation fails. But the blur vaporizes almost instantly. It is hard to catch that moment. Like interviewing people dancing. This is all affect.

FREEZE

Blast the present moment out of its complacent continuity. Ruffle the smooth surface of capitalist time. Denormalization! This is the work of the dialectical image: both the goal and the method of a politics of the impasse.

The "relationship between what has been to the now" is not progression, but image, "suddenly emergent" (Benjamin 1999, 462 [AP N2a,3]). The image in the now of its (mis)recognition cracks the ground of legibility itself. For Benjamin the image is a monad, a constellation, a crystal, a diagram. It is a collective dream-fragment that defies the linear temporality of historical narrative. The dialectical image thus enacts the "appropriately perverse refusal that characterizes queer theory . . . of history as a linear narrative . . . in which meaning succeeds in revealing itself—as itself—through time" (Edelman 2004, 4).

Today, in the age of the meme, awash in viral replication, we need new ways to be shocked, to encounter the potential released by broken time, to crack the kernel of the now out of its shell (Hardesty, Linz, and Secor, 2019). The GIF with its repetitions from two to infinity (never one) isolates a quick gesture, a moment, and extends it infinitely, promising an unending yield of enjoyment (jouissance). Groups of people form tableaus of frozen action filmed by a moving camera: this is a viral internet trend called "the manne-quin challenge." The more movement that the tableau arrests —half-falls, half-leaps, improbably interrupted gestures—the better the "challenge" has been met. The mannequin challenge doesn't look like anything if you photograph it. You have to use mobility to capture the elaborately staged stasis. EVERYBODY FREEZE! That flâneur, the camera, roves through the tableau of resisted momentum. This is how we will encounter stasis and movement, the constellation and the way in which it is taken up into the grind of history.

Freeze! Let's become shocked out of our continual motion long enough to realize that we do not need to keep doing it. The mobility of static. Look at the screen that is receiving no signal. What do you see, composing and decomposing in the flickering light-dark? Let your eyes blur and your mind empty. Let the emergent phantasmagoria shock you.

DIG A BURROW

We have tactics, not strategies. We are squatters and nomads, cowbirds and hermit crabs. We are giant armadillos digging burrows for all manner of occupants. "There is no longer anything but movements, vibrations, thresholds in a deserted matter: animals, mice, dogs, apes, cockroaches are distinguished only by this or that threshold, this or that vibration, by the particular underground tunnel in the rhizome or the burrow. Because these tunnels are underground intensities" (Deleuze and Guattari 1986, 13). These holes are opportunities. Boundaries are not walls; they are permeable membranes, entrances through which small things may slip. Ambivalence to genealogy allows for this kind of border crossing, much in the way fungus helps itself to spaces across the forest floor, disrespecting defined entities, sharing nutrients sometimes and smothering life at other moments (Tsing 2012, 143).

Our burrow doesn't shut some in and some out. It has the topology of a Klein bottle: the opening is a cut that, like Fortunatus's purse that contains all wealth by virtue of its having been sewn *the wrong way*, makes "the outer surface continuous with the inner surface" (L. Carroll 1893, 579) so that *everything* is at once inside it and outside it. This "twisted, uncomfortable, uncanny-looking" aperture has no boundary, no orientation. Our burrow is a zone of indistinction between in and out, included and excluded. It is not a house: do not demand a deed, a debt, a foundation, or an insurance policy. Maybe we live like the Lost Boys, a queer family of orphans living in a hole in the ground, disconnected from context and from linear temporality. They are what J. Jack Halberstam (2011) calls "forgetful subjects," subjects who "forget, among other things . . . family and tradition and lineage and biological relation and live to create relationality anew in each moment and for each context and without a teleology and on behalf of the chaotic potentiality of random action" (80). The Lost Boys in the burrow of their eternal now make kin "in lines of inventive connection"; they are, as Donna J. Haraway (2016) would put it, *Staying with the Trouble*. Their queer subterranean dwelling is just an example, not a blueprint, of how we might live in the upside down. This is a spatial politics of and for the impasse.

GIVE WHAT YOU DON'T HAVE

The impasse is the land of strange bedfellows and solidarity based in action, not genealogy. The old blocks that seemed so solid and understandable

LINZ AND SECOR

(class, gender, race, etc.) dissolve. Instead, solidarity is finding who is "adjust[ing]" in the same way to the topography of the impasse despite having radically different ontologies or histories (Berlant 2011, 202). In the impasse, solidarity is not what you think. We don't come together. We don't make each other whole or solid. We are not what we want each other to be, and we have nothing to give each other. Here solidarity is like love: it's giving what you don't have (Lacan 2015). We check in to Standing Rock without believing that it matters. We are all disillusioned, beyond hope. We don't need to pretend here. The important thing is that *we give it anyhow*. We give this stuff we don't have to an imperfect movement, to a vision of a just society that will not be just, to a cause that will fail. Not only that, but we *receive* solidarity knowing that what we are receiving is not what we want. That those who come in solidarity do not have what they are offering to us and are not who we imagine them to be. And everyone is doing the same. No one is certain or satisfied. No one knows what they're doing. Even the ones who talk very loudly. There is no certainty, no guarantee, no external point from which to anchor our politics. We don't pretend to know ourselves. We renounce ourselves in the name of our own failure.

It is all about reverberations, not intention. The best allies are the ones who say, when the time is right, "Absolutely, I get it, boycott me," and who step aside in recognition that their presence is not always a mark of their solidarity. Sometimes your contribution is to remove yourself, to offer your-self for effacement. Don't disappear but become invisible. Show up by not showing up. In the impasse, self-effacement is solidarity. "Self-interruption, self-suspension, and self-abeyance" are all best practices (Berlant 2011, 27). As Beyoncé sings, "Your love was stronger than your pride" (Beyoncé 2016; see also Sade [1998], "Love Is Stronger than Pride").

FORGET

Forgetting is the crowbar we use to open a tiny space—enough for a beam of light to stream in, enough for the ruptures and contradictions to come pouring out. Forgetfulness—like the field of holes in the weave of a fabric—arrays a multitude of little gaps, tiny deaths, fleeting orgasms, imperceptible openings of discontinuity in the stifling logic of the already-made. There is something psychotic in the multitude (Deleuze and Guattari 1987). Forget the one. Forget your mother and father! Have you forgotten your place? Amnesia answers: Yes, I have, and I will forget it again and again. I've lost the plot. I've mislaid my keys. I've forgotten where I was going and why, wandering off and starting a new life. Forgetting enables a step out of history, allowing us to feel unhistorically (Nietzsche 2010). Cleansed of the self-justifying past and its promise of (future) happiness (Ahmed 2010), the present unfurls its immanent potentiality in the gaps we pry open by forgetting. This is not the same as the forgetting that allows the dominant culture to push aside the past in order to maintain a fiction of progress. The history that erases and justifies the present as an inevitable telos is the one to forget.

> BENJAMIN (1968) (*quoting Nietzsche*): "We need history, but not the way a spoiled loafer in the garden of knowledge needs it." (260)
> HALBERSTAM (2011) (*nodding*): Forgetfulness can be a useful tool for jamming the smooth operation of the normal and the ordinary. (70)

IMPROVISE

Begin to play without knowing what will be played, how it will unfold, where it will end or start up again. Become absorbed. Detach from conventions of judgment, aesthetic and moral. Forget about consequences. Push in the direction of your listening, find something to follow and shadow it without imitation. Do not fall back on the coherent discourse of composition— the promise of order, the illusion of a pure line between the score and the performance, the plan and its execution (Toop 2016). "Be open to the one who comes up to you. Be changed by an encounter. Become a poet of the episode, the elision, the ellipsis" (Berlant 2011, 34). Remember that there are always potentialities latent in the script. There is no repetition without difference. Strange anomalies proliferate, "anything is possible—anything can be changed—now" (Rzewski 1999, 385). Because "time is not just a linear sequence . . . in each moment a new universe is created" (382). Insert yourself and make new universes: there is room for your creation because causality is only justified in reverse.

WONDER

When the policeman calls "hey you!" we know better than to turn, to consent to (mis)recognition as though it is inevitable. To turn, to accept this interpellation, is mortifying. This is symbolic death. But let's face it. When the Other issues that "hey you," if you freeze without turning, or if you keep walking, or if you run, you could be shot. A lot depends on what kind of body you are. And this is death death. Wonder is what you use to hover between these two deaths (the living one and the dead one). Jam the codes. Jam the gun. Neither refuse the hail nor accept it: instead, force yourself to be confused and then do something confusing, forgetful. If need be, play dead—becoming-opossum. Become unrecognizable. Lengthen this interval endlessly so you can continue to live. Take a quarter turn away from the Master's discourse and encompass the scene in the Hysteric's discourse (Lacan 2007). Vomit, bleed, ejaculate: do what you can to bring on a more visceral catastrophe (Benjamin 1999, 473 [AP N9a,1], 474 [AP N10,2]). And when the other steps forward, confused, into the breach of your illegibility, greet them with wonder. Wonder is a relation to the other that refuses the old codes of recognition, that has nothing to do with being, imitating, or opposing. Wonder puts us *in* difference, in pure difference. It opens up relationality instead of closing it down. Wonder is improvisational; it says, "yes, and. . . ." And . . . yes, this is how we become-hummingbird, beating our wings in a blur as we hover between a symbolic and a real death, between the sleeping and the waking dream, between accepting and refusing, sipping the nectar of serendipity. To wonder is to read anew, to suspend judgment, to receive impression, to encounter. Wonder is the suspension of the known order such that we become open to receiving impulses and reading them out of context (Irigaray 1993, 75). In the impasse, a turn toward the other is a revolution of wonder.

Bundle It Together

Those are some of the tools we found. There are an impossible number more of them. It's like dividing by zero. We use them here in the interstice to keep that space open, to arrest ourselves in it, to "stay with the trouble" with Haraway (2016), to slow down and appreciate the irrational with Isabelle Stengers (2011), to stick with the nothing of queer failure in order to find a radical new way of being in the world and in relation to each other with Halberstam (2011). It isn't easy. You're going to want to patch up the gaps in the structure of the universe with your hat (Lacan 2007), to mend "each tear . . . in reality's dress with threads of meaning" (Edelman 2004, 35). You are going to want to go home. You are going to want, at least, a destination. How do we freeze our momentum? How do we stay in this savage place? How do we shut ourselves into the impasse to let it do its work on us?

Blast our present moment, our now, out of its inscription within dominant narratives that situate the current catastrophe as the telos of an unfolding determination. Temporal decontextualization (forgetting) undermines the legibility of our present, extracts it from all justification, forces its immediate reality into view. This can happen by way of what Benjamin calls shock, or what Luce Irigaray calls wonder. Shock and wonder are the affects of the impasse; they are ways of intra-acting (Barad 2007) that expand capacities and unleash unexpected intensities. By short-circuiting expectations, they evade the closures (identity, recognition, judgment, normalization) that limit our capacity for creative lines of flight. All of the tools we found work to discharge or extend this kind of shock wave.

Set free latent combinatory forces that do not require or produce a new order. Release the energies of our times by enacting emergent solidarities without regard for genealogy or teleology, origin or aim. Make improvisational alliances that unfold without a script or a score, that tap out heterogeneous rhythms. Resist the urge to demand certainty or commitment, to ground your actions on futurity, on promises or hopes. Do not expect to reach a destination. Allow failure, accident, and disappointment to incite you. These orientations are important because they spur movement, creativity, and risk-taking. Some of our tools (solidarity, improv, snacks) work this way, to keep us from just staring at our shoes in this place beyond hope.

Create subterranean openings and connect them to others. Tunnel out a burrow, seep through foundations, pry open portals. Become a rhizome: engage in transversal pullulation and help yourself to spaces. Follow the aleatory and microscopic movements of the nonhuman. Using these tools we tunnel tactically across-beneath the territory of the big Other, tracing a minor expression whose "trajectories form unforeseeable sentences and partly unreadable paths across a space" (de Certeau 1988, xviii). Porosity and strange topologies keep our dwellings and networks open, incapable of exclusion.

This is politics for the impasse. Politics in a backpack that is there to be homeless with you. We do not have answers. We do not want answers. We are beyond hope, and we want more problems. We can bundle it back together like this, but it is already coming apart and full of holes. That's how we like it. It is all about orientations and affects. A politics for the impasse resists the demand not only for closure, but also for certainty—we don't have it, and we don't need it. We act without grounds for action. We give what we don't have. We expect failure, but that doesn't mean we do not dissolve ourselves into some imperfect action. We know that failure is generative. When the tire blows, when you sprain your ankle, it makes you take a break. Extend the interval. Here in the impasse we kick up some dirt and create new pluriverses.

References

Ahmed, Sara. 2010. *The Promise of Happiness*. Durham NC: Duke University Press.

Barad, Karen. 2007. *Meeting the Universe Halfway: Quantum Physics and the Entanglement of Matter and Meaning*. Durham NC: Duke University Press.

Benjamin, Walter. 1968. *Illuminations*. Edited by Hannah Arendt. Translated by Harry Zohn. New York: Schocken Books.

———. 1999. *The Arcades Project*. Translated by Howard Eiland and Kevin McLaughlin. Cambridge MA: Harvard University Press.

Berlant, Lauren. 2011. *Cruel Optimism*. Durham NC: Duke University Press.

Beyoncé. 2016. "All Night." *Lemonade*. CD/DVD. New York: Parkwood Entertainment and Columbia Records.

Carroll, Lewis. 1893. *Sylvie and Bruno Concluded*. London: Macmillan.

Carroll, Sean. 2010. *From Eternity to Here: The Quest for the Ultimate Theory of Time*. New York: Dutton.

de Certeau, Michel. 1988. *The Practice of Everyday Life*. Berkeley: University of California Press.

Deleuze, Gilles, and Félix Guattari. 1986. *Kafka: Toward a Minor Literature*. Translation by Dana Polan. Minneapolis: University of Minnesota Press.

———. 1987. *A Thousand Plateaus: Capitalism and Schizophrenia*. Translation by Brian Massumi. Minneapolis: University of Minnesota Press.

Edelman, L. 2004. *No Future: Queer Theory and the Death Drive*. Durham NC: Duke University Press.

Halberstam, Judith (J. Jack). 2011. *The Queer Art of Failure*. Durham NC: Duke University Press.

Haraway, Donna J. 2016. *Staying with the Trouble: Making Kin in the Chthulucene*. Durham NC: Duke University Press.

Hardesty, Robby, Jess Linz, and Anna J. Secor. 2019. "Walter Benja-Memes." *GeoHumanities*, 1–18. https://doi.org/10.1080/2373566x.2019.1624188.

Irigaray, Luce. 1993. *An Ethics of Sexual Difference*. Translated by Carolyn Burke and Gillian G. Gill. Ithaca NY: Cornell University Press.

Katz, Cindi. 1996. "Towards Minor Theory." *Environment and Planning D: Society and Space* 14, no. 4: 487–99. https://doi.org/10.1068/d140487.

Lacan, Jacques. 2007. *The Seminar of Jacques Lacan, Book XVII: The Other Side of Psychoanalysis*. Edited by Jacques-Alain Miller. Translated by Russell Grigg. New York: W. W. Norton.

———. 2015. *The Seminar of Jacques Lacan, Book VIII: Transference*. Edited by Jacques-Alain Miller. Translated by Bruce Fink. Cambridge: Polity.

Nietzsche, Friedrich. 2010. *On the Genealogy of Morals*. Translated by Walter Kaufmann. New York: Vintage.

Rzewski, Frederic. 1999. "Little Bangs: A Nihilist Theory of Improvisation." *Current Musicology* 67/68: 377–86. https://openmusiclibrary.org/article/48504.

Sade [Adu], Andrew Hale, and Stuart Matthewman. 1998. "Love Is Stronger than Pride." *Stronger than Pride*. Los Angeles: Epic Records.

Smyth, Araby, Jess Linz, and Lauren Hudson. 2019. "A Feminist Coven in the University." *Gender, Place and Culture* 27, no. 6: 1-27. https://doi.org/10.1080/0966369X.2019.1681367.

Stengers, Isabelle. 2011. *Cosmopolitics II*. Minneapolis: University of Minnesota Press.

Toop, David. 2016. *Into the Maelstrom: Music, Improvisation, and the Dream of Freedom, before 1970*. New York: Bloomsbury.

Tsing, Anna Lowenhaupt. 2015. *The Mushroom at the End of the World: On the Possibility of Life in Capitalist Ruins*. Princeton NJ: Princeton University Press.

Weatherall, James Owen. 2016. *Void: The Strange Physics of Nothing*. New Haven CT: Yale University Press.

12 Raising Sasquatch to the Place of the Cryptozoological Thing

Oliver Keane and Paul Kingsbury

An increasingly prominent site where Bigfoot or Sasquatch organizations and individual researchers meet to share and discuss their findings are the now dozen or so annual Sasquatch conferences located across the United States.[1] Given the lack of academic research on Sasquatch investigation cultures, however, we know very little about who attends these events, why they attend, and what they do there (Jenzen and Munt 2013). To address this gap in the literature, our chapter explores the case study of the 2016 Sasquatch Summit (hereafter the "Summit"), which took place during the long weekend of November 20–22 at the Quinault Beach Resort and Casino on Quinault Indian Nation land in Grays Harbor, Washington. One of the most striking features of the Summit was the extent to which it resembled a conventional academic conference in terms of the prominence of nametags, swag-filled tote bags, speakers' PowerPoint presentations, workshops, and late-night theory debates in the hotel lobby bar. What distinguished the Summit from a conventional academic conference, such as the American Association of Geographers Annual meeting, was the extent to which it revolved around an inescapable and fundamental absence: the lack of data or a material artefact capable of definitely proving the existence of its main object of study. This raises an intriguing question: how exactly, under the aegis of a "research conference" (to use one of the Summit's webpage monikers), is it possible to represent, debate, and share knowledge about a living entity that science and the vast majority of people regard as nonexistent? (Chapman University 2018).

Following Jacques Lacan (1992), we argue that the Summit situates or, more precisely, "raises" Sasquatch to the "place" of "the Thing" (*das Ding*), that is, an inaccessible yet invasive and alluring void. This Thing, however, is not simply nothing nor an absence. Rather, in Lacan's (1992) crypto-metaphysical vein, it is a generative and captivating negativity that both creates and is retroactively created by various imaginary and symbolic representations or stand-ins, which Lacan calls the "Other thing" (118). We argue that the Summit's proliferation of Other things—Sasquatch footprint casts, video and audio clips, merchandise, and so on—transforms and concretizes Sasquatch into what we call the "cryptozoological Thing" via the process of sublimation. Specifically, we illustrate how two interrelated paradoxes of sublimation concretize the void of the cryptozoological Thing at the Summit. First, we discuss how the processes of signification, which comprise the Summit's Other things, encircle and carve out the alluring place of the cryptozoological Thing. Such a process is paradoxical because it entails making something out of nothing. And second, we map the spatial concentration of at least two seemingly irreconcilable discourses between Native and non-Native attendees about the ontological status of Sasquatch. While an impasse would seem to preclude a relationship with the crypto-zoological Thing, these very differences are already the cryptozoological Thing itself. Here, the paradox concerns how a relationship can be main-tained by obstruction. Before elaborating in-depth on exactly how these processes occur at the Summit, we first discuss the field of cryptozoology and Lacan's concepts of the Thing and sublimation.

What Is Cryptozoology?

The term *cryptozoology*, which was coined during the 1950s and is etymo-logically derived from the Greek words for "hidden" (*kryptos*), "animal" (*zoion*), and "study" (*logia*), concerns "the study of unknown, legendary, or extinct animals whose existence or survival to the present day is disputed or unsubstantiated" (OED 2019). Some of these animals or "cryptids" have

KEANE AND KINGSBURY

been allegedly observed for centuries and are thus culturally significant (Coleman and Clark 1999; Regal 2011). By combining scientific and cultural discourses, cryptozoology disrupts the ideological distinction between science and society that ossified during the late nineteenth century. At this time physical anthropologists believed that humans were the only extant hominoid species. Subsequent discoveries, however, of hominoid fossils in many locations around the world and the discovery of the mountain gorilla in 1902 prompted some scientists and amateur researchers to question this belief (Krulos 2015). These doubts, coupled with numerous oral testimonies and historical records of observations, encounters, and even interactions with simian-like creatures among Indigenous, settler, and migrant populations gave rise to the cryptozoological movement. Early cryptozoologists argued that large, bipedal, and hair-covered hominoids were extant and living in remote wilderness regions of the earth. These creatures are said to exist in remote forest and mountain areas, especially the Himalayan region where they are known as "Yeti" (the Anglicization of an indigenous Sherpa term), "Abominable Snowmen," or "Meetoh Kangmi" (a Tibetan term), as well as across western Canada and the northwestern United States, where they are known as "Sasquatch" (the Anglicization of a First Nations phrase) (Deis, Coleman, and Doyle 2015) or "Bigfoot" (popularized by a journalist in 1958) (Coleman and Clark 1999; McLeod 2009).

Today cryptozoology is widely dismissed as a pseudoscience because its objects of study are considered to be the products of folklore, hoaxing, or simple misidentification. Yet cryptozoology remains a prominent topic in popular culture, especially in the context of paranormal investigation cultures (Jenzen and Munt 2013). Spurred on by the now-iconic one-minute long "Patterson-Gimlin" film shot in 1967 in northern California, consolidated by 1970s docudramas such as *The Legend of Boggy Creek* (1972) and *Sasquatch, the Legend of Bigfoot* (1976), and internationally disseminated by popular television documentaries in the early 2000s such as *Finding Bigfoot* on Animal Planet, interest in searching for and proving the existence of Sasquatch has grown in recent years (McLeod 2009). In the past several decades there has also been a steady increase in the number of local

22. The Great Hall. Source: Keane and Kingsbury.

(e.g., the British Columbia Scientific Cryptozoological Club, founded in 1989) and international (e.g., the Bigfoot Field Researchers Organization, founded in 1995) organizations that study alleged evidence of Sasquatch activity using field methods such as tracking, footprint casting, and video and audio recordings. In the past decade or so the growth of these organizations has been propelled by online discussion forums, photo- and video-sharing websites such as YouTube, and the organization webpages and social media channels that disseminate map data, images, and discussions of purported Sasquatch sightings.

One of the consequences of the rise of online cryptozoological communities is the growth of conferences such as the Summit. The Summit was founded in 2013, and according to its main organizer, Johnny Manson, "over 600" people attended the 2016 event (fig. 22).[2] Attendees were predominantly white, mainly working class and non-college-educated, typically male, and residents of nearby states (Washington, Oregon, California, and Idaho). This particular demographic reflects the historical

KEANE AND KINGSBURY

and geographical context of Sasquatch research more generally, wherein the rural locations in which the expeditions take place are predominantly white and working class. In addition, their remote and rugged topographies have been historically and culturally regarded as the domain for men rather than women. Numerous researchers, however, supported the increased participation of women researchers in the past decade or so. We also learned that the main reason why someone would attend the Summit was because they or someone they knew had an extraordinary encounter or numerous extraordinary encounters with something they believed to be or in many cases were utterly convinced was a Sasquatch or a group of Sasquatches. The heady combination of the concrete and the incredible is central to Lacan's notions of the Thing and sublimation.

The Thing and Sublimation

Lacan introduced the concept of the Thing (*das Ding*) in his seventh annual public seminar, *The Ethics of Psychoanalysis* (hereafter "*Seminar VII*"), which took place on a fortnightly basis during the 1959–1960 school year in the Hôpital Sainte-Anne, Paris. The Thing is intimately related to the register of the real, that is, a part of psychical life that disturbs from within and without psychical and social reality, which for Lacan consists of language and social codes (the symbolic), as well as meanings, values, and visual images (the imaginary). As part of the real, the Thing is the trace of a "prehistoric, unforgettable Other, that later no one will ever reach" (Lacan 1992, 56) and "characterized by the fact that it is impossible for us to imagine it" (125). From a Lacanian perspective, then, human subjectivity is borne out of traumatic encounters with the Thing, which are "strange and even hostile on occasion, or in any case the first outside" (52). The psychical boundary between the outside and the inside is established through the dyadic interactions between the child and the maternal Thing: the primordial (m) Other. According to Joan Copjec (2002), the child's separation from the Thing "opens up a hole in being . . . not that the mother escapes representation or thought, but that the jouissance [intense libidinal enjoyment] that attached me to her has been lost and this loss depletes the whole of my being" (35–36). This encounter inaugurates what Lacan provocatively calls "castration" wherein the intervention of language inaugurates the social subject via her separation from a once complete being. One way to recuperate this lost jouissance (enjoyment) is through sublimation.

Sigmund Freud established the conventional psychoanalytic understanding of sublimation and conceptualized it as one of the vicissitudes of the drives. For Freud, sublimation involves the redirection or modification of the aim and object of the drives toward socially and ethically prized goals and achievements. In contrast, Lacan theorized sublimation as a process that transforms the object of the drives insofar as it is changed from a mundane object into a sublime object, that is, an object that exceeds its material dimensions and radiates mesmerizing though potentially terrifying jouissance. Lacan's (1992) "most general formula" for sublimation is that it "raises an object . . . to the dignity of the Thing" (112). A key point here is that any object can be "elevated" (another preferred term of Lacan's) to the place of the Thing (see Kingsbury 2011a, 2011b). As a sublime object, the Thing is intensely desirable though impossible to attain because it is located in the real. Yet the Thing can "drop" or "fall out" of the real and threaten the psychical stability of the subject. We expand on this point below and how it informs two aspects of sublimation at the Summit.

Encircling the Cryptozoological Thing

Throughout *Seminar VII* Lacan (1992) likens the structure of the Thing to vases, canons, matchboxes, macaroni, as well as honey and mustard pots. At first glance these everyday objects would seem to possess wildly different structures. Yet each of them, like the Thing, is topologically the same insofar as they are created around an initial emptiness, introducing "the possibility of filling it" (121). Crucially, the Thing is made out of "the fashioning of the signifier," which involves the intensive localization of numerous "signifying units," which Lacan likens to the processes of "flocculation" and "crystallization" (118). To illustrate his point Lacan tells an anecdote about being overwhelmed by the "truly imposing multiplicity" (114) of the artistic arrangement of a friend's matchbox collection that

23. Sasquatch prints leading to registration. Source: Keane and Kingsbury.

24. Bottles of Sasquatch attractant. Source: Keane and Kingsbury.

sprawled along a mantelpiece, wall, molding, and door. Similarly, much of the Summit consisted of the conspicuous proliferation and spatial concentration of signifying units of Sasquatch.

Even before arriving at the conference venue, during the car journey we encountered numerous signifiers of Sasquatch: yellow and black Sasquatch crosswalk signs and strategically placed wooden silhouettes of Sasquatch peeking from behind roadside trees. Upon entering the Quinault Beach Resort and Casino building, we checked in and followed a path of Sasquatch-sized footprint stickers on the floor (fig. 23). Conference registration took place in a small room chockablock with more Sasquatch signifiers, which operate as the Other thing, such as a life-sized statue, stickers, patches, cupholders, T-shirts, posters, holiday greetings cards, "Sasqrunch" baked caramel corn snacks, and even spray bottles of simulated "authentic Sasquatch pheromone" called "Desire" (fig. 24). Having registered for the Summit, we left the cramped room and went into the main conference room called the "Great Hall." This room would soon become a weekend-long packed scene of eight hour-long talks, numerous impassioned town hall–style witness testimony sessions, looped audio and video clips of alleged Sasquatch encounters, and table displays of more "Squatchy" objects such as books, trucker caps, beanie hats, tape measures, stickers, patches, buttons, T-shirts, koozies, footprint casts, and so on.

In their "wholly gratuitous, proliferating, superfluous and quasi absurd" (Lacan 1992, 114) numbers, all these signifiers intensified the fascination of Sasquatch and helped "colonize the field of *das Ding*" (99). That is to say, all these Sasquatch signifiers not only generated an aura (*Erscheinung* [114], to use Lacan's phrase); they also carved out "the space or central place in which the Thing as such presents itself" (118). Here, the Summit's "fashioning of the signifier and the introduction of a gap or a hole [the Thing] in the real is identical" (121) because its Thing—the cryptozoological Thing—is instantiated as real: an as yet unproven, uncaptured, and unsubstantiated object that both evades and invades the symbolic and imaginary schemes of cryptozoology. As something that evades and invades, this place of the cryptozoological Thing is not only empty because it demarcates a void; it

25. Dunes and beach lit up at night. Source: Keane and Kingsbury.

is also topologically structured insofar as it is both inside and outside the conference site as an "intimate exteriority" (Lacan 1992, 139). Specifically, the cryptozoological Thing is located in "both the real of the subject and the real he has to deal with as exterior to him" (118). Though devoid of empirical matter, the Thing coagulates as a pressure point in the real—the source and summit of jouissance—lurking in the warm and brightly lit interiority of the conference and in the looming primeval pine forests surrounding it on the outside. Adding to this topological twist were the swathes of woodland camouflage clothes circulating inside the building and the oceanfront rooms enticing its guests (including ourselves) to look outside onto the gale-blown vegetated dunes and beach (permanently illuminated at night by huge floodlights) and scene of multiple Sasquatch sightings (fig. 25).

While the Great Hall provided an arena for attendees to talk about the ultimately failed attempts to definitively prove the existence of Sasquatch, these attempts nonetheless succeeded as iterations of a "repetitious, con-

26. The Olympic Project's Sasquatch footprint casts. Source: Keane and Kingsbury.

stant, cyclical return to an initial point of attachment" (Johnston 2005, 317), that is, to an all-too brief and fleeting encounter with Sasquatch. As the T-shirt for sale stated: "Sasquatch ☯ you complete me." Along two walls of the room, parallel to the rows of hundreds of chairs, were the vendor, speaker, and Sasquatch organization tables. Many tables were laden with collections of Sasquatch footprint casts (fig. 26). Just like the potter, the cryptozoologist creates a cast using their hands out of an emptiness. Like a vase or matchbox, the casts are formed around a hole. They materialize the impression of a void just like the marks in three sets of deer and elk rib bones on another table. According to the researcher (during a lecture at the Summit) who found them at Mount St. Helens in Washington, the "masticatory impression" evinced the "enclosure of the [Sasquatch] teeth." Other casts included the mold of a Sasquatch clitoris, anus, thighs, and buttocks.

KEANE AND KINGSBURY

The cryptozoological Thing's power of fascination is generated not by its immediate properties but rather by the place it occupies in fantasy space, that is, the space where desire and jouissance is organized. Its allure is contingent upon cryptozoologists apprehending their Thing from a specific distance that maintains a gap between, on the one hand, the real, that is, the impossible and inaccessible place of a non-empirical object (the cryptozoological Thing) and, on the other hand, the symbolic and imaginary, that is, the empirical realm of objects such as casts and bones (Other things). This distance demarcates a difference between jouissance and pleasure. Freud theorized the psyche as a dialectical relationship between the reality principle, which is a "call to order" and the pleasure principle, which "naturally tends toward deception and error" (Lacan 1992, 28). The pleasure principle aims to increase pleasure, which is defined as a reduction in excessive excitation (jouissance), while the reality principle, which is not objective because it ultimately is made "out of pleasure" (225), aims to correct erroneous attempts at reducing excitation by the pleasure principle. Central to Lacan's (1992) argument is the idea that the function of the pleasure principle is to "lead the subject from signifier to signifier, by generating as many signifiers as are required to maintain at a low level as possible the tension" (119) of the psychic apparatus. By generating a smooth movement from signifier to signifier, the pleasure principle prohibits the subject from getting too close to the Thing. Exemplifying the collapse of the distance between reality and the real was Mitchel Townsend's lecture at the Summit, which began with a recollection of his "spirit journey" during a Sasquatch expedition: "I had a vision in a dream, a waking dream that I needed to go to a certain spot on a certain river and the truth would be revealed to me. . . . I went to the spot on the river and on the ground were thousands of artifacts, thousands, that had been exposed as the river had risen and fallen." These artifacts allowed Townsend to emphatically declare the following: "Ladies and Gentlemen, I give you, I can't give it to you, you own it, we all own it. Yes, I own them, but, they're ours. Ladies and Gentlemen, this is the only morphologically correct hybrid hominid scaled footprint carved into solid rock in the history of this world."

While the rock mimics the structure of the footprint casts insofar as it is the material impression of a void, Townsend claimed he has definitely proved the existence of Sasquatch: "There it is. You wanted proof? There it is. Go ahead take pictures." In an interview shortly after the talk, Townsend told us: "Bigfoot is solved! I solved it today. I actually solved it two months ago. I've proven it through verifiable, impossible-to-fake, impossible-to-hoax, microscopically verifiable forensic dental impression. . . . I also have the only anatomically correct Bigfoot print, hybridized Bigfoot print chipped into solid rock 80,000 years old that's the Crown or the Queen's Jewel. Done deal. Solved!"

By offering up the "Queen's Jewel" on stage, which he did so by slowly lifting it out of a small wooden box and carefully unwrapping it out of protective paper, as the cryptozoological Thing itself, Townsend disrupts the pleasure principle because he terminates the movement of the subject along a path of signifiers. As a result, Townsend ushers in an overproximate and threatening encounter with the Other thing. It is threatening because it obliterates the distance between the Other thing and the cryptozoological Thing, that is, between signification and the void. Notably during the hour-long Q&A session, which closed the Summit's proceedings, Townsend was the only presenter not to get a question from the audience. What, then, are we to make of Townsend's claim? Our contention is that he tells the truth in the form of a fiction. His presentation recalls Slavoj Žižek's (2014) interpretation of the disappearance of the former police detective John "Scottie" Ferguson's desire in the experience of losing Madeleine Elster (who was originally impersonated by Judy Barton as part of a murder plot) in Alfred Hitchcock's *Vertigo*: it "is not simply that Judy is a fake (he knows that she is not the true Madeleine, since he recreated a copy of Madeleine out of her), but that, because she is *not* a fake—she *is* Madeleine; Madeleine *herself* was already a fake—*objet a* disintegrates, the very loss is lost, we get a negation of negation" (99; emphasis in the original). The Queen's Jewel is not simply fake; it is fictional but not as a symbolic falsehood or imaginary deception. Townsend in a twisted irony told the truth: Sasquatch is real because it is the cryptozoological Thing: it is the sum of its signifiers that encircle it and is never itself.

Obstructing the Cryptozoological Thing

Earlier we stated that the making of signifiers and the localization of the Thing as hole in the center of the real occurs simultaneously. Here, the Thing is the result of a gap "between the thing-in-itself (the noumenal) and the thing as it appears (the phenomena)" (Secor 2008, 2625). Crucially the Thing is located in the very gap that demarcates the difference between the noumenal and phenomenal, which can be localized and apprehended in everyday practices and objects. As Žižek notes, the Thing "*is* this particular object, but that this object is strangely split . . . the split is within the object itself" because it "is both itself and, at the same time, something else" (Žižek and Daly 2004, 67). Addressing the Thing's paradoxical status as something that is at once accessible and inaccessible, Lacan (1992) asserts that "the whole of psychic life is obliged, to encircle it or bypass it in order to conceive it . . . it always presents itself as a veiled entity" (118). That is to say, the Thing is concretized because it is *as if* something were hidden behind representation, *as if* something were inaccessible to us. As if, because "this radical antinomy which seems to preclude our access to the Thing is already the Thing" (Žižek 2006, 26). That is, the Thing is an unobtainable object not because it lies beyond our reach or because it is hidden out of our view in a zone of inaccessibility. Rather, the Thing *is* precisely this very obstacle. This is why Lacan (1992) designates courtly love with its seemingly inaccessible lady as "an exemplary form, a paradigm, of sublimation" (128).

Anna Secor (2008) has usefully illustrated the above paradoxes via Žižek's notion of the "parallax gap" or the antinomic differences that comprised the 1995 O. J. Simpson trial (was he guilty or innocent?) and the U.S.-led war on Iraq (was the conflict the result of global capitalism or military territorial power?). The parallax gap comprises the truth of each situation, but it cannot be discerned by digging for or unveiling a hidden, deeper truth (whether Simpson was *really* guilty or innocent or whether the Iraq War was *really* about money or territory). Rather, the truth is in "*the difference itself*" that comprises the two opposing positions (Secor 2008, 2625;

emphasis in the original). In this section we illustrate how the alluring power of the cryptozoological Thing, which is comparable to the parallax gap, is concretized as a result of the differences that comprise seemingly irreconcilable discourses about the ontological status of Sasquatch. According to Manson:

> You have the science-based blood and guts kind of thinkers or believers, if you know, they can't touch it or feel it. And then you have the paranormal, they call it the "woo-woo" and they're the ones that claim that Sasquatch can mentally communicate with you, can cloak. Some, depending on how down the rabbit-hole you go, link them to UFOs and other kinds of supernatural things. I don't necessarily support those theories. I just think it should be represented. If it's there, if it has a major impact in the research community then it should be represented. I swear some of these conferences will only have the "para" or the "woo" or will only have the blood and guts. But I wanted a mixture, so let the guests decide for themselves.[3]

Echoing Žižek's (1993) discussion on how the consolidation of a social group depends on the unique way it *"organizes its enjoyment"* (201; emphasis in the original) around its Thing and the protection of this enjoyment from being stolen by another social group, the (to use Johnny Mason's categorizations) "blood and guts" and "woo" camps each affirmed and defended their particular ways of researching and thus enjoying their Thing. One such way was to undermine the opposing party's viewpoint. Here the scientific position criticized the paranormal position for not gathering evidence carefully enough, while the paranormal camp ridiculed the science camp for not taking seriously enough the singularity of people's encounters with Sasquatch. Perhaps the most prevalent and contentious difference over the cryptozoological Thing concerned debates over whether Sasquatch was an undiscovered human or nonhuman primate. One researcher at the Summit told us, "I'm learning something about their habits, something about how they interact with humans." The distinction between "them" and "humans" implies that Sasquatch is nonhuman. Similarly, D. Jeff Meldrum (2007), a speaker at the Summit and professor of anatomy and anthropology at

KEANE AND KINGSBURY

Idaho State University, suggested that Sasquatch might be related to the thought-to-be extinct giant ape *Gigantopithecus blacki*, which according to the fossil record possessed teeth of "clear hominoid design" (100).

In contrast to the nonhuman camp, Native American attendees asserted that Sasquatch was human. As one Native American (a member of the Quinault Indian Nation) investigator put it: "[Sasquatches are] an ancient people . . . we're all hybrid hominids, different heights, different colored hair, different body types. We are it and it is us. That's why there's so many different kinds." According to Manson, "I approached the Quinault and they were very supportive of [the conference] and this is their realm and they have grown and lived with the Sasquatch people for centuries." Another member of the Quinault tribe also announced during a brief speech before the prayer that opened up the conference proceedings that all the attendees should "have a respect for those people . . . we call them people out there." This difference has been entrenched by previous scientific discourses about Native Americans. According to Meldrum (2007), "geographically restricted surveys [of Native American cultures] do present an emerging consensus of a . . . humanlike animal . . . Just how humanlike are these animals in the Native American mind? Clayton Mack [a renowned First Nations hunter and guide] concluded, 'Half man, half animal, I think'" (87). Our findings, however, challenge this claim insofar as it was the Native investigators who posited Sasquatch as fully human and the non-Native investigators as half animal. We should also note the certainty that accompanied the Native American researchers' claims of the human status of Sasquatch. One of these researchers told us the following: "knowing" that Sasquatch are "a people" means that "the veil's been pulled back because our intentions and our heart is true."

Instead of attempting to reconcile the differences between the human and nonhuman positions, Summit attendees respectfully disagreed with or simply ignored the other's point of view (recall the repression of Townsend's claim during the Q & A session). We believe this lack of engagement is because the real difference between these two opposing views is "not an external difference between two positively identified logics" (Secor

2008, 2626). That is to say, the scientific nonhuman position is not simply the flip side or Other of the Native human position and vice versa. Rather, the fundamental difference between these positions is a minimal difference that emerges out of the shared impossibility of ever catching or ontologically containing Sasquatch, that is, closing the gap between knowable phenomena (the Other thing qua the signifiers "nonhuman," "human," "people," and so on) and an unknowable thing-in-itself (the cryptozoological Thing). This impossibility is not an impediment to each side's research agenda. Rather, the impossibility constitutes a creative relation or perhaps, more accurately, a nonrelation with the cryptozoological Thing. Why? Because this very impossibility enables both parties to create something out of nothing, that is, to create Other things out of the cryptozoological Thing. This nothing, however, is not an absence or something missing from reality. It is not the lack of concrete hard evidence qua a scientific specimen that would prove the reality or positive existence of Sasquatch. Rather, this nothing *is* part of reality because reality itself *is* incomplete: it is the hole of the real around which signifiers circulate, and so it can never be captured or fully known by a scientific discourse, or any discourse for that matter.

Mobilizing the differences between the blood and guts paradigm (Sasquatch is actually a biological being) versus the woo paradigm (Sasquatch is actually a paranormal entity) or the animal paradigm (Sasquatch is actually a nonhuman primate) versus the human paradigm (Sasquatch is actually a person) sublimates or elevates Sasquatch to the place of the cryptozoological Thing. Again, this Thing is not unobtainable because it is buried deeper and rendered inaccessible as a result of the disjunctions between the opposing viewpoints. Rather, the Thing *is* their very difference or shift in perspectives from one to another that comprises the reality of the Summit. This reality is "'non-All'. It is not all there is, but there is nothing beyond it, and this Nothing is Being itself" (Secor 2008, 2625). Or, to put it in the words of the renowned YouTube cryptozoologist "ThinkerThunker" with all the connotations of a Lacanian negation of the negation, the Summit is a testament to why "Bigfoot doesn't not exist."

The Dignity of the Cryptological Thing

In this chapter, we argued that the Summit allows attendees to enjoy and believe in their cryptozoological Thing insofar as it is "represented by something else" (Lacan 1992, 118), that is, Other things. As part of the process of sublimation, this Thing concerns the "oblig[ation] . . . to encircle or bypass it in order to conceive it. Wherever it affirms itself, it does so in domesticated spheres" (118). Conference events such as the Summit exemplify such spheres because they are highly structured contexts in which communities can rally around their Thing and enjoy it from a safe distance, "avoiding the destructive encounter with the real and allowing desire to proceed in a domesticated environment" (Neill 2011, 139). Exposing somebody to the horror of the real could result in a psychotic breakdown, that is, the disintegration of a subject's beliefs, agency, and, perhaps most significantly, desire. In the context of the Summit, it would be tantamount to proving once and for all why Sasquatch cannot or does not exist.

Such a position, of course, is embraced by mainstream scientists, particularly in reaction to the Patterson-Gimlin film. Scientists frequently appear on Sasquatch television documentaries using the falsification of DNA samples as a means of implicitly stating that it is ultimately wrong to believe in the existence of Sasquatch (see Buhs 2009; Evans 2017; Davis 2017). Countering such statements, Meldrum (2004) claims to have validly deduced the existence of Sasquatch based on the Patterson-Gimlin film and footprint evidence. This claim has been published in the semiannual "peer-reviewed" *Journal of Scientific Exploration*. While the journal is regarded by academics as a Fortean and pseudoscientific outlet, to date no scientific peer-reviewed study has disputed the truth or validity of Meldrum's contentions (see also Dixon 2007). One reason for this is because Meldrum's paper presents a basic paradox for mainstream scientists who cannot accept the existence of Sasquatch given the "basic tenet" of science that "neither rejects nor accepts anything without examining the evidence" (Sykes et al. 2014). What, then, are we to make of the scientific assertion that the "advocates in the cryptozoology community have more work to do in order to produce convincing evidence for anomalous primates" (Sykes et al. 2014)?

If anything, the cryptozoological Thing has much to teach us about what counts as legitimate knowledge in contemporary society. We also believe that the Summit and the research practices of cryptozoology more generally should not be understood as delusional or pathological, but rather as creative because like the other "three forms of sublimation, art, religion and science" (Lacan 1992, 129), they are an attempt, and a dignified one at that, to apprehend an object and raise it to the empty place of the Thing.

Notes

We are grateful to Johnny Manson and all the 2016 Sasquatch Summit participants who assisted us with our research. This research is supported by the Social Sciences and Humanities Research Council of Canada (Grant No. 435-2015-0355).

1. Because we focus on the *Sasquatch* Summit, we use the term *Sasquatch* for the remainder of the chapter.
2. Johnny Manson, email message to author, January 31, 2018.
3. Johnny Manson, email message to author, January 31, 2018.

References

Buhs, Joshua Blu. 2009. *Bigfoot: The Life and Times of a Legend*. Chicago: University of Chicago Press.

Chapman University. 2018. "Paranormaly America 2018: Chapman University Survey of American Fears" (blog). October 16. https://blogs.chapman.edu/wilkinson/2018/10/16/paranormal-america-2018/ (accessed September 25, 2019).

Coleman, Loren, and Jerome Clark. 1999. *Cryptozoology A to Z: The Encyclopedia of Loch Monsters, Sasquatch, Chupacabras, and Other Authentic Mysteries of Nature*. New York: Simon and Schuster.

Copjec, Joan. 2002. *Imagine There's No Woman: Ethics and Sublimation*. Cambridge MA: MIT Press.

Davis, Nicola. 2017. "DNA Sampling Exposes Nine 'Yeti Specimens' as Eight Bears and a Dog." *Guardian*. November 29. https://www.theguardian.com/science/2017/nov/29/dnasampling-exposes-nine-yeti-specimens-as-eight-bears-and-a-dog (accessed November 29, 2018).

Deis, Robert, David Coleman, and Wyatt Doyle, eds. 2015. *Cryptozoology Anthology: Strange and Mysterious Creatures in Men's Adventure Magazines*. [USA]: New Texture.

Dixon, Deborah. 2007. "A Benevolent and Sceptical Inquiry: Exploring 'Fortean Geographies' with the Mothman." *cultural geographies* 14, no. 2: 189–210.

Evans, Mark. 2017. "Bigfoot Files." Mark Evans website. https://www.markevans.co.uk/television/bigfoot-files/ (accessed November 29, 2017).

Jenzen, Olu, and Sally R. Munt, eds. 2013. *The Ashgate Research Companion to Paranormal Cultures*. Farnham, UK: Ashgate.

Johnston, Adrian. 2005. *Time Driven: Metapsychology and the Splitting of the Drive*. Evanston IL: Northwestern University Press.

Kingsbury, Paul. 2011a. "Sociospatial Sublimation: The Human Resources of Love in Sandals Resorts International, Jamaica." *Annals of the Association of American Geographers* 101, no. 3: 650–69.

———. 2011b. "The World Cup and the National Thing on Commercial Drive, Vancouver." *Environment and Planning D: Society and Space* 29, no. 4: 716–37.

Krulos, Tea. 2015. *Monster Hunters: On the Trail with Ghost Hunters, Bigfooters, Ufologists, and Other Paranormal Investigators*. Chicago: Chicago Review Press.

Lacan, Jacques. 1992. *The Seminar of Jacques Lacan, Book VII: The Ethics of Psychoanalysis*. Edited by Jacques Alain Miller. Translated by Dennis Porter. New York: Routledge.

McLeod, Michael. 2009. *Anatomy of a Beast: Obsession and Myth on the Trail of Bigfoot*. Berkeley: University of California Press.

Meldrum, D. Jeffrey. 2004. "Midfoot Flexibility, Fossil Footprints, and Sasquatch Steps: New Perspectives on the Evolution of Bipedalism." *Journal of Scientific Exploration* 18, no. 1: 65–79.

———. 2007. *Sasquatch: Legend Meets Science*. New York: Forge.

Neill, Calum. 2011. *Lacanian Ethics and the Assumption of Subjectivity*. New York: Palgrave Macmillan.

Oxford English Dictionary (OED) *Online*. 2019. S.v. "Cryptozoology." https://www.oed.com/.

Regal, Brian. 2011. *Searching for Sasquatch: Crackpots, Eggheads, and Cryptozoology*. New York: Palgrave Macmillan.

Secor, Anna J. 2008. "Žižek's Dialectics of Difference and the Problem of Space." *Environment and Planning A* 40, no. 11: 2623–30.

Sykes, Bryan C., Rhettman A. Mullis, Christophe Hagenmuller, Terry W. Melton, and Michel Sartori. 2014. "Genetic Analysis of Hair Samples Attributed to Yeti, Bigfoot and Other Anomalous Primates." *Proceedings of the Royal Society B: Biological Sciences* 281, no. 1789: 1–3.

Žižek, Slavoj. 1993. *Tarrying with the Negative: Kant, Hegel, and the Critique of Ideology*. Durham NC: Duke University Press.

———. 2006. *The Parallax View*. Cambridge MA: MIT Press.

———. 2014. *Event: A Philosophical Journey through a Concept*. London: Penguin.

Žižek, Slavoj, and Glyn Daly. 2004. *Conversations with Žižek*. Malden MA: Polity.

PART 4 Voids

13 O(void)

Excerpts from *Lot*, a Long Ethnopoetics Project about the Colonial Geographies of Haida Gwaii

Sarah de Leeuw

"Into the void" is a suggestive turn of phrase. It suggests Black Sabbath songs and complete emptiness, outer space and negation, draining (especially of liquids) and a serious situation in the card game Bridge when a player is dealt no cards. In the spirit of geography's creative re-turn (Hawkins 2013; de Leeuw and Hawkins 2017), the growth of geohumanities in the discipline (Cresswell et al. 2015; Dear 2015), and the expanding interest in and production of poetry by geographers (Acker 2013, 2015; Cresswell 2013, 2014, 2015; de Leeuw 2013, 2015, 2017; Magrane and Cokinos 2016), I responded poetically to the invitation evoked by "into the void."

Poetry is, in great part, about tricking language, about interrogating and exploding relationships between words so they summon new orientations to ideas, places, or objects. Poetry often *evokes* something as opposed to didactically *conveying* it. How to trick and transform the word *void* so it evokes something unexpected then? Plunk an *o* in front of it was my answer. Very different for evocations invited by the word *void*, according to most English language dictionaries *ovoid* is a simple (perhaps even somewhat dull) word denoting a rather humble entity. An egg shape. Having the form of an egg.

Within Northwest Coast Indigenous art practices, however, the ovoid form is the most basic and foundational shape in all visual languages (Townsend-Gault, Kramer, and Ki-Ke-In 2013). Its shape is the constraint around which the vast majority of Northwest Coast Indigenous art is formed, a fundamental space, a geography, that produces a specific way of seeing and being in the world. In conversations with First Nations artists across northern British Columbia, I have been reminded many times that the ovoid is a shape artists working in the Northwest Tradition need to eat, sleep, and breathe: artists need to see the shape everywhere, need to ingest it into their very being. The ovoid is a constraint that literarily *forms* worlds. It has done so since time immemorial (Townsend-Gault, Kramer, and Ki-Ke-In 2013). The ovoid continues its worlding work, despite the omnipresence of colonial settlers.

I grew up a settler on the northwest coast of British Columbia, just under the Alaskan panhandle, on Haida Gwaii (the Queen Charlotte Islands). For more than three years now I have been working on a single long poem produced through a series of constraints. These constraints—while not specifically copying the ovoid, because I think that would rightly be critiqued for possible cultural appropriation— inform a long poem *formed* and *constrained* by a collection of edges, lines, and restrictions not unlike those of the ovoid form. Like the ovoid my (poetic) lines loop back on each other and bend: they can be (and are) extended and stretched, collapsed and constricted. Then they dilate again, bend again. The lines are open-versed with concentrated focus on internal rhyme. So, in openness they are also closed.

The poem is crafted entirely in couplets, a dualist structure formed to mirror both the two main islands that comprise the archipelago and a kind of "two-eyed" seeing (see Marshall, Marshall, and Bartlett 2015) of Haida Gwaii geographies, contact/postcontact, Haida/non-Haida, colonial-violence/something beyond. I experiment throughout with other restrictions and constraints: forming entire collections of couplets out of words extracted from the single word *Charlotte*, running word-reduction equations through computer software on texts about the islands that then render and order new words from longest to shortest. Overt repetition offers sound mirroring of the subject. And more.

Readers do not necessarily need to be aware of these constraints, especially when reading excerpts of the poem *Lot*. But it might help to be aware that the echoes of an ovoid sit behind this work.

Know too that the work is a conscious effort to extend conversations about violence and colonialism in British Columbia, violence that I think is too often *voided* from mainstream geographies and conversations. Finally, the poem follows recent discussions about Queen Charlotte, the British monarch for whom the islands were (re)named, possibly being a Black woman (see Giscombe 2012). Poetry, I think, opens new spaces through which to consider this and other aspects of the complex colonial geographies that are Haida Gwaii, geographies where I grew up.

LANDED

Virgin fur.
Cap.

Pelt.
Labret.

A type of
adze, toes.

After cloaks
inlet, for

King George
the *Queen Charlotte.*

Distinguish
this land

for his queen
otter, a fortune.

FORTUNE QUEEN[1]

emphasized
appearance

speculated
movement

Margarida
genealogy

frontline
charlotte

magazine
antislave

ancestry
ancestry

scottish
portrait

descent
episode

claimed
mulatto

support
african

african
ramsay

queens
painter

alleged
claims

castro
valdes

mario
cocom

sousa
allan

trade
that

TRADE THAT

charlotte otter charlotte
otter charlotte otter

charlotte
otter charlotte

otter charlotte
otter charlotte otter

charlotte otter charlotte
otter charlotte

otter charlotte otter
charlotte otter

charlotte otter
charlotte otter

charlotte otter
charlotte otter

charlotte otter
charlotte otter

charlotte otter
charlotte otter

My father makes up a story.
All the black stones, wind blasted.

On the shore. At the tide line.
Are bears who jumped here.

From the mainland.
And missed.

He does not know
about a stone woman.

STONE WOMAN

And the woman   was half stone
And the woman   had a face marked with stone

And the woman   was a woman made partly of stone
And the woman   rose from the salt and felt stone

And the woman   faced stone and breathed stone
And the woman   was a stone woman

And the woman   made stone of which she was made
And the woman   had a face made partly of stone

And the woman   had a jaw of stone
And the woman   had one eye of stone

And the woman   held stone in an arm made partly of stone
And the woman   looked and her look was stone

And the woman	cradled a baby who was a girl who would become stone too
And the woman	wept and she wept tears of stone
And the woman	was a stone woman
And the woman	dove down under water and met stone
And the woman	felt stone too
And the woman	and stone
And the woman	and stone
And the woman	and stone
And the woman	stone
And the woman	stone
And the woman	in stone
And the woman	and stone
And the woman	was stone
and woman and	the woman was stone woman

(FROM) C H A R L O T T E

i
Oh oracle.
Oh latch.

Oh cater
    colt coral.

Oh alter.
Oh hero.

Oh arch.
Oh core.

Oh tale.
Oh tear.

O(void)   241

Tear.
Oh trace.

ii
Her alert trot.
Her ace.

Throe role.
Ratchet.

Ratchet her ha
her eh.

Each hale act.
Her let, her care.

iii
Halter cheat.
A leach.

Torch her ear, her hat
      her rattle rot role.

Tet a tet, rat a tat tat.
A chore.

iv
Rotate her.
A clear clatter cotter.

Hot earth char   otter   orca.
Lace to roe. A heart. Her trace.

That throat-toe chortle. Lore.
Harlot. Tart. Coal era. Cloth.

The ache, later. Alone.
Heal heart, heal.

Etch each echo.
An oath.

MAKING A GIRL

Be careful. Be careful   seaweed slips   be careful.
Be careful. Be careful   with the cradle and the baby   be careful

Be careful. Be careful   because killer whales are the most powerful. Be careful.
Be careful. Be careful   of nests but also of snares.   Be careful.

Be careful. Be careful   when small birds lift off together. Be careful.
Be careful. Be careful   your mother and father, your sister and son. Be careful.

Be careful. Be careful   to dry fish, to set out red meet, to flatten salal berries.
Be careful. Be careful. Be careful also with other berries. And with leaves. Be

careful. Be careful. Be careful you will always run fastest, but with care. Be careful.
Be careful. Be careful   with your caring breath, with your hands. Be

careful. Be careful. Be careful   when you dress the dead be careful.
Be careful. Be careful   steamed ceder is so fragile   be careful.

AS IN LOT

as in   to cast
as in   to draw

as in   an act of divination
as in   a curse or spell

as in   a game of chance
as in   a portion, a share

as in   a person's destiny
as in   rare

as in   royalty paid to mine owner, ore
as in   forming part of a larger whole

O(void)   243

as in	person regarded as having a special quality (bad lot)
as in	plot of land
as in	front of a house
as in	small enclosure
as in	site of film studio
as in	a number, amount
as in	very much, with modifier 'a'
as in	allocate, appoint
as in	Charlotte, diminutive of Charles
	shortened. Lottie. Oh Lot.

My sister is a sleepwalker.
Also, she is terrified.

Of tsunamis.
For two years.

She calls out before bed.
Mum! Dad!

Where will we go
after we have washed away?

WE IMAGINE DISASTER

We imagine disaster, hoping for kindness.
We look for that kindness. We imagine disaster.

We arrive at the earth, quake split and see sea spit froth and balance, rock mush
bull frogs and fog with starfish. In tide pools that are not tributaries, we wait.
We wade

wishing, imagine disaster.
We also fish. Fins are what we carve crave, imagining disaster, the tsunamis that will

deliver docks and mounds, moles from ocean-under, an unknowable global, warming, we wait, fishing, lines cast tide-ward, the pull of abdomens, sea abalone

salal green our nets bobbing, looking for kindness in the bears or wasps, egg pollination we wait, sharkskin, imagine disaster.

We awake cranky, grumble but are kindred with yew trees and ewes that are not trees, the laurel and gorse and heather and alder. All kindness to us, we imagine

disaster, walking in sand agate sunshine shipwrecked cloud trout and also newts who try to speak, a raven's beak, we hope for kindness. Seaweed televisions, how

walruses and sea-lions have begun to Skype, the world is there, whales are there, yelling is there the yip of blue, of orange and white and brown. We are a stream and

the banks of a stream and gulls, something sticky tricky, we imagine disaster. We count and we learn. Still quaking warmth millimeter by millimeter the stub of a

log spiky knot snag loud a quirky eagle leaf needle. We also hold onto mushrooms in moss, hoping for kindness rooted in cohos' scales and spring-salmon too, marching

toward the mainland now. Grey orchids our pillows clutched because we did learn kindness, and now we imagine disaster.

We are layered, chubby beetles war-torn hemlock berries and longhouses abscessed with our toothy dismissal. Even whittled cedar is canoe-hate slipshod sideways
smacking down satellites and maps, we imagine ourselves. Terrified white seaweed, weed, a shell with no mollusk. Such ships moon floating tugging we mistook

O(void)

kindness, imagine disaster.
We search for fresh water. Long lists lingcod willow songbird a chainsaw of
seals,

the layers of blubber something like new butter like pirates. We trade
beads, copper plugs a volcano, beach a dragonfly walking leashed by a
caddisfly ripple the dogs

join us too, our cats, our stuff stuffed trunked tack, dry barrels, wool, sugar
and the flowering *menziesia*. These are just the beginnings of our cata-
logues, barnacles

black cottonwood with riffle debris insects landing. We also want to sing
with strings and clapping drums, voices lift but also lie down with our
hearts we craft

jetliners gently, gentle now, and steam with engines tea and say kindness,
kindness again, and imagine disaster.

We knowingly loved, hoping for kindness on Twitter and after the holocaust, with eyes fixed on pine orb drops of crab oil highway trail automobiles to the stars

combustion halibut a dollyvarden electroshocker sampling on open fire
pits, bridges, we bring tents, the stench of tuberculosis or a plague. Holding
the eye, the

ovoid eye of beaver and mouse and orca, something above our feet we feel
kindness but imagine disaster.

We say whenever they are illuminated how ships are named for queens
not nearly as black as mining for stones, argilite animals underneath, not
spoken, bottom of

totem strong, our arrival, we imagine disaster happy for kindness, for
waves, marriage, our children and our children's children with new
tongues the taste of a

balancing rock packages, FedExed friends waving, plotting out anchors, planning and planting fields and crops from stern to bow new files and claims, a resting

colony, a nap of migrating birds with our plastic pellets beak-throat lodged, the world wide web, also with our hands and those we hold dear, slipping, we imagine

disaster, hoping for kindness.
We imagine disaster. We hope for kindness.

Note

1. A "snowball constraint" poem, based on "Charlotte of Mecklenburg-Strelitz," *Wikipedia* entry, lasted edited September 16, 2019, https://en.wikipedia.org/wiki/Charlotte _of_Mecklenburg-Strelitz (accessed September 24, 2019).

References

Acker, Maleea. 2013. *Air-Proof Green*. St. Johns NL: Peddler Press.

———. 2015. "Two Poems (Hook and Going West)." *GeoHumanities* 1, no. 1: 185–87.

Cresswell, Tim. 2013. *Soil*. London: Penned in the Margins.

———. 2014. "Geographies of Poetry/Poetries of Geography." *cultural geographies* 21, no. 1: 141–46.

———. 2015. *Fence*. London: Penned in the Margins.

Cresswell, Tim, Deborah P. Dixon, Peter K. Bol, and J. Nicholas Entrikin. 2015. Editorial. *GeoHumanities* 1, no. 1: 1–19.

Dear, Michael. 2015. "Practicing Geohumanities." *GeoHumanities* 1, no. 1: 20–35.

de Leeuw, Sarah. 2013. *Geographies of a Lover*. Edmonton AB: NeWest Press.

———. 2015. *Skeena*. Sechelt BC: Caitlin Press.

———. 2017. "Writing as Righting: Truth and Reconciliation, Poetics, and New Geo-Graphing in Colonial Canada." *Canadian Geographer/Le Géographe canadien* 61, no. 3: 306–18.

de Leeuw, Sarah, and Harriet Hawkins. 2017. "Critical Geographies and Geography's Creative Re/turn: Poetics and Practices for New Disciplinary Spaces." *Gender, Place & Culture* 24, no. 3: 303–24.

Giscombe, C. S. 2012. "Queen Charlotte Meets Haida Gwaii." *Chronicle of Higher Education*, October 23. http://www.chronicle.com/blogs/linguafranca/2012/10/23/queen -charlotte-meets-haida-gwaii/ (accessed September 24, 2019).

Hawkins, Harriet. 2013. *For Creative Geographies: Geography, Visual Arts and the Making of Worlds*. New York: Routledge.

Magrane, Eric, and Christopher Cokinos, eds. 2016. *The Sonoran Desert: A Literary Field Guide*. Tucson: University of Arizona Press.

Marshall, Murdean, Albert Marshall, and Cheryl Bartlett. 2015. "Two-Eyed Seeing in Medicine." In *Determinants of Indigenous Health in Canada: Beyond the Social*, edited by Margo Greenwood, Sarah de Leeuw, Nicole Marie Lindsay, and Charlotte Reading, 16–24. Toronto: Canadian Scholars' Press.

Townsend-Gault, Charlotte, Jennifer Kramer, and Ki-Ke-In, eds. 2013. *Native Art of the Northwest Coast: A History of Changing Ideas*. Vancouver: UBC Press.

14 Playing with Plenitude and Finitude
Attuning to a Mysterious Void of Being

Mikko Joronen

Throughout his thinking, one of the most seminal philosophers of the twentieth century—Martin Heidegger—kept approaching the deep embeddedness of the question of being to nothingness, concealment, death, and finitude. Dasein facing the emptiness of death as an anxious moment of nullification and existential possibility; being as hyphenated (be-ing), archaic (beyng), crossed over (~~being~~), or "abyssal ground" (that grounds by staying away); *Ereignis* (happening of being) as an appropriation of revealing via inappropriable; finite dwelling of "Mortals" sheltering the concealed plenitude of possibilities. All these formulations voice an effort to think of the relationship between the finitude and the possibility of being as a site, which "ontological void" operates as a force of openness—as a groundless (*an-archic*) reservoir of plenitude for things to emerge. Although the geographical literature on Heidegger has been (justly) keen to elaborate the potentials of Heidegger's more straightforwardly geographical notions, such as place/topology (e.g., Elden 2005; Malpas 2006; Joronen 2016), dwelling (e.g., Rose 2012; Wylie 2002), space and world (Pickles 1985; Schatzki 2007), globalization (Joronen 2008), and the event (Strohmayer 1998; Joronen 2013; Simonsen, de Neergaard, and Koefoed 2017), less attention has been paid to what might constitute an *attunement* to things that is capable of opening up such plenitude, and so mobilizing it as a ground for a *political action*.

In this chapter I look at the different ways of relating and attuning to the ontological void. I ask in particular how these attunements (*Stimmung*) open up a space for what I suggest could be seen as a political action playing with the ontological finitude and plenitude. I start by looking at the question of attunement, but also of resoluteness and receptivity, with regard to Heidegger's different takes on the relationship between being and void, revealing and concealment. I ask in particular, what happens to the attunement/mood early Heidegger considered fundamental to our "there-being" (Dasein)—anxiety—when revealing is granted through the "event of being" (*das Ereignis*) centered around the "site of the thing" rather than through the place and temporality of human Dasein? By elaborating Heidegger's late notion of *Gelassenheit*—an attunement that lets-*things*-be—I argue that while the positivity of void and the movement from Dasein to things may have been so properly articulated, as a modality of (ontological) freedom Gelassenheit creates several problems that need further explication. I suggest a different attunement is needed—one that is entangled with the particular uses of things via active play simultaneously attuned to the ontological void of open being. Such play, instead of anxiety or Gelassenheit, has the capacity, as Giorgio Agamben (2015) holds, to render inoperative different uses and relations of meaning through the "impotentiality of being"; that is, through the impossibility of being to ever fully reveal itself.

Resoluteness and Receptivity: Being, Void, Attunement

In his early works, such as *Being and Time* (1927) and the following *What Is Metaphysics?* (1929), Heidegger approaches *anxiety* as a specific mood with a capacity to open up what he calls a "momentary vision" (*Augenblick*) to a nothingness (of ontological void). Though achievable only "momentar-ily," and thus via events passing by like a "blink of an eye" (Augenblick), such 'vision' is not to be considered as a peculiar way of seeing, but rather as an attunement (*Stimmung*), a mood fundamental in kind: the one of existential anxiety (Guignon 2009, 196; see also Heidegger [1929] 1993). In Heidegger's early works it is precisely anxiety that serves as the most fundamental existential attunement of Dasein, separated from the subjective feelings, affects, and less profound moods such as fear, grief, anger or shame ([1927] 1996, 317).

Although Dasein—referring to the "there-being" that one is always thrown into—is always attuned to some mood, what makes existential attunement in general, and anxiety in particular, distinctive is the way in which they relate Dasein to the world and finitude. Anxiety is an attunement related not to this or that innerworldly *thing/object* but to the *being-in-the-world* as such, to its finitude in particular. In anxiety it is the world that gets taken away—the world collapses and becomes insignificant, leaving Dasein with the uncanny feeling of not being at-home in-the-world. Such ontological unhomeliness, however, does not merely align Dasein to nothingness in such a way that Dasein is fetched back from its everyday absorption in the world; it also disrupts prevalent ways of being-in-the-world by affording a view of their absence and temporariness through Dasein's own finitude, its own mortality. Anxiety is thus a disclosive attunement of a special kind, where Dasein, by momentarily understanding its own finitude and death, opens up the possibility to be otherwise through the nothingness and void it so encounters.

When facing death, one is of course not-yet dead. It is rather Dasein's potentiality-for-being-in-the-world that comes forth in anxiety; it is void constituting, not a *total nothing* of nihilism, but a condition for unlocking the *world as a world* (see Heidegger [1927] 1996, section 40; emphasis mine). In anxiety, with Dasein projecting itself upon its own possibilities through the uncanny feeling of not being at-home in-the-world, a future-orientated potentiality for being-in-the-world opens up. Anxiety is a world-disclosing mood, a mood that opens up the world through its disappearance, insignificance and void. Confronting such a void is never about the complete isolation of Dasein from the world, but a moment where potentiality for being-in-the-world opens up through Dasein's anxious not-being-at-home in the world.

Facing the nothingness (of death) thus operates as a force nullifying Dasein's "fallenness" (*Verfallen*) into familiar everyday routines and significance (of the world) characterized by what Heidegger calls the average social figure of "common man" ("the They"; *das Man*). And yet the force of nothingness is not a mere negation, but a route to potentiality revealed and given for Dasein to be-ahead-of-itself (Heidegger [1927] 1996, 179). What Dasein finds in its anxious facing of the nothingness of death is eventually the truth about Dasein itself: the openness to being it is able to give a place for (as the *Da* of *Sein*; the "there" of open "being"). It is for this reason Dasein becomes authentic when attuned to anxiety: it absorbs what is ownmost to it; namely, the openness to being. Such anxiety is not a fearful angst about losing what one presently has, but a moment of understanding those possibilities that the nullification of the prevailing intelligibility of the world entails. When released from the shattering weight of dying and the imminent disappearance of the world in its attunement to a void, Dasein can turn rapturous and ecstatic about the open *future* that is so brought to the situation to act upon (Heidegger [1927] 1996, 311, 352). It is in such a "moment" (Augenblick) that anxiety turns into rapture and a "potentiality for existence" opens up so that Dasein can genuinely *care* about its being. What the anxiety about nothingness of death ultimately reveals is thus Dasein's concern or care (*Sorge*) about its own being. As Piotr Hoffman (1993) puts it, "if we were not threatened by death, our basic state would not be care; but if our basic state were not care, our death would not be felt as threatening" (201).

Heidegger's ([1927] 1996) early talk about resolute Dasein, which frees itself for the world in anxious nullification and the opening up of the world (as world), should not be understood as a willful subject detaching himself or herself from the world as a free-floating ego (274). The analysis of Dasein rather underlines the deep interconnection between being-in and nothingness, anticipation of death and the concrete action in reso-lute moment. A disagreement prevails, however, on how to consider such resoluteness: as an ownmost *decision* where Dasein withdraws itself from the routines and patterns defined by the familiar world (e.g., Polt 1999), or in terms of openness to being that Dasein *receives* due to anxious nul-lification (e.g., Vallega-Neu 2003). Some go even as far as to claim that the possibilities opened up by our attunement to a void have nothing to do with the actual choices Dasein makes when coming back to the world (Mitchell 2015, 225–26). While the latter can surely be said about the death and nothingness that first unlock the potentiality for being-in-the-world, it is dubious why the moment of openness would not have any actual effect to Dasein's coming-back-to-the-world. Heidegger ([1927] 1996), for instance, speaks about the authentic retrieving of possibilities as an *act* of "Dasein choosing its heroes," also adding that such choosing is "existentially grounded in anticipatory resoluteness," which first frees oneself for the "struggle to come" (352). Although the receptivity is surely part of the analysis of Dasein, as Heidegger ([1927] 1996) explicitly writes in *Being and Time*, "it would be a complete misunderstanding of the phenomenon of resoluteness if one were to believe that it is simply a matter of receptively taking up possibilities" handed to Dasein (275).

It is the nature of this reception and the proper attunement it requires that, I argue, constitutes the most crucial questions in defining the positive role a void can play in political action. In what follows I thus look at the question of void and its relationship to action from a particular angle: the one of receptivity. Instead of approaching the relationship between openness (or the void) and action through the notions of willing/decision, I pay particular attention to the mechanism of opening that being allows, and that we, as the ones to whom being is allowed, thus receive. I hence look at the question of the void from the perspective of being (instead of human Dasein), starting not from Dasein's moods but from the "full sphere," which I show that "being," together with the "void," constitutes.

The Full Sphere: Plenitude of Void

In the short text "What Are Poets For?" Heidegger (2001) refers to the unity of being and a void, or "revealing" and "concealing," by quoting Rainer Maria Rilke's poem: "like the moon, so life surely has a side that is constantly turned away from us, and that is not its opposite but its completion to perfection, to plenitude, to the real, whole, and full sphere and globe of being" (Heidegger 2001, 121).

As Julian Young (2000) argues, the comprehension of the void as an element *completing* being to a full sphere of plenitude and openness differs significantly from Dasein's attunement to a *nullifying* void. In *Being and Time*, Young writes, "being is nothing other than 'the meaning of being,'" so that beyond it "lies only the empty, complete negative, absolute and abysmal nothing" (Young 2000, 191; see also Heidegger 1996 [1927], 240–41). The ultimate goal in facing such a "negative void" may be the opening up of potentialities for being-in-the-world, but the role the *void* plays in *Being and Time* consists in nothing but negating and nullifying the prevailing configuration of the world—of making things insignificant and unhomely to Dasein. In other words even though "the insignificance of the world disclosed in *anxiety* reveals the nullity of what can be *taken care* of," the role of the void remains clear: to negate (Heidegger [1927] 1996, 315; second emphasis mine).

As Levinas's famous critique of Heidegger underlines, to guard anonymous "being" brings forth nothing but the barbaric horrors of nothingness, where the face of the other is lost under the brute impersonality of the empty and the void (Abbott 2014, 91–95). Such, however, is not the case in Heidegger's later discussion of being as *Ereignis* (translated as the "event of revealing," or the "Appropriation"). Here being is understood as a horizon of concealing-revealing, capable of overcoming the prevailing clearing of revealing through its transformative "happening" (Ereignis). The void is no more the negative empty about which Levinas was so frightened. Instead it creates what Heidegger already called in his signposting midperiod work *Contributions to Philosophy (from Ereignis)* (1936–1938) the *ab-ground*: a ground that grounds, like the dark side of the moon in Rilke's poem, by "staying away." The void hence grounds; it enables. It is "the primary clearing for what is open as emptiness," a "sheltering that lights up" and lets *Ereignis* (event of being) rise (Heidegger 2000, 265–67). It forms a reservoir of plenitude, which as a lack of ground allows for being to remain open and for ontological configurations to reach their finitude. As a constitutive part of the "full sphere" of being, the role of the void is no more to negate, or to allow an empty absolute, but to operate as a concealed groundlessness, as a plenitude and positive *reservoir of not-yet-uncovered* (Young 2000, 196).

The turn from the negative empty to the positive plenitude of the void is a crucial change for a number of reasons. Firstly, the relationship between "being" and "human beings" is now defined in terms of granting and reception, where being gives and Dasein receives. In revealing "prevails a giving, the giving that gives presencing," Heidegger writes in 1962, further adding that such giving does not refer to things (that are present) but to the mechanism of "letting-presence," where being happens by "opening and concealing" things (Heidegger 1972, 5, 16, 19). The distance to resoluteness (*Entschlossenheit*) of Dasein could not seem much wider, the notion of reception offering almost an antithesis of, rather than a complementary perspective to, the resolute decision of *Being and Time*. And yet, it would be misleading to assume that receptivity simply parallels with passivity and indecision, with things merely emerging out of their own (vital) powers (see Joronen 2011). The fundamental giving (of being) and the receptivity (of human beings) are not signs of passivity, lack of action, or inability to decide, but positive conditions enabling us to attune to a void as an abundant reservoir, which gives being and allows its revealing(s) to occur anew. The void is "the highest gift of being" (Heidegger 2006, 263), as it grants being in its endless plenitude of happening. As Heidegger aptly writes in a lecture course held three decades after *Being and Time*, this groundless abyss of the void is "neither empty nothingness nor murky confusion, but rather: the event of appropriation [Ereignis]" (Heidegger 2002, 39). It is the *happening* of being (das Ereignis), the "event of concealing-revealing," that now reveals a site (or a clearing) of things for us to dwell in, simultaneously concealing the open reservoir that being in its fullest sphere constitutes. It is this positivity and abundance of the void one receives, albeit as concealed, in the event.

Secondly, comprehending being as a horizon of concealing-revealing—as a site and clearing, rather than Dasein—also sets aside *human* "there-being" from the center of revealing, replacing it with a coming-to-presence of *things* (Malpas 2006; Schatzki 2007; Joronen 2013). Human beings, whom Heidegger later on called the "mortals," of course play a crucial part in the revealing of "the thing," but now as *participants* of its site of revealing. What the abyss of void gives in concealing-revealing is not first and foremost the presence of thing(s), but their way(s) of coming-to-presence (that is, their revealing, or presencing). The presences of things, like our capacity to participate at the happening of revealing, are not irrelevant byproducts, but neither are they what is first given out of the abyss. It is rather the way of revealing, the coming-to-being (the "letting-presence"), which the void grants in Ereignis. What remains given is of course the coming-to-being of *things*; yet the giving itself refers primarily to the process of *coming-to-being*, to the event of revealing that occurs. The void hence does not denote an ontic absence of this or that thing but names the inexhaustible plenitude of ontological possibilities hidden in the midst of things.

As the above-mentioned conditions underline, comprehending a void as a positive reservoir of plenitude brings to the fore the site of concealing-revealing (rather than Dasein) and the giving of being (rather than resoluteness). What then is our role in this giving? What part can resoluteness and decision play when Dasein is no more at the center of revealing (its place, the *Da-* of Dasein) but receiving what it participates with? What happens to Dasein's attunement, when being happens as a letting-presence of things rather than through the Dasein? Can attunement to a positive void remain anxious?

Attunement That Shelters: Shrine of Nothing

In order to ponder the question of attunement from the perspectives opened up by the giving of being (Ereignis) and the primacy of the thing (as a site of concealing-revealing), it is perhaps more appropriate to ask what is left, if nothing, from the process leading from the anxiety of nullifying insignificance to the rapturous care of resolute Dasein? Anxiety does not seem to fit in well together with a positive void, particularly since such a void grants a plenitude of revealing, not a total insignificance and nullification putting Dasein into an unhomely state of not-being-at-home. In fact, in his late thinking Heidegger redefined Dasein as Mortals, not only shifting the focus from being (Da-*sein*) to dying but also comprehending human beings as elementally opposed to living beings (Mitchell 2015, 212–16). Surely, just as Mortals live, also Dasein dies. Yet, Mortals are no longer beings momentarily anticipating their death in anxious attunement, so that a transition from one mode of existence to another becomes possible. Mortals are rather beings capable of entering and finding their place—their dwelling—*in* death. Death is no longer a concern of a particular Dasein at a particular moment (a "momentary vision"), but a "shrine of nothing" that has the ability to constantly shelter in itself the openness for "presencing of being" (Heidegger 2001, 176). Again, we can see a reference to the convergence of a positive void and being (as the full sphere), which Mortals can now shelter to what is elemental and accessible to them: their death and finitude, the "shrine of nothing." To shelter the full sphere of being and its inexhaustible giving to such a "shrine" means thus the ability to be open, not only to whatever is given (as a revealing of things) but also to the finitude of all such ways of giving.

It is crucial to notice that what Mortals relate to is the finitude intrinsic for the full sphere of being. Mortals receive and preserve being as an abyssal mystery and secret of the groundless opening that is able to allow an inexhaustible amount of unpredictable revealing(s). Death of Mortals is not a force of negation momentarily unlocking potentialities of being for Dasein; death is rather a "refuge of being" that shelters concealed potentialities of open being (Heidegger 2012, 54). It is in this context that we can return to the question how to attune to being in such a way that the abyss of the void is let to maintain sites in their positive richness of finitude and plenitude? What kind of attunement is needed for more steady, active, and persistent sheltering of the "mystery of being" to our "shrine of nothing," the "refuge of being"?

To go through all the existential attunements, moods, and basic dispositions, even as they emerge in Heidegger's corpus, would be simply beyond the scope of this chapter. Heidegger, for instance, discussed the role of wondering as a basic disposition of early Greek thinking, its existential capacity to bring forth the extraordinariness of the ordinary, the usual and familiar as the most wondrous things, and thus to open up the gap between things (the familiar) and their way of being (the unfamiliar) (Heidegger 1994, 135; 1995, 153–55). And still, although wondrous thinking had the ability to become surprised and enchanted about the uncanniness of things in their familiar everyday existence, wonder was too attached to things (and their "beingness"), hence belonging to the inauguration of the long history of the Western "oblivion of being" (for more detailed discussion, see Heidegger 2000; Joronen 2012).

Curiously, in an interview given to *Le Monde* in 1980, Michel Foucault defines his motivation in a manner very similar to wonder. He refers to a special kind of "curiosity" that evokes in him a "care one takes for what exist and what could exist," adding that such "readiness to find what surrounds us strange and odd" allows us to "to throw off familiar ways of thought and to look at the same things in a different way" (Foucault 1997, 325; Foucault 1990, 8; see also McGushin 2007). Although Foucault's brief take on curiosity, surprisingly close to wonder, may provide a way to unlock the unfamiliarity of things and so to grant a possibility to consider things in new terms, the question remains, whether the constant avidity and breathless excitement of curiosity—seeking "novelty only to leap from it again to another novelty" as Heidegger ([1927] 1996) wrote in *Being and Time* (161)—has the calmness for ontological consideration. In fact, it seems to have such little interest in the question of *being*, that as soon as it catches sight of one *thing*, it is already looking for the next one. It lacks what Heidegger (2006) called in his midperiod work *Besinnung* (1938–1939), the "mindfulness" about being and its happening (116–17). Instead of focusing on the newness of *things* alone, such mindfulness situates human beings *in-between* being and things. As mindful "guardians" of this "in-between," we do not simply look over and care for things and their proper modes of revealing. As guardians, we rather prepare the decision that turns ontological tides by staying open (that is, by *not* looking at things), the "de-cision" itself arriving from the abyss of being as a form of event/appropriation (that is, as Ereignis) (Heidegger 2006, 38–39). By interestingly swaying between active human awareness and Ereignis (as what *determines* revealing), mindfulness takes a step forward in properly recognizing the receptivity of being.

However, it was not until Heidegger's late discussion of Gelassenheit, the "letting-be" and composure toward things, that all the aspects discussed above were properly acknowledged. Accordingly Gelassenheit denotes an attunement open to the unfathomable openness—the "mystery of being"—

hidden among the gatherings of things. It consists of "releasement toward things," not as their abandonment, but as an awareness of the "mystery of being" hidden within them. Such letting is not a form of passivity, since the "releasement toward things and openness to the mystery" do not "befall us accidentally" but "flourish only through persistent, courageous thinking" (Heidegger 1966, 54–55, 61). What the Gelassenheit (as a thought, attunement, and action) allows for is the "presencing of things" to take place through the abyss of the void, but in such a way that also the plenitude of the void becomes sheltered within the things so revealed. "Letting-be," then, does not merely let things emerge of their own accord; rather, it shelters abyssal groundlessness, the *an-arkhe* of being, to things as their horizon of openness. And yet this requires human comportment—pondering and action, thinking and building—which as a "shrine of nothing" safeguards the openness of being to things through human composure.

As the discussion above indicates, Gelassenheit is not a mere attunement to things, but human comportment emerging out of the composure, receptivity, and consideration toward the secret hidden within things: the play between revealing and concealing that being (as finite Ereignis and open site) constitutes. As an openness to mystery, Gelassenheit is attuned to wait for the appropriation to happen by allowing room for something to take place (Heidegger 1998, 144). It opens up the "shrine of nothing" for the new events of revealing to occur and thus underlines the mortal way of becoming attuned to what allows the fundamental power of transformation through a particular way of thinking and acting in, with, and out of what is revealed in Ereignis. Mortals can shelter the possibility of the abyss and thus let being transform—not through the decisive power of willing, nor by approving transformation as a plain fate to adopt, but through a receptive sensibility toward openness and the affirmation of what may (and has) occur(ed).

Playing with Impotentiality

As the underlining of receptivity indicates, for late Heidegger it is the groundless abyss of the void, and the *an-archic* openness it grants, that operate as a primary source for ontological freedom. It is this an-archic/groundless opening from which the freedom for acting also stems, so that, as Peter Trawny (2015) writes, "whomever closes himself off from the open . . . not only cannot think, he also cannot act" freely (23). And yet one does not have to go far to realize a fundamental problem in the otherwise so subtle Gelassenheit: the letting that does not respond to but merely safeguards the openness for the presencing of things to happen. With all its active functions, such "courageous thinking" responds to revealing with nothing other than by leaving the backdoor open for the coming events (Ereignis) (Heidegger 1966, 56). No wonder Heidegger (1976) suggested in the posthumously published *der Spiegel* interview (2017) that "only a god can save us": with our "shrine of nothing," we are only left with a divine waiting for the new event to eventuate and allow its giving. We can "move near" the open, but only "wait" and "listen" for the answer humming from the "mysterious region" of the open (Heidegger 1966, 71, 79, 89).

Gelassenheit, it seems, leaves open how exactly the receptivity (of the full sphere of being) is connected to the particularities and manifoldness of acting in the world. As Peter Sloterdijk aptly writes, by turning around Heidegger's famous quote of Hölderlin's poem: "where the saviors are, grows the danger too" (Sloterdijk 2018; Alt 2016, 232). Unlike Heidegger (1977), who had used the passage to emphasize the possibility of a "saving power" growing precisely where the "dangers" of forgetting the "openness of being" come to the fore in their most obscene forms (that is, "where the danger is, grows the saving power also") (see also Agamben 1998, 75), Sloterdijk reminds us that the opposite also holds true: one also needs to stay aware of the "dangers" each new appropriation of revealing brings along. Accordingly, and what I wish to argue in the remaining part of the chapter, a proper attunement should cherish the ability to respond to what is "let" to eventuate in Ereignis (as concealment and revealing), but also to act upon it through what I call the *response-ability* (see also Joronen 2017; Joronen and Häkli 2017). Such response-ability creates a unity between being and acting, and so brings forth a *play* between receptivity and responding, ontology and politics, eventually sheltering the "mystery of being" within what I call a *playful attunement* to being and things.

Interestingly, in his recent work *The Use of Bodies*, Agamben (2015) also suggests abandoning Gelassenheit, proposing instead a form of action that is capable of using what he calls the "impotentiality of being": namely the inability of being to fully reveal itself (168). Unlike Heidegger, who claims that the mysterious openness should be sheltered to Mortals' "shrine of nothing," Agamben thus maintains that it is the use of what he calls "destituent power"—a power finding its potentiality from this original impotentiality of being—which can keep life ungovernable by properly attuning us to the void's positive plenitude and ontological freedom (see Joronen 2017).

To speak of the original impotentiality of being as a fundamental condition of possibility for our "ability to respond" may sound contradictory at first. What could response-*ability* that faces the *inability* of being signify? First of all one needs to recognize that such ability does not denote a capacity to master being but brings to the fore the opposite, the impossibility of all such efforts. The impossibility to master and close being with definitive statements—to own being as such—is not a condition we could choose or decide on, but epiphenomenal to the fact that being cannot ever fully reveal what it fundamentally signifies: an openness to (finite) revealing(s). As open and groundless, being always contains a sense of concealment, of mystery, and a void; hence being always gives itself as finite, impartial, and (partly) hidden. For Agamben this "inability of being" is the original ontological source of potentiality—the impotentiality behind all that is potential. Impotentiality hence does not mean being has no effect on things whatsoever, but rather the opposite: that being is unable to bring itself fully to the fore (as revealing) and precisely as such constitutes an infinitely inexhaustible reservoir for things to emerge (concealment). Impotentiality denotes a positive condition that functions as the original source of all potential, or what Agamben calls politics: an action that "corresponds to the essential *inoperativity* of humankind" (Agamben 2000, 140–41; emphasis mine; see also discussion in Agamben 2015, 278).

Agamben's notion of impotentiality, it seems, covers well the positive and abundant side of open being but also makes void's positive plenitude part of the use of *things* with a manner missing, not only from Heidegger, but also from Foucault's take on curiosity (McKenzie 2008). With the help of Agamben, politics can be thus located, not only within the *play* between revealing (singular) and concealing (abundant), but also within a playful *use* of things. Just as being takes place as irreparably consigned without being ever exhausted to its singular revealing(s), also political action is consigned but never limited to its own situation (or site of revealing), both conditions making room for a playful attunement of response-ability.

Considering the above, our possibility to act politically (that is, our ability to respond) relies on a possibility to cut oneself loose from those limit-conditions that first merge to action. Yet response-ability does so, not through the power of willing, but by playing with the original impotentiality of being. The letting-presence of Ereignis may thus prevail and constitute our fundamental possibility to "be there," but what follows is not merely the letting-be of Gelassenheit, which answers to the dangers and limiting power of revealing(s) merely by safeguarding the concealed openness for coming events. Instead we have an action that brings to the fore the original inability of being (to fully reveal itself), and so makes it possible to render inoperative the prevalent structures of identity, vocation, separation, domination, and so forth. Unlike Gelassenheit, such action plays, profanes, and renders inoperative the prevailing operations, that it so transforms into possibilities and new uses.

What is at stake in inoperative action, I suggest, is thus not a mindful thinking but a *playful attunement*. The inoperative response-ability is a play with being—not just a play between the concealing and revealing *of* being, but play *as* an ability to respond to revealing by playing *with* the uses of things. The relationship of political action to revealing should hence be settled in such a way that what is enabled in action is not merely an *understanding* of what is given by revealing, nor merely a *waiting* of what the Ereignis could bring about. Action finds its power, not from the *an-archic* waiting, but from the *an-archic action* that renders inoperative the effects of prevalent ontological structures by playing with them. Response-ability is thus a movement between an-archic void (incapable of emerging as such) and an-archic action (capable of inoperativity via impotentiality). Such playful attunement does not simply overrule and dismantle all the operations of power that have an effect on it, but rather makes itself something on which these operations do not have the desired effect. Ungovernability of life, so reached, does not mean a life that simply destroys all the governing structures affecting it, but rather a life that is not ontologically reducible to any framing, vocation, or governmental purpose (Joronen 2017; cf. Gordon 2017). Instead of Mortals capable of dying, such ungovernable life abandons itself to the improper and inappropriable, not for the sake of facing sheer nothingness, but for the sake of grasping particularities of everydayness in an existentially modified way.

What is the most fundamental trait here is neither the heroic nor the vitalist strength to tease out new potentialities (Casarino and Negri 2004; Esposito 2008) but a destitute ability not to flee impotentiality: that is, the active way to play with our own ability to inability. Such play, the ability to respond, is neither about making nor waiting Ereignis, but something that, in order to bring ontological change in relation to (uses of) things, needs to become engaged with the impotentiality of being, its inability to be more than finite singulars. This requires that the full sphere of being (the open plenitude for finite singularities) and destitute action (which can use the an-archic impotentiality of being) properly come together in a playful attunement. The void denotes a possibility to experience finitude and to play with the groundless plenitude of being, so that it can become part of the praxis as an inoperationalizing force of the open.

References

Abbott, Mathew. 2014. *The Figure of This World: Agamben and the Question of Political Ontology*. Edinburgh: Edinburgh University Press.

Agamben, Giorgio. 1998. *Homo Sacer: Sovereign Power and Bare Life*. Translated by Daniel Heller-Roazen. Stanford CA: Stanford University Press.

———. 2000. *Means without End: Notes on Politics*. Translated by Vincenzo Binetti and Cesare Casarino. Minneapolis: University of Minnesota Press.

———. 2015. *The Use of Bodies: Homo Sacer IV, 2.* Translated by Adam Kotsko. Stanford CA: Stanford University Press.

Alt, Suvi. 2016. *Beyond the Biopolitics of Development: Being, Politics and Worlds.* Rovaniemi, Finland: University of Lapland.

Casarino, Cesare, and Antonio Negri. 2004. "It's a Powerful Life: A Conversation on Contemporary Philosophy." *Cultural Critique* 57, no. 1: 151–83.

Elden, Stuart. 2005. "Contributions to Geography? The Spaces of Heidegger's *Beiträge*." *Environment and Planning D: Society and Space* 23, no. 6: 811–27.

Esposito, Roberto. 2008. *Bios: Biopolitics and Philosophy.* Translated by Timothy Campbell. Minneapolis: University of Minnesota Press.

Foucault, Michel. 1990. *The Use of Pleasure.* Vol. 2 of *The History of Sexuality.* Translated by Robert Hurley. Essential Works of Foucault, 1954–1984, vol. 1. New York: Vintage Books.

———. 1997. "The Masked Philosopher." In *Ethics, Subjectivity and Truth*, edited by Paul Rabinow. New York: New Press.

Gordon, Neve. 2017. "Palestinian Resistance and the Fallacy of Destituent Play." *Political Geography* 56: 101–3.

Guignon, Charles. 2009. "The Body, Bodily Feelings, and Existential Feelings: A Heideggerian Perspective." *Philosophy, Psychiatry, & Psychology* 16, no. 2: 195–99.

Heidegger, Martin. (1927) 1996. *Being and Time: A Translation of* Sein *and* Zeit. Translated by Joan Stambaugh. Albany: State University of New York Press.

———. (1929) 1993. "What Is Metaphysics?" In *Basic Writings*, edited by David Farrell Krell. New York: HarperCollins.

———. 1966. *Discourse on Thinking.* Translated by John M. Anderson and E. Hans Freund. New York: Harper & Row.

———. 1972. *On Time and Being.* Translated by Joan Stambaugh. New York: Harper & Row.

———. 1977. *The Question concerning Technology, and Other Essays.* Translated by William Lovitt. New York: Garland.

———. 1994. *Basic Questions of Philosophy: Selected "Problems" of "Logic."* Translated by Richard Rojcewicz and André Schuwer. Bloomington: Indiana University Press.

———. 1995. *The Fundamental Concepts of Metaphysics: World, Finitude, Solitude.* Translated by William McNeill and Nicholas Walker. Bloomington: Indiana University Press.

———. 1998. *Pathmarks.* Edited by William McNeill. Cambridge: Cambridge University Press.

———. 2000. *Contributions to Philosophy (From Enowning).* Translated by Parvis Emad and Kenneth Maly. Bloomington: Indiana University Press.

———. 2001. *Poetry, Language, Thought.* Translated by Albert Hofstadter. New York: Harper & Row.

———. 2002. *Identity and Difference.* Translated by Joan Stambaugh. Chicago: University of Chicago Press.

———. 2006. *Mindfulness*. Translated by Parvis Emad and Thomas Kalary. New York: Continuum.

———. 2012. *Bremen and Freiburg Lectures: Insight Into That Which Is and Basic Principles of Thinking*. Translated by Andrew W. Mitchell. Bloomington: Indiana University Press.

———. 2017. "'Only a God Can Save Us.' The Spiegel Interview (1966)." In *Heidegger: The Man and the Thinker*, edited by Thomas Sheehan, 45–68. New York: Routledge.

Hoffman, Piotr. 1993. "Death, Time, History: Division II of *Being and Time*." In *The Cambridge Companion to Heidegger*, edited by Charles Guignon, 195–214. Cambridge: Cambridge University.

Joronen, Mikko. 2008. "The Technological Metaphysics of Planetary Space: Being in the Age of Globalization." *Environment and Planning D: Society and Space* 26, no. 4: 596–610.

———. 2011. "Dwelling in the Sites of Finitude: Resisting the Violence of the Metaphysical Globe." *Antipode* 43, no. 4: 1127–54.

———. 2012. "Heidegger on the History of Machination: Oblivion of Being as Degradation of Wonder." *Critical Horizons* 13, no. 3: 351–76.

———. 2013. "Heidegger, Event and the Ontological Politics of the Site." *Transactions of the Institute of British Geographers* 38, no. 4: 627–38.

———. 2016. "Politics of Being-Related: On Onto-Topologies and 'Coming Events.'" *Geografiska Annaler: Series B, Human Geography* 98, no. 2: 97–107.

———. 2017. "Few Notes on Ontology and Destituent Power: A Reply to Gordon." *Political Geography* 56: 104–5.

Joronen, Mikko, and Jouni Häkli. 2017. "Politicizing Ontology." *Progress in Human Geography* 41, no. 5: 561–79.

Malpas, Jeff. 2006. *Heidegger's Topology: Being, Place, World*. Cambridge MA: MIT Press.

McGushin, Edward F. 2007. *Foucault's Askēsis: An Introduction to the Philosophical Life*. Evanston IL: Northwestern University Press.

McKenzie, Jonathan. 2008. "Governing Moods: Anxiety, Boredom, and the Ontological Overcoming of Politics in Heidegger." *Canadian Journal of Political Science* 41, no. 3: 569–85.

Mitchell, Andrew J. 2015. *The Fourfold. Reading the Late Heidegger*. Evanston IL: Northwestern University Press.

Pickles, John. 1985. *Phenomenology, Science and Geography: Spatiality and Human Science*. Cambridge: Cambridge University Press.

Polt, Richard. 1999. *Heidegger. An Introduction*. Ithaca NY: Cornell University Press.

Rose, Mitch. 2012. "Dwelling as Marking and Claiming." *Environment and Planning D: Society and Space* 30, no. 5: 757–71.

Schatzki, Theodore R. 2007. *Martin Heidegger: Theorist of Space*. Stuttgart: Franz Steiner Verlag.

Simonsen, Kirsten, Maja de Neergaard, and Lasse Koefoed. 2017. "A Mosque Event: The Opening of a Purpose-Built Mosque in Copenhagen." *Social & Cultural Geography* 20, no. 5: 649–70.

Sloterdijk, Peter. 2018. "Ist die Welt noch zu retten?" *Das Philosophische Quartet*. Posted by morallyb4nkrup, November 9, 2012. YouTube video. https://www.youtube.com /watch?v=7-qtu4fsn3a (accessed January 20, 2018).

Strohmayer, Ulf. 1998. "The Event of Space: Geographic Allusions in the Phenomeno- logical Tradition." *Environment and Planning D: Society and Space* 16, no. 1: 105–21.

Trawny, Peter. 2015. *Freedom to Fail: Heidegger's Anarchy*. Cambridge: Polity Press.

Vallega-Neu, Daniela. 2003. "Thinking in Decision." *Research in Phenomenology* 33, no. 1: 247–63.

Wylie, John. 2002. "An Essay on Ascending Glastonbury Tor." *Geoforum* 33, no. 4: 441–54.

Young, Julian. 2000. "What Is Dwelling? The Homelessness of Modernity and the World- ing of the World." In *Heidegger, Authenticity, and Modernity*, vol. 1, *Essays in Honor of Hubert L. Dreyfus*, edited by Mark Wrathall and Jeff Malpas, 187–204. Cambridge MA: MIT Press.

15 In the Void of Formalization

The Homology between Surplus Value and Surplus *Jouissance*

Ceren Özselçuk and Yahya M. Madra

The void is where Jacques Lacan's formalization of psychoanalysis encounters Marx's critique of political economy. The void, in the historicity of this particular encounter between psychoanalysis and the critique of political economy, emerges as a structuralist concept that designates the empty place of the signifier. Lacan's well-known formula, "a signifier represents the subject to another signifier," summarizes this performative and retroactive nature of signification that rests on the void of meaning and the empty place of the subject. In a rather accurate reading of Marx's *Capital*, Lacan identifies a homology between this structuralist emphasis on the primacy of signifier over signified and the primacy of the regime of value as that which stamps and retroactively constitutes objects of human labor as commodities in a relational system of (exchange) value.

More precisely, in this turn toward structuralism, Lacan (2006, 14) uses the Marxian concept of surplus value in order to introduce "the place" of object *a* and to situate its "essential function." In *Seminar XVI*, titled *From an Other to the other*, he brings together his earlier work on the graph of desire (already a formalization of the process of signification and identification) with the mathematical logic of set theory and introduces the concept of *plus-de-jouir* (surplus *jouissance*) as "a new design" (Regnault 2010, 131) for the object cause of desire, the object *a*. In Lacan's trajectory from structuralism to topology, this "new design" will lead to a shift of focus from the partial objects (for example, breasts, feces, gaze, voice) to an impossible object, to what Jacques-Alain Miller (2007) calls a "topological hole" found as a "third term" between "corporeal specimen" and "logical consistency" (29). Especially in the first four sessions of this twenty-five-week-long seminar, in an explicit reference to Althusser's "structural" reading of Marx's *Capital*, Lacan characterizes the relationship between surplus value and surplus jouissance as one of homology and uses the phrase "being of thought" to describe the "essential function" that both concepts play in their respective discursive fields.

Lacan's structuralist reading of psychoanalysis and the critique of political economy has wide-reaching consequences throughout his discourse moving forward. Indeed, it constitutes a key moment in his turn toward the formalization of psychoanalysis. Lacan (2002) marks this turn toward mathemes on the very first day of *Seminar XVI*, when he writes on the board the formula, *"the essence of psychoanalytic theory is a discourse without words"* (I 1). Yet, we identify two distinct threads in his discourse that we wish to disentangle. On the one hand he articulates an *epistemological analysis*, which underlines the structural sameness of analytical discourse with the discourse of Marxian critique of political economy. On the other hand he brings up a *historical analysis*, developing throughout the seminar a conjunctural and institutional critique of "the market that is called the University" (II 14).[1]

Lacan would revisit and play with this line of historical analysis again in *Seminar XVII*, when he produces the concept of four discourses and deploys the movement in social links from master's discourse to the discourse of the university to discuss transitions both *into* and *within* capitalism. Such emphasis on historical shifts opens Lacan's discourse to historicist interpretations (which periodize social formations as homogeneous units synthesized around a particular consciousness or power and assign to them a unified temporal direction). Nonetheless Lacan again and again inflects these kinds of historical statements with ambiguous temporal qualifications that more often than not give off the effect of a myth rather than the reflexive knowledge of historicist periodization.[2] Furthermore Lacan, again in *Seminar XVII* and later on in *Seminar XX*, consistently would try

ÖZSELÇUK AND MADRA

to distance himself from the structural necessity of historicism associated with Hegel (Feltham 2006) and note that the four discourses are "not in any sense to be viewed as a series of historical emergences—the fact that one may have appeared longer ago than the others is not what is important here" (Lacan 1998, 16).

In any case, already in *Seminar XVI* Lacan tackles the question of historicity of the concept of surplus value as well as the relationship between structuralism and historical materialism. "Was surplus value there before abstract labour . . . resulted from something that we will call . . . the absolutisation of the market?" asks Lacan. And his answer hinges on the homology: "It is more than probable, and for a good reason which is that we have, for that, introduced the *surplus enjoying*" (Lacan 2002, II 8). But there is something that is not working in the homology here. Lacan begins this discussion of the dimension of history by exploring the thorny problem of squaring the historicity of mathematical logic with his structuralist argument on the consequences of mathematical logic regarding one's existence as a subject whether one knows it or not. He hedges his answer: even if one could retroactively identify the existence of a discourse of logic in the representations of some facts regarding the existence of a subject, the consequences of discourse will not be the same once the discourse of mathematical logic has been put forward at a given historical moment. In other words, while the psychoanalytical concepts (for example, *surplus enjoying* or the enjoyment derived from the renunciation of enjoyment) can be applied retroactively, the introduction of psychoanalysis, as "a discourse without words," constitutes "a turning point of the incidence of knowledge in History" (Lacan 2002, III 2). Once a discourse is inaugurated, it will have consequences.

Precisely at this point the homology breaks down. For Marx's concept of surplus value is a concept that is articulated to read, specifically, the capitalist relations of production and reproduction for exploitation (that is, the extraction of surplus value through the mediation of value). Lacan (2002) seems to recognize this when writes "absolutisation of the market is only a condition so that surplus value can appear in discourse . . . absolutisation of the market to the point that it encompasses labor itself" (II 8). However, surplus value is tied to absolutisation of the market not only genetically but also conceptually. The proper question, therefore, should have been, "Was surplus labor there before Marx invented abstract labour?" This is not hairsplitting as what is at stake is the failure to repeat Lacan's turn toward formalization on the side of Marx's critique of political economy. The fidelity to the void of the encounter requires us to be as precise as possible with respect to the terms of the homology. If the structuralist homology between psychoanalysis and the critique of political economy enabled Lacan to substitute object *a* for the phallus by completely inscribing the former within a reference to jouissance, we should also be able to honor Marx's formalizing gesture: by distinguishing between surplus labor and surplus value—even if we were to grant that Marx arrives at surplus labor retroactively, after inventing surplus value—Marx gains the capability of theorizing noncapitalism, both in its precapitalist and postcapitalist forms. If Lacan's formalization of psychoanalysis, by leading him toward a clinic of the *sinthôme*, expanded the domain of psychoanalysis to the treatment of nonneurotic patients, Marx's formalization (the critique of political economy) led him not only toward situating capitalism in its historicity but also to exploring "associationism" as a form of postcapitalism that foregrounds class justice.

Formalization and Discourse

Instead of getting sidetracked by the imaginary guarantees of historicism, we would like to highlight the historicity of Lacan's turn toward formalization (and not formalism) through mathemes structured around the void of impossibility. While Lacan has been using graphs and mathemes since the 1950s, it is in the period of 1960s that he began to comment more explicitly on formalization. A significant moment in this respect is the encounter between Lacan's formalizations of Freud and Althusser and his students' "structural" reading of Marx if what we mean by an encounter is a contingent meeting where each discourse is moved to respond toward the "other" and provoked to address an "internal" difficulty, and as a con-

ÖZSELÇUK AND MADRA

sequence is transformed in the process. From this perspective our thesis is that this encounter, which is a constitutive part of the debate on the scientific claims of structuralism, has pushed Lacan toward interrogating the social and thinking about the place of object *a* in social links and has pushed Althusserian Marxism toward qualifying the function of the subject and the unconscious and clarifying the philosophical conditions of the scientificity of Marx's (historical) materialism respectively.[3]

In *Seminar XVI* Lacan himself theorizes the precise nature of this encounter when he emphasizes the term *homology*, pointing to a similarity in the structural place and function of the concepts of surplus value and surplus jouissance: "This *surplus enjoying* appeared, in my last talk, in function of a homology with respect to Marxist surplus value. Homology, clearly means—and I underlined it—that the relation is not one of analogy. It is indeed the same thing that is at stake. It is a matter of the same stuff in so far as what is at stake is the scissors' mark of discourse" (Lacan 2002, III 1).

There are a number of important points to unpack in this dense paragraph. First, the "sameness" of homology needs to be strictly distinguished from that of analogy, which we interpret Lacan to associate with the harmony of proportionality, thus, in conformity with an imaginary sense of similarity (Regnault 2010, 118), whereas the similarity in homology pertains to the way in which both concepts mark in their respective discourses a structural relation to the limit, to the impossible Real. In other words, homology pertains to the way each concept orients their respective discourses toward a formalization structured around the void of impossibility.

Second, and directly following from this first point, is the way both surplus value and surplus jouissance are related to the "scissors' mark" or "cut" of discourse.[4] This invokes the idea of the epistemological cut, or the epistemological break, the Bachelardian explanation of scientific beginnings of which Althusser also famously makes use in order to distinguish Marx's "discourse-object unity" (Althusser and Balibar 1997, 15) from the discourse-object unity of classical political economy of Adam Smith and David Ricardo. It also invokes the cut of the master signifier that marks the joining of the body with the symbolic that inaugurates the (four) formations of social link. Remaining at this epistemic level, we can argue that what "place" and "function" the concepts of surplus jouissance and surplus value share is their status as master signifiers that set in motion a discourse around them. For Althusser (2018), this is how "Marx's thought . . . proceeds . . . by *positing* a concept that initiates the exploration (analysis) of the theoretical space opened up and closed off by this positing" (14–15). These are respectively the analytical discourse and the critique of political economy.

This discussion gives us another homology to propose between Althusser's practice of symptomatic reading (which stands in a certain tension with the idea of epistemological break) and Lacan's practice of analytical discourse, if, on this idea of discourse, we broadly follow Lacan's references in *Seminar XVI* to a dynamic structure that produces consequences encircling an impossibility. What we want to emphasize here is the topological status of the "scissors' mark," which, as a cut, delineates the spatial extension in the field of the symbolic Other of what is only imaginable in the intersubjective field as an interior (that is, the space of extimacy). In Althusser's symptomatic reading, conceptual discovery as the practice of theorization—in this case Marx's theorization of historical materialism (when read along with linguistic and psychoanalytical theoretical innovations) and his innovative distinctions between value and use value and his invention of surplus value (Althusser and Balibar 1997, 80)—threads the border of this extimate space. These conceptual inventions are both inscribed (even when they are critical of capitalism) in the ideological practice of aiding the essential functioning of the capitalist social formation as a whole, yet at the same time, as conceptual apparatuses of scientific practice, they work on it, deconstruct it, and render it non-all, thus, opening it up to contingent and diverse beginnings and imminent transformations.[5]

For Lacan, on the other hand, and in a similar move at elaborating a discursive structure, "scissors' mark" names the location of extimacy in which surplus jouissance can be worked on: while it remains unknown to the subject, and in its unknown and unconscious status gives the subject its symptomatic consistency, surplus jouissance is also what simultaneously opens the subject to the possibility of traversing the stuckness in her relation to enjoyment (that is, subjectivation) through the practice of analytical discourse. (Let us hold for the moment how this topological structure diverges from the homology with Althusser's symptomatic reading in that it points to a different dimension of extimacy that combines, in a disjunctive manner, knowledge and being.) That is, "scissors' mark" refers to the extimate space in which the subject, unknowingly, comes into being at once by way of being divided by and intruding into the field of the Other (of language), and gaining consistency through its encirclement around the object *a* that stands both as the "hole" in the Other and as "what comes to fill it in" through phantasmatic projections (Miller 2007, 25).

Object *a* is the "obscure object" of Lacan's invention that he produced from his reading of Freud based on elaborating the problematic relationship between "a divided subject and a non object" (Nobus 2013, 163). In Miller's (2007) suggestive explanation, object *a* "imposes a topological structure on the Other, which is made from a hole, and thus has borders, and at the same time it is here as an attraction, condensing, capturing—the word is Lacan's—*jouissance* . . . Petit a, a whole hole with a border, imposes a form on *jouissance*" (Miller 2007, 23; emphasis in the original). And "this is because the *objet a* is *extime*, and purely in the relationship established by the institution of the subject as effect of the signifier, and as itself determining a structure of border in the field of the Other" (Lacan 2006, 249; emphasis in the original; cf. Miller 2007, 55–56).

Lacan seems to argue that movement around this location is only possible as an effect of the analytical discourse (that is, different from the function of surplus jouissance as master signifier, he points to its "real" function as the remainder of signifier's inscription on the body that is brought into relief in the relation of analytical discourse). Nonetheless, to give consistency to this place of surplus jouissance and to be able to write object *a* in the discourse whose effect it is, homology with surplus value seems to be of crucial aid to Lacan.

Surplus Value as a Boundary Concept

Let us repeat the question: In what way does surplus value occupy a location and function in Marx's critique of political economy that is the same as surplus jouissance? Or in more precise terms: To what extent can Lacan's treatment of object *a* as an ambivalent "thing" in the topologically ambivalent sense described above, in terms of "how the subject is formed through internal exclusions and external inclusions" (Blum and Secor 2011, 1030), be said of surplus value? To begin to answer we need to make a brief turn to Althusser's reading of surplus value as Marx's "basic discovery" (Althusser and Balibar 1997, 80). First thing to recall once more is that Althusser characterizes this discovery of Marx not as a new object per se, but rather as a "discourse-object." With this combinatory, Althusser presses on the fact that the "'object' studied or discovered by Marx . . . , fully different from the 'object' studied by Smith or Ricardo, can be identified only on the condition of rectifying Marx's own epistemology" (Balibar 2011, 6), including the philosophical question of what is cause. Althusser theorizes Marx's "epistemological break" with classical political economy, as well as with both Hegelian and Cartesian modes of causality, in order to bring into visibility Marx's invention of a new idea of "cause" that is symptomatic of the text of *Capital* (see also Cullenberg 1996). It is in this sense that Althusser underlines the status of surplus value as a complex structure and insists that surplus value is "not a thing" but rather "the concept of a relationship . . . an existing social structure of production . . . visible and measurable *only in its 'effects'* . . . only present there, as a structure [in the total movement of its effects, in what Marx calls the 'developed totality of its form of existence'], in its *determinate* absence" (Althusser and Balibar 1997, 180–81).

In his attempt to formalize surplus value as the place of absent cause, Althusser tries to distance Marx's discourse on capitalist mode of production from those problematics of value that are based on "measurable economic facts" and that establish deterministic relations among them and ground their "essence" on imaginary identifications secured by an anthropology

ÖZSELÇUK AND MADRA

of "needs" (*homo oeconomicus*). In contradistinction to the constructions of such homogeneous and economistic space of value, as Étienne Balibar (2011) argues, Althusser reads surplus value "as a *boundary-notion* between the economic and the social, which allows Marx to include a complexity of historical forces and instances in the 'reproduction' of the capitalist framework" (7).

If we follow up on this idea of the surplus value as a boundary notion between the economic and the social, we can introduce the overdetermination of value through the processes of production and circulation on the one hand and the processes of (social) reproduction and distribution (class struggle over surplus value) on the other hand. Yet nested in this complex topology is another one that pertains to the place of surplus value, in this instance *within* the economic, inside the circuit of capital. In this regard recall Marx's own rather curious description of the (impossible) place of surplus value: "Capital cannot therefore arise from circulation, and it is equally impossible for it to arise apart from circulation. It must have its origin both in circulation and not in circulation" (Marx [1867] 1990, 268).

Precisely for this reason surplus value is not a thing, much less a corporeal object, but rather a complex relation, an absent cause that exists only in its effects, a discourse-object with consequences. Surplus value, therefore, when conceived as the "absent cause" of a complex of relations existing and visible only in its effects, rather than a fixed quantity (of unpaid labor-time) from which other magnitudes, such as prices, are unilaterally derived, opens up a conceptual space for exploring the contingent and contradictory conditions of its re/production and distribution that only retroactively give surplus value a sense of consistency (for example, analysis of value-forms) (Roberts 1996).

The Impossibility of Value

Many commentators who trace the intersection between Lacanian psychoanalysis and Marxian critique of political economy have investigated the homology between the logic of signifier and the analysis of value-form (Kordela 2006; Tomšič 2015). Ultimately, the structural homology between surplus jouissance and surplus value rests on the homology between these two representational systems (sign and value) and their respective retroactive logics. This homology is indeed a very productive one and should further be explored—if only to see the limits of the project of articulating Marxian critique of political economy and Lacanian psychoanalysis (more on this below). Yet, if we are to push the homology between the value-form and the logic of signifier beyond the confines of structuralism and give it a properly psychoanalytical twist, we must locate the void not only as an absent cause but also as the impossibility of its reconciliation. We now turn our attention to explore the nature of this constitutive and ineradicable impossibility of value.

According to George Henderson (2013), Marx provides an account of the impossibility of value across all three volumes of *Capital*, and he does this by recurrently invoking the "specter of associated labor . . . as the unexpected underlay and warrant of value" (60). It is as if for Marx value is a category that exceeds capitalism, and even commodity production, and pertains to all social formations where some minimal form of division of labor necessitates the presence of a mode of distribution and gives laboring activity its social character (Hussain 1979, 94). Marx begins *Capital* with an analysis of the commodity form by comparing it with noncapitalist forms: Robinson on his island, feudal estate, (patriarchal) peasant household and "an association of free men" (Marx [1867] 1990, 169–73). And in volume 3 of *Capital* Marx begins to articulate the failure of value under "capitalist production as a whole" by juxtaposing it with an image of communism, "genuine, prior control of society" where "the connection between the amount of social-labor-time applied to the production of particular articles, and the scale of the social need to be satisfied by these" (Marx [1894] 1991, 288–89) is established. Assumed in this definition of communism is a correspondence between the productive *abilities* and the social *needs* of this community.

Let us bracket for the moment the possible failures of value under associated production as a question that needs to be attended to and turn our attention to the void of impossibility of value under capitalism that this fantasmatic notion of communism fills in. Throughout volume 3 of *Capital* Marx carefully distinguishes between different value-forms (*exchange value* and *prices of production*) in order to render visible the effectivity of the sphere of circulation over the sphere of production. Prices of production, in contrast to exchange value, are the social-labor-times attached to each commodity under the competitive tendency of equalization of the rates of profit for each capital. Yet paradoxically, due to this competitive tendency, the prices of production of commodities tend to systematically deviate from their values (the amount of social-labor-time necessary for producing them), and as a result surplus value gets redistributed among competing production units in proportion to their relative productivity. Marx describes this process as "a tendency to equalization, which seeks the 'ideal' mean position, i.e. a mean position which does not exist in reality. In other words, it tends to shape itself around this ideal as a norm" (Marx [1894] 1991, 273).

This ideal position where all production units achieve the same rate of profit does not exist, and precisely for this reason competitive process ensues. In this very fundamental sense, precisely because (surplus) value does not get realized where it is produced, "capitalist production as a whole" is always internally dislocated, always thrown into crises. Henderson (2013) traces out two important consequences (among others) of this point that function as the key to reading the rest of volume 3. The first consequence pertains to the tendency of the profit rate to fall where rising labor productivity (due to the competitive drive described above) leads to a decline in the mass of living labor applied in relation to the mass of objectified labor that it sets in motion. This prospect leads capitalist firms either to shift their focus from profit rate to mass of profit as centralization and concentration of capital proceeds or to substitute living labor with more productive technology that depreciates faster. This, for Marx and Marxists, is a failure of value to allocate the resources in the right way—a failure that could be remedied, as the standard case for socialism goes, under planned economy.[6]

The second consequence pertains to "the tendency for revenues in capitalist society to be distributed in such a way that the origins of value and surplus value become hopelessly obscured" (Henderson 2013, 59). Here we find the "other" reference to fetishism found in *Capital,* as if bookending Marx's critique of political economy. As the "threads of the inner connection get more and more lost" (Marx [1894] 1991, 967), the trinity formula (capital—profit, land—ground-rent, labor—wages), "as the connection between the components of value and wealth in general and its sources, completes the mystification of the capitalist mode of production" (969). In other words fantasies of reconciliation fill the void of the impossibility of value.

Value is only possible with a concrete institutional device that will function as a "mode of distribution." In other words value does not precede its "mode of representation"; it exists only in and is visible through its effects. Yet there is no social-institutional mechanism or *dispositif,* including that of associated production, that can reconcile it. What is the status of Marx's positing of associated production as an institutional device that can render value possible? Is it an ideal that does not exist? Or is it a regime of value from which the distraction of the profit motive with its inhibiting effects (competition) is subtracted? Assuming for a moment that competition can indeed be eliminated, would that mean that this new communist regime of value can fully reconcile the productive abilities and the social needs of the community? To the extent that neither abilities nor needs can be treated as stable categories, we cannot answer this question in the affirmative.

Limits of Homology

So, is the absent cause of surplus value that renders the capitalist framework of value contingent, contradictory, and bereft of the anthropological guarantees of theoretical humanism the "same" as the real of surplus jouissance, the void of desire that object *a* both embodies and covers over? A significant number of scholars engaged either explicitly or implicitly with the debate on homology would respond in the negative, pointing to the obstacle of the strictly distinct and opposed problematics that each thinker has pursued, and that inevitably led to their eventual parting of ways: purportedly,

Althusser's Spinozist problematic of immanence, that is, subjectivation premised on the process without a subject, and Lacan's Cartesian problematic of divided subject, that is, subjectivation premised on the faculty of judgment (Gillot 2016, xxv). While this widely shared reading of their relation has its merits, it needs to be qualified on both sides. On the side of Lacan, his formulae of sexuation brings the problematic of immanence, through his logic of non-all, on the same topological surface with the transcendent logic of exception. And on the side of Althusser, even though he himself rejected the nomination of structuralism (as Lacan recognizes in *Seminar XVI*), starting with "symptomatic reading" and "absent cause," we find a series of concepts (in an associative and equivalential chain, we can recall "structural cause," "metonymic cause," "overdetermination," "*Darstellung*," and "immanent cause") circulating in his and his collaborators' discourses that resonates strongly with the key Lacanian formula, "unconscious is structured like a language."

What is common in both cases is that the formalization involves rendering the absent presence of a constitutive impossibility (qua discourse-effect). In this sense it is quite distinct from the positivist tendency to find the true essence of what appears to be a complex phenomenon—formalism. While the latter (formalism) universalizes what is at best a particular figuration of the structure, the former (formalization) formalizes the impossibility around which different figurations can be elaborated.

However, for Lacan, formalization constituted the path to encircle the real in a precise manner (in his words, "The real can only be inscribed on the basis of an impasse of formalization" (Lacan 1998, 93)), and this cannot be thought independent of the "practical and pedagogical value" (Peden 2012, 10) to theorize and act upon the different modalities through which subjects "enjoy" and relate to the real both in the clinical as well as metapsychological contexts. In other words Lacan's turn toward formalization was an attempt to develop a conceptual framework for the analysts both to make sense of, and strategically intervene in, the discursive structures that entrap the subject. Indeed, in the next seminar, *Seminar XVII*, Lacan would not only write the different relations to object *a* in terms of four discourses but also prioritize, in *Seminar XX*, the unique relation of analytical discourse to other discourses by positioning it "whenever there is a movement from one discourse to another" (Lacan 1998, 16).

So if Lacan's use of homology is formulated within the scope of analytical discourse to give shape and intervene into our relations of stuckness to enjoyment, then turning our attention to the other pole of the homology, what is a corresponding space of social transformation that the discourse of Marxian political economy renders effective? We think this question presents in front of us a rather different obstacle in extending Lacan's homology to the Marxian critique of political economy, which also circles back to our starting concern with Lacan's oscillation between a historical analysis and an epistemological analysis. When a homology is established between surplus jouissance and surplus value, that is, between analytical discourse and the logic of capitalism (or capitalist discourse), a correspondence is drawn between a formal structure of dislocation on the one side and a historically contingent formation structured around a constitutive dislocation on the other side. This correspondence courts the risk of hypostatizing the historical formation of capitalism as a universal form. Put differently, in this formulation surplus jouissance and surplus value are not at the same level of formalization, or more precisely, there is not enough formalization on the side of Marxian theory. In concluding we want to propose that the proper formalization should rather be at the level that cuts across all organizations of surplus labor, whereby surplus value is the particular form it takes under capitalism, and where the impossibility of value is addressed both at the void of reconciling value (both in its capitalist and associational modes) as well as its complex structural displacements and condensations (for example, absent cause). Marx's critique of political economy, by extracting surplus labor and its antagonistic constitution from its capitalist figuration in surplus value, repeats Lacan's gesture of formalization of object *a* (through extracting it from its oedipal figurations [McNulty 2014]) and projects the categories of surplus labor to a more-than-capitalist world, here and now (Gibson-Graham 2006).

Notes

1. We should mention that reading (the unedited version of) *Seminar XVI* is especially arduous as Lacan expresses himself, in Jacques-Alain Miller's (2007) characterization, "midway between the clear and the obscure" (42). Due to the politically charged environment his aim seems to be as much to strategically seduce his "new" audience (of radical students) in the agitated atmosphere of 1968 as to address the "turmoil surrounding the reform of university education and the serious rifts in the *Ecole Freudienne* about the validation of psychoanalytical formation" (Gallagher 2010, 2; see also Samo Tomšič's (2015) discussion of Lacan's critique of "the Anglo-American model of the valorization of knowledge" [212]).

2. For instance, while Lacan (2007) does explicitly refer to the time of his writing as the moment when "this society called capitalist society can afford to allow itself a relaxation of the university discourse" (168), elsewhere he notes that, even in 1960, "we were a long way away—are we any closer? that's the question—from challenging authority" (40). See Yahya M. Madra and Ceren Özselçuk (2014) for an extensive discussion of the problem of historicism in the contemporary readings of the four discourses.

3. Important in this respect are Louis Althusser's (2016) two lectures on the problematic nature of human sciences, his study of ideology and ideological interpellation (Althusser [1969] 1971), his notes on discourses (Althusser [1966] 2003); Michel Pêcheux's (1983) work on discourse; Alain Badiou's ([1967] 2012) work on structure and subject, as well as the various contributions of the *Circle d'Épistémologie* to the journal *Cahier pour l'Analyse*—in particular Miller's ([1968] 2012) "Action of the Structure." Nonetheless, this encounter needs to be regarded to instigate not a convergence of these two structural inquiries, but on the contrary the desire to push to its radical consequences the articulation of their different objects and divergence, which in the final instance led not only to their parting ways, but also a separation of positions within the field of Althusserian Marxism itself. See also the introductions to the two volumes of Peter Hallward and Knox Peden (Hallward 2012) and Tom Eyers (2015) for succinct accounts of this encounter.

4. For an overview of Lacan's uses of the cut, see Sidi Askofare et al. (2001).

5. In this formulation we are inspired by our conversation with Étienne Balibar, Friedman's Café, New York City, November 21, 2016.

6. For a more general and theoretical treatment of the impossibility of value under capitalist competition, see Stephen Resnick (2001).

References

Althusser, Louis. (1966) 2003. "Three Notes on the Theory of Discourses." In *The Humanist Controversy and Other Writings, 1966–67*, edited by François Matheron, translated by G. M. Goshgarian, 33–84. London: Verso.

———. (1969) 1971. "Ideology and Ideological State Apparatuses (Notes towards an Investigation)." In *Lenin and Philosophy, and Other Essays*, translated by Ben Brewster, 127–86. New York: Monthly Review Press.

———. 2016. *Psychoanalysis and the Human Sciences*. Translated by Steven Randall. New York: Columbia University Press.

———. 2018. "Preface to Le Concept de loi économique dans 'Le Capital,' Gerard Duménil." Translated by G. M. Goshgarian. *Rethinking Marxism* 30, no. 1: 4–24.

Althusser, Louis, and Étienne Balibar. 1997. *Reading Capital*. Translated by Ben Brewster. London: Verso.

Askofare, Sidi, Christiane Alberti, Michel Lapeyre, and Marie-Jean Sauret. 2001. "The Cut." Translated by Dominique Hecq. In *A Compendium of Lacanian Terms*, edited by Huguette Glowinski, Zita M. Marks, and Sara Murphy, 51–54. London: Free Association Books.

Badiou, Alain. (1967) 2012. "The (Re)commencement of Dialectical Materialism." In *The Adventure of French Philosophy*, edited and translated by Bruno Bosteels, 133–70. London and New York: Verso.

Balibar, Étienne. 2011. "Marx's 'Two Discoveries.'" Keynote address, World of Capital: Conditions, Meanings, Situations, April 29, Institute for Comparative Literature and Society at Columbia University.

Blum, Virginia, and Anna Secor. 2011. "Psychotopologies: Closing the Circuit between Psychic and Material Space." *Environment and Planning D: Society and Space* 29, no. 6: 1030–47.

Cullenberg, Stephen. 1996. "Althusser and the Decentering of the Marxist Totality." In *Postmodern Materialism and the Future of Marxist Theory: Essays in the Althusserian Tradition*, edited by Antonio Callari and David F. Ruccio, 120–49. Hanover NH: Wesleyan University Press/University Press of New England.

Eyers, Tom. 2015. *Post-Rationalism: Psychoanalysis, Epistemology, and Marxism in Post-War France*. London: Bloomsbury Academic.

Feltham, Oliver. 2006. "Enjoy Your Stay: Structural Change in Seminar XVII." In *Jacques Lacan and the Other Side of Psychoanalysis: Reflections on Seminar XVII*, edited by Justin Clemens and Russell Grigg, 179–194. Durham NC: Duke University Press.

Gallagher, Cormac. 2010. "From an Other to the Other: An Overview." http://www.lacaninireland.com/web/wp-content/uploads/2010/06/FROM-AN-OTHER-TO-THE-OTHER.pdf (accessed January 21, 2018).

Gibson-Graham, J. K. 2006. *A Postcapitalist Politics*. Minneapolis: University of Minnesota Press.

Gillot, Pascale. 2016. Foreword to *Psychoanalysis and the Human Sciences*, by Louis Althusser, vii–xxviii. Translated by Steven Rendall. New York: Columbia University Press.

Hallward, Peter. 2012. "Introduction to Volume One: Theoretical Training." In *Concept and Form*, vol. 1, *Key Texts from Cahiers pour l'Analyse*, edited by Peter Hallward and Knox Peden, 1–55. London: Verso.

Henderson, George. 2013. *Value in Marx: The Persistence of Value in a More-than-Capitalist World*. Minneapolis: University of Minnesota Press.

Hussain, Athar. 1979. "Misreading Marx's Theory of Value: Marx's Marginal Notes on Wagner." In *Value: The Representation of Labour in Capitalism*, edited by Diane Elson, 82–101. London: CSE Books.

Kordela, A. Kiarina. 2006. "Capital: At Least It Kills Time (Spinoza, Marx, Lacan, and Temporality)." *Rethinking Marxism* 18, no. 4: 539–63.

Lacan, Jacques. 1998. *The Seminar of Jacques Lacan, Book XX: On Feminine Sexuality, The Limits of Love and Knowledge, 1972–1973 (Encore)*, Edited by Jacques-Alain Miller. Translated by Bruce Fink. New York: W. W. Norton.

———. 2002. *The Seminar of Jacques Lacan, Book XVI: From an Other to the other, 1968–1969*. Translated by Cormac Gallagher from unedited manuscripts. Publisher unknown. https://esource.dbs.ie/handle/10788/165 (accessed September 26, 2019).

———. 2006. *Le Seminaire de Jacques Lacan [livre XVI, D'un Autre à l'autre, 1968–69]*. Paris: Le Seuil.

———. 2007. *The Seminar of Jacques Lacan, Book XVII: The Other Side of Psychoanalysis*. Edited by Jacques-Alain Miller. Translated by Russell Grigg. New York: W. W. Norton.

Madra, Yahya M., and Ceren Özselçuk. 2014. "Affective Economies: Lacan's Four Discourses against the Historicism of Capitalist Abstraction." In *States of Crisis and Post-Capitalist Scenarios*, edited by Heiko Feldner, Fabio Vighi, and Slavoj Žižek, 141–66. Surrey: Ashgate.

Marx, Karl. (1867) 1990. *Capital: A Critique of Political Economy*. Vol. 1, *Process of Production Capital*. Translated by Ben Fowkes. London: Penguin Books.

———. (1894) 1991. *Capital: A Critique of Political Economy*. Vol. 3: *Process of Capitalists Production as a Whole*. Translated by David Fernbach. London: Penguin Books.

McNulty, Tracy. 2014. *Wrestling with the Angel: Experiments in Symbolic Life*. New York: Columbia University Press.

Miller, Jacques-Alain. (1968) 2012. "Action of the Structure." In *Concept and Form*. Vol. 1. *Key Texts from Cahiers pour l'Analyse*, edited by Peter Hallward and Know Peden, 69–83. London: Verso.

———. 2007. "A Reading of the Seminar *From an Other to the other*." Translated by Barbara Fulks. *Lacanian Ink* 29: 8–61.

Nobus, Dany. 2013. "That Obscure Object of Psychoanalysis." *Continental Philosophy Review* 46, no. 2: 163–87.

Pêcheux, Michel. 1983. *Language, Semantics and Ideology: Stating the Obvious*. Translated by H. C. Nagpal. London: Palgrave Macmillan.

Peden, Knox. 2012. "Introduction: The Fate of the Concept." In *Concept and Form*. Vol. 2, *Interviews and Essays on the Cahiers pour l'Analyse*, edited by Peter Hallward and Knox Peden, 1–14. London: Verso.

Regnault, François. 2010. "Lacan's Marx." Translated by Asunción Alvarez. *Lacanian Ink* 36: 117–45.

Resnick, Stephen. 2001. "Class, Contradiction and the Capitalist Economy." In *Phases of Capitalist Development: Booms, Crises and Globalizations*, edited by Robert Albritton, Makoto Itoh, Richard Westra, and Alan Zuege, 179–94. London: Palgrave Macmillan.

Roberts, Bruce. 1996. "The Visible and the Measurable: Althusser and the Marxian Theory of Value." In *Postmodern Materialism and the Future of Marxist Theory: Essays in the Althusserian Tradition*, edited by Antonio Callari and David F. Ruccio, 193–211. Hanover NH: Wesleyan University Press/University Press of New England.

Tomšič, Samo. 2015. *The Capitalist Unconscious: Marx and Lacan*. London: Verso.

16 Localizing the Void

From Material to Immaterial Materialism

Lucas Pohl

> Everything that remains of what has come down to us
> from a tradition that is termed *philosophical* accords a
> major place to the void.
>
> —JACQUES LACAN, *Talking to Brick Walls*

Toward a Class Struggle in Geography

In 2015 the filmmaker Robert Zemeckis (2015) tried something challenging. In *The Walk* he tells the story of Philippe Petit and his world-famous high-wire walk between the Twin Towers of the World Trade Center in 1974. The story is told by Petit, played by Joseph Gordon-Levitt, who stands on top of the Statue of Liberty, the New York skyline of the 1970s in the background. The most interesting aspect of this movie is not the plot itself, but the way it deals with the obvious fact that the World Trade Center has been destroyed thirty years after Petit's walk. While the main plot of *The Walk* tells the nice little story about how Petit became a high-wire artist and how he secretly broke into the World Trade Center to do his walk, the final scene demonstrates the impossibility of this kind of storytelling. In the final scene Petit speaks to the viewer and says that after his performance he got a free ticket to the observation deck of the Twin Towers, which would be valid "for ever." Thoughtfully Petit looks into the camera and suddenly is clear: he knows it. During the whole length of the movie, he knows what will happen. At this moment the camera moves away from Petit to the World Trade Center. Slowly the sunlight moves, and two holes appear, one at each building. Then the outlines start to blur, and the whole screen starts to darken. For a few seconds just the holes light up, so that one can imagine them as two fields of explosion, then the screen becomes completely dark, and the credits begin. While the ending of *The Walk* points to the impossibility of going back in time and watching the World Trade Center as it was before 9/11, it confronts us more generally with the fact that here something is given a place in a setting that cannot be represented from the standpoint of the setting itself and therefore appears only as a strange form of present absence. The movie confronts us with a reality that is shaped by something that only appears through its in-existence, yet it is precisely this appearance that reveals the incompleteness of this reality.[1]

The basic premise of this chapter is that a similar insight applies to materialist geographies. To proclaim such thing as a "materialist geography" sounds like a strange endeavor. Is not every geography today a materialist geography? Isn't materialism itself already something like a theory of everything today? Terry Eagleton (2016) writes in his book *Materialism*: "Materialism is a remarkably capacious concept. It stretches all the way from the mind-body problem to the question of whether the state exists primarily to defend private property. It can mean a denial of God, a belief that the Great Wall of China and Clint Eastwood's ankles are secretly interrelated, or an insistence that the Golden Gate Bridge continues to exist when nobody is looking at it" (Eagleton 2016, 33).

This remarkable capaciousness counts also for the influence of materialism in the geographic discipline. From historical-geographical materialism à la David Harvey to new vitalist materialisms, a vast amount of materialist approaches spread in geographies from all angles. While materialism in this sense became "irreproachable" for geography today (Kirsch 2012, 435), it also became obsolete to proclaim such thing as a materialist geography.

As a way to avoid that materialism simply becomes the common sense of all geographies, this chapter looks for a possibility to differentiate between two kinds of materialism in order to distinguish two different ways of approaching materialism geographically. In the following pages I seek to formulate what I call, in an Althusserian manner, a *class struggle in geog-*

raphy, which means proposing a split of materialist geographies into two camps.[2] To capture the theoretical underpinnings of this class struggle I encounter geography through two philosophical positions.

We can assume that there are (at least) two great living (French) philosophers of our time. The first is Bruno Latour, whose actor-network theory (ANT) is acknowledged by Graham Harman (2016) as "the most important philosophical method to emerge since phenomenology in 1900" (1). The second philosopher is Alain Badiou, whose philosophy "truly marks the beginning of the twenty-first century," if we follow Bruno Bosteels (2011, 210). While a comparative reading of Latour and Badiou already contributes to an academic void mentioned by David Harvey (2006), who references Badiou in a short comment as an "outsider" of geography who should start to "be as carefully read as Latour" (411), in the following pages I furthermore propose that these two philosophers help us accentuate two kinds of materialisms: *material materialism*, which takes matter as primary and leads to *material geographies*, and another materialism that I call *immaterial materialism*, which is organized around the void and encourages us to proclaim such a thing as a *materialist geography*.[3]

Material (Materialist) Geographies

Over the last years one can witness an increasing tendency in human geography to link materialism with matter. Geographic materialism therefore "accords ontological priority to the material conditions of existence, and rejects non-material (e.g. spiritual, metaphysical, and other transcendent) prime causes" (Kirsch 2012, 435). Ultimately what matters for geographers is "the figure of matter that underpins a materialism" (Anderson and Tolia-Kelly 2004, 673). The massive increase of geographers who consider themselves materialists can therefore be read as a response to a call for rematerializing human geography (Jackson 2000). It is the attempt "to take things seriously" that turns a geographer into a materialist today. This perception is majorly inspired by the works of Latour.[4] In his essay "Can We Get Our Materialism Back, Please?" (2007) Latour argues that "something has happened to materialism" throughout the last years

(138). Today materialism is not inherently related to Marx anymore; it has finally gotten rid of its idealist remnants and has become a truly "material materialism" (141). Such a materialism finally does justice to matter. It stops offering "thin descriptions of objects" and rather starts with "thick descriptions of things." This transition from objects to things is crucial for Latour's overall project: "Long before designating an object thrown out of the political sphere and standing there objectively and independently, the *Ding* or Thing has for many centuries meant the issue that brings people together" (Latour 2005a, 23; emphasis in the original).

The critical encounter Latour takes from Heidegger is to problematize any understanding that takes materiality simply as a static and uniform matter of fact. Against such objectifications, which locate the object outside the realm of politics, the thing derives from an "ontological pluralism" (Latour 2013, 142), emerging "at the heart of an assembly" (Latour 2004a, 54): "There are many . . . types of gatherings which are not political in the customary sense, but which bring a public together around things: scientific laboratories, technical projects, supermarkets, financial arenas. . . . All these phenomena have devised a bewildering set of techniques of representation that have created the real political landscape in which we live, breathe, and argue" (Weibel and Latour 2007, 99).

It seems clear why Graham Harman (2009) proposes that "Latour is the ultimate democrat in philosophy" (91), as his call "back to things" (Latour 2005a) is a call to follow its gatherings, its parliaments. In this respect Latour (2004b) discharges two fundamental figurations of matter: he first denies any notion of things as simply "out there" and unquestionable (233), and he then refuses any assertion that there is only one type of matter in the world, because "if there really is one thing that materialism has never known how to celebrate, it is the multiplicity of materials" (Latour 2013, 220).

Well, Latour's prayer for a material materialism was heard. Following the "vast spillage of things" (Thrift 2008, 9), geographies from all angles today acknowledge that matter is "never apprehensible in just one state" (Anderson and Wylie 2009, 332), or, briefly, that "things matter" (Kirsch 2012, 435). *Material geographies* therefore became a common framework to designate geographies that take things seriously. In their review paper Ian Cook and Divya Tolia-Kelly (2010) remarkably acknowledge that material geographies are more than a simple subdiscipline. To write "a review of these geographies is therefore a difficult task . . . because arguments about 'materiality' have become central to a disparate variety of geographical studies" (100). Matter in this sense is not restricted to particular ways of geographic thought. In fact, the whole discipline seems to tend "towards geographical analyses that get inside things, their meaning and uses, and tease out their role in the production of the places and spaces we inhabit" (Crang 2014, 289). To "follow the thing" therefore became a widespread approach all over the geographic discipline (see Christophers 2011; Cook and Harrison 2007; Cook et al. 2004; Gregson et al. 2010; Pfaff 2010). But what does it mean to follow a thing? If we take Latour seriously, "a thing is so utterly concrete that none of its features can be scraped away like cobwebs or moss" (Harman 2009, 14). That is why material geographers cannot simply refer to the material qualities of objects if they really want to follow the thing all the way. To "get inside the thing" they have to deal with "economic, political, social, cultural, agricultural and other pro-cesses" (Cook et al. 2004, 642) as well as "constellations of people, plants, bugs, diseases, recipes, politics, trade agreements, and histories" (Cook and Harrison 2007, 40). Against this background, material geographies tend to become geographies of every*thing*, and every material geographic research circulates around an irrevocable question: does it describe the thing thickly enough? Latour himself admits at one point: "We still don't know how to assemble, in a single, visually coherent space, all the entities necessary for a thing to become an object. . . . When we have learned how to do that, we might finally get our (material) materialism back" (Latour 2007, 142).

While on the one hand the thing appears to be a "full set of features" (Harman 2009, 14), on the other hand (material) materialism struggles to capture this fullness. What we can do, if we follow Latour, is only to describe as thickly as possible, because then we might get what we want: a "full" account of the thing itself. But can we really get what we want? Is material materialism able to depict all the relations of things? Or is there an irredeemable promise at the heart of it?

The Trouble with Plasma

Multiple times throughout his work Latour suggests that not everything can be covered through the assembling of things. He even states, "This empty space 'in between' the networks, those *terra incognita* are the most exciting aspects of ANT" (Latour 2006, 19). In the following part of this chapter, I engage with this space in between the actor-networks, not only because this space is for the most part neglected by material geographies, but also because it is the blind spot that pushes material materialism to its limit.

In *Paris, ville invisible* (Latour and Hermant 1998), one of the few works in which Latour is writing on the city, he and Emilie Hermant claim that a city can become visible just through the illusion of a *panorama*, which pictures the city as a whole and at the same time masks the variety of actors that the city assembles. They propose to grasp the city as invisible to promote the impossibility of its full representation. In contrast to the panorama-view the city here appears as virtual, shapeless, and powerful— what Latour calls *plasma*. In an extract of *Paris, ville invisible*, he writes: "I use the term plasma for this space—but it is not a space—in which lie—but there is no rest—the various circulations of totalizations and participations waiting for explication and composition" (Latour 2012, 93).

Almost ten years after *Paris, ville invisible*, Latour continues to write about the relationship of panorama and plasma. In *Reassembling the Social* (Latour 2005b), he follows his course, now to theorize society in general. Here Latour (2005b) tries to dissolve the concept of society (in the Hobbesian sense of a Leviathan) and to renew social theory. After the panorama-city, the panorama-society—a "decaying monster" that is "stranded like a whale" (163–64)—must be overcome. Latour again introduces plasma as the missing masses that cannot be covered by the panorama: as "that which is not yet formatted, not yet measured, not yet socialized, not yet engaged in metrological chains, and not yet covered, surveyed, mobilized, or subjectified" (244).

By reading both works—*Paris, ville invisible* and *Reassembling the Social*—together, we are able to capture the limit of material materialism.[5] While the ultimate aim of material materialism is to come up with thick descriptions of things, plasma refers to the limit of description. Since material materialism has not yet been able to properly fulfill its task and "to assemble, in a single, visually coherent space, all the entities necessary for a thing to become an object"—it has to find a way to capture the excess of matter that exceeds its horizon. Therefore, Latour invents the concept of plasma to capture the strange space outside the actor-networks, a formless mass that exists prior to every relation, untouched and unaffected, to mark the inexhaustible and unknown potential for further descriptions. It is not surprising that material geographers tend to neglect the existence of plasma, because what plasma basically points to is that no thick description is ever thick enough, and that all assemblings of things are possible only against the background of plasma.

Latour himself presents a way out of this deadlock. As a "truly vast space of unsocialized material" (Harman 2009, 133), Latour's plasma becomes a figure of *dark matter*, an unknown territory "much like the missing masses for a cosmologist trying to balance out the weight of the universe" (Latour 2005b, 244). For Badiou this seems to be an easy solution typical for scientific epistemology. In his short essay *Black* (2017), Badiou dedicates himself to cosmological metaphors, describing them as scientific attempts to fill a gap in thought. Dark matter would therefore simply provide a "name for any possible perception as well as for everything that ought to exist" (78–79). If we take up this claim and transfer it to Latour's missing masses, we are able to proclaim that Latour introduces plasma only to fill the gap of material materialism. The rest of this chapter is dedicated to formulating a materialist account that resists filling this gap.

Localizing the Void

After retracing the limit of material materialism and picturing how Latour himself accounts for this limit through his concept of plasma, in the following pages I go one step further and transcend material materialism.

Through Badiou's materialist dialectic I want to picture a materialism that is not founded on the premise of matter, and that exceeds the materiality of things through an immaterial kernel at the heart of every situation, a materialism that I therefore call immaterial materialism. Such a materialism not only does justice to the problem raised by Latour's notion of plasma; it also encourages us to sketch a program for material*ist* geographies. To use a phrase from Badiou's (2009) *Logics of Worlds*, in the following I claim that a (immaterial) materialist geography "only exists to the extent that it ploughs the gap" (7) instead of filling it.[6]

But before we change from material to immaterial materialism, let us first point out their similar point of departure. We should insist that it is not Badiou's point to simply ignore the question of matter. Therefore let us first go back to the *thing*. Like Latour, Badiou also refers to the thing as the category, which underlies his materialist approach.[7]

> What is a thing qua a "there is" without any determination of its being, except precisely its being qua being? We can speak of an object of the world. We can distinguish it in the world by its properties or predicates. In fact, we can experiment with the complex network of identities and differences that render this object manifestly non-identical to another object of the same world. But a thing is not an object. A thing is not yet an object. . . . We need to think a thing before its objectivation in a specific world. (Badiou 2011, 46)

What we see here is again the claim that a turn from objects to things is necessary to understand how the ontic reality appears as a single and visually coherent space or *world*. In worlds, things appear as objects—the object is always already "being-there" in a world. In contrast to the object, which is always counted *as one*, Badiou (2005) follows the thing, as his whole mathematical ontology is based on the premise that "the one is not" (23). Just like Latour, Badiou (2011) rejects the "being as one" to proclaim that being is *multiple*, or that "being is thing," because the thing "is nothing other than a multiplicity" (47). Through this, Badiou's philosophy acknowledges the multiple entanglements on which every consistent presentation of an object is based. But if there are only things as multiplicities, do we not end up facing a never-ending nexus of things of things of things and so on? Is there any limit, a Badiousian plasma? "Yes, there is an endpoint. But this endpoint is not a primitive object or an atomic component; it is not a form of the One. The endpoint is also, necessarily, a multiplicity. This multiplicity is the multiplicity of no multiplicity—the thing which is also nothing, the void" (Badiou 2011, 47).

Similar to Latour, Badiou also reaches a limit in his approach to things. But instead of introducing a category of pure matter that denotes everything, which is not yet part of the assembling of things, Badiou's limit is immanently inscribed into the thing itself. In a sense Badiou is even closer to Heidegger than Latour. Already Heidegger proclaims that the void (which for him also takes place at the heart of the thing) is not a mere illusion that in fact is only a different kind of matter. Just as the jug is made to create an empty space for liquid, the void opens up the possibility for a space to assemble (Heidegger 2001, 163–80). In a similar vein Badiou states in an interview that "the void is not a space. It is rather the basic opening of any possible space" (Constantinou and Madarasz 2009, 792). While the void in this sense appears to be the indivisible remainder immanent to things, it also disturbs the task "to assemble, in a single, visually coherent space, all the entities necessary for a thing" (Latour 2007, 142), because the void itself remains placeless, a present absence that both enables the thing to gather its entities and prevents the thing from being "fully" materialized. In a mathematical manner Badiou (2008a) therefore states: "The absolutely initial point that assures the chain of ordinals of its being is the empty set 0, decided axiomatically as secularised form, or number-form, of Nothingness [the void]. This form is nothing other than the situation-name of being qua being, the suture of every situation-being, and of every language, to their latent being. The empty set being an ordinal, and therefore a natural multiple, we might say: the point of being of every situation is natural. Materialism is founded upon this statement" (83).

Here, we arrive at the kernel of the difference between material and immaterial materialism. What is crucial about both kinds of materialism is the way they deal with a certain lack of representation. Both problematize that there is something missing in their attempts to assemble a thing. For Latour this is an epistemological problem. He therefore introduces the plasma, which appears as the unformatted matter (of knowledge) deriving as a (scientific) blind spot—a giant and unknown space full of dark matter that is waiting for us to be discovered. To switch between material and immaterial materialism, we simply have to go one step further and ontologize this plasma. Badiou's problem is not that we cannot offer a full description of the thing, but that the thing already contains its own negation. He transfers the excess of things into the thing itself. Plasma, in a Badiousian sense, is therefore not a *terra incognita* outside of the social, but a certain unknown territory *inside* of it: "At the heart of every situation, as the foundation of its being, there is a 'situated' void, around which is organized the plenitude (or the stable multiples) of the situation in question" (Badiou 2001, 68).

Now we also understand why the void contains a need to reintroduce dialectics. As dialectical "thinking tracks down the unrepresentable point in its field" (Badiou 2018, 85), it encourages us to grasp the excess as an immanent contradiction of the thing itself. Such a dialectic is missing in Latour's material materialism, which relates the unrepresentable point to a lack of knowledge and not to being as such. While plasma, for Latour, is also matter, but in a different epistemological state (unsocialized matter), the void, for Badiou, is rather an indivisible remainder between the thing and nothing; an unsolvable tension inherent to the thing itself. This way of transposing the obstacle into the thing itself changes the whole aim of materialism. The starting point is no longer to foster a form of representation that enables us to capture the ontological complexity of things, but to insist on the void as the ontological impossibility of a full representation of the thing itself. As Badiou (2005) states, "In truth, this is where the entire question lies. Taking a short cut through what can be inferred as common to Descartes, to Lacan, and to what I am proposing here . . . I would say that the debate bears upon the localization of the void" (432).

To localize the void as the unlocalizable point at the heart of every situation is the ultimate aim of Badiou's philosophy. This is how he does justice to Lacan, who is for him the "educator of all future philosophers" (Badiou 2008b, 129).[8] For Lacan (2017), philosophy always circulates around the void after Plato "made his entire idea of the world revolve around that" (82). As Lacan points out with regard to the allegory of the cave, Plato's whole thinking was based on the premise that our world is shaped by something that only appears through its absence. While Badiou can therefore certainly be called a philosopher in the full (Platonian) sense, it seems questionable what that means with regard to materialism. Is Plato not *the* idealist, if there ever was one? How should someone like Plato serve us to call for a materialist geography? While this sounds like the ultimate paradox, philosophers such as Slavoj Žižek (2014) have in fact stated that "the only way to be a true materialist today is to push idealism to its limit" (31). Against this background one could say that Badiou only becomes a "true materialist" by pushing the concept of the void, as the cornerstone of idealism, to its limit, which means by making it the ultimate category of (his) materialist thinking. While Latour's project aims "to cure materialism of its idealistic tendency" (Noys 2012, 84) by doing justice to matter, Badiou's materialism leads to the ultimate break of the link between materialism and matter, and thus enables us to call for a materialism of the void.

Nevertheless, to reduce Badiou to the void does not do justice to his philosophy. On the contrary: a lot needs to be said before we can truly tackle his influence on rethinking materialist geographies, not only reconciling other key terms of Badiousian philosophy, such as *truth*, *event*, or *subject*, but also, for instance, Badiou's suspicious opinion about social science. This chapter can be read as a small step toward a geographical grounding—or better, ungrounding—of Badiou's materialist dialectic through his approach to the void. Based on such a minimal version of Badiou, we can start to take up the thread for reaching the potential and limits of relating philosophy with geography through materialism.[9]

(Immaterial) Materialist Geographies

After capturing the difference between material and immaterial material-ism, we are now able to translate these arguments back into the geographic landscape. It is the void that draws a division line between material and materialist geographies. By introducing the void as immaterial, materialist geographies avoid negotiating it with an epistemological obstacle. The void is not simply the missing mass we do not see because of lacking measuring devices; it is no dark matter in the cosmological sense. The void is imma-terial in the way that it ontologically deprives itself of being (ac)counted (for) in a situation. There is something—or better, there *is* nothing—that exists solely through its inexistence; that is the primary starting point of materialist geographies. Instead of searching for thick descriptions, mate-rialist geographers therefore search for lacks of description; they rely on the premise that something escapes positive experience. For materialist geographers, "what counts in any genuine creation, whatever its domain, is not so much what exists as what in-exists" (Badiou 2012, 68). The aim of materialist geographies is to insist that not everything matters (relative to a world), or that negativity matters. It is not so much the *masses* we emphasize in reconciling the missing masses, but the fact that they are *missing*. Not "absent matter(s)" (Anderson and Tolia-Kelly 2004, 669), but absence matters! In this sense materialist geographies do not try to plug the hole, but to plough it.

What is the relevance of such a negative geography for doing empirical research? Do we not end up with an abstract theory that does not tell us anything about reality? The only answer to this question is that there is no reality without abstraction. This point is often illustrated by Badiou through a view on today's world of globalized capitalism. If we approach capitalism solely based on what it materially (ac)counts (for), we overlook what Badiou considers to be the most important aspect of capitalism, the *inexistent*, all those who "are counted for nothing by capital, meaning that from the point of view of the structural development of the world, they are nothing" (Badiou 2016, 36). Since the inexistent are unrepresentable from the standpoint of capitalism, they do usually not appear in the world, so that one is tempted to believe that there is no exclusion and that capitalism does indeed includes everyone. Sometimes, however, it happens that the inexistent gain visibility, so that we are suddenly confronted with this supernumerary element that renders our world incomplete.

An example of how the inexistent suddenly appeared at the heart of capitalism was the fire that destroyed the Grenfell Tower in London a few years ago. On June 14, 2017, the public housing block in one of the city's most prosperous districts burned down. While the identities of the seventy-two people who died in the accident remained unclear for a long time, the burning tower building immediately turned into a symbol of what is wrong with capitalist urban development. The fact that a public housing block was in flames right in the middle of such a hypergentrified city and financial flagship as London "made clear what many have felt for years: London has become a city for capital not people," as Rowland Atkinson (2017) aptly puts it. Grenfell Tower, therefore, opened up a space of visibility for all those who are "counted for nothing" with regard to the functioning of capitalist urban development; it pointed to the repressed and exploited kernel of negativity on which capitalist strongholds like London are based.

Consequently this enables us to proclaim that materialist geographies are not isolated from reality but on the contrary seek to *fully* account for reality *through* abstraction. This becomes particularly clear in *The Walk*, in which 9/11 enters the scene only in the subtracted form of two holes. The two formal shapes that appear shortly before the movie ends are there to show us that something has not taken place, that 9/11 is present absent in the movie, but instead of telling the "full" story (i.e., showing how the airplanes crashed into the towers, etc.), the greatness of the movie consists in the fact that it does not even try to offer us a "thick description" and instead solely captures the unrepresentable point at the heart of the situation. The moment when the viewer is confronted with the traumatic absence that the film has kept at a distance throughout the rest of its plot, this moment when the void is given a place in the story and thus ruins the whole picture, it is precisely this moment that completes *The Walk* as such.

Notes

1. It is not surprising that the movie was a financial flop, especially in the United States, as it considers 9/11 as an object of anxiety. For a broader discussion of this argument, see also Lucas Pohl (2018, 79–82).

2. I refer to an interview that Louis Althusser gave in 1968, where he proclaims that "philosophy represents the people's class struggle in theory" (Althusser 2001, 8).

3. Even if this is by far not the first geographic attempt to work on and with Badiou (see Bassett 2008; Constantinou 2009; Dewsbury 2007; Hannah 2016; MacCannell 2009; Madarasz 2009; Mould 2009; Plotnitsky 2012; Shaw 2010a, 2010b, 2012).

4. Bruno Latour is of course not the only theoretical influence that animates geographies to become materialized. Jane Bennett's (2010) vital materialism, for example, in a similar manner contributes to "the force of things." For a geographic overview see also Divya Tolia-Kelly (2011).

5. Such a reading is recommended by Latour himself in a footnote to *Reassembling the Social* (Latour 2005b, 1).

6. Originally, Badiou (2009) describes here how the materialist dialectic resists becoming part of its theoretical environment, "on its right flank, from the diktats of authenticity, and on its left, from the humilities of Critique" (7).

7. In this way Latour and Badiou take the thing as their starting point from Heidegger, which may come as no surprise if Heidegger is, as Badiou (2005) acknowledges in *Being and Event*, "the last universally recognizable philosopher" (1), although we probably should add "of the twentieth century."

8. For a discussion of the triangle of Badiou, Lacan, and Descartes, see also Frank Ruda (2015, 83–116).

9. In this sense my argument is more moderate than, for instance, that of Ian Shaw (2012), who references Badiou to call for an "evental geography." For his convincing attempt to relate Badiou's philosophy and geography, Shaw has "to situate geography as the preeminent philosophical condition" (616), therefore manipulating one of Badiou's fundamental points of departure: that events take place only in love, art, politics, and science (whereby the latter primarily refers to mathematics). While Shaw's approach is therefore in a way already *post*-Badiousian, my argument seeks to show, step by step, how far geography can go, if we stick to Badiou's own way of thought.

References

Althusser, Louis. 2001. *Lenin and Philosophy: And Other Essays*. New York: Monthly Review Press.

Anderson, Ben, and Divya Tolia-Kelly. 2004. "Matter(s) in Social and Cultural Geography." *Geoforum* 35, no. 6: 669–74.

Anderson, Ben, and John Wylie. 2009. "On Geography and Materiality." *Environment and Planning D: Society and Space* 41, no. 2: 318–35.

Atkinson, Rowland. 2017. "London, Whose City?" *Le Monde diplomatique.* July. http://mondediplo.com/2017/07/06london (accessed September 26, 2019).

Badiou. Alain. 2001. *Ethics: An Essay on the Understanding of Evil.* Translated by Peter Hallward. London: Verso.

———. 2005. *Being and Event.* Translated by Oliver Feltham. London: Continuum.

———. 2008a. *Numbers and Numbers.* Translated by Robin Mackay. Cambridge: Polity Press.

———. 2008b. *Conditions.* Translated by Steven Corcoran. London: Continuum.

———. 2009. *Logics of Worlds: The Sequel to Being and Event.* Translated by Alberto Toscano. London: Continuum.

———. 2011. *Second Manifesto for Philosophy.* Translated by Louise Burchill. Cambridge: Polity Press.

———. 2012. *The Rebirth of History: Times of Riots and Uprisings.* Translated by Gregory Elliott. London: Verso.

———. 2016. *Our Wound Is Not So Recent: Thinking the Paris Killings of 13 November.* Translated by Robin Mackay. Cambridge: Polity Press.

———. 2017. *Black. The Brilliance of a Noncolor.* Cambridge: Polity Press.

———. 2018. *Can Politics Be Thought? Followed by Of An Obscure Disaster: On the End of the Truth of the State.* Translated by Bruno Bopsteels. Durham NC: Duke University Press.

Bassett, Keith. 2008. "Thinking the Event: Badiou's Philosophy of the Event and the Example of the Paris Commune." *Environment and Planning D: Society and Space* 26, no. 5: 895–910.

Bennett, Jane. 2010. *Vibrant Matter. A Political Ecology of Things.* Durham NC: Duke University Press.

Bosteels, Bruno. 2011. *Badiou and Politics.* Durham NC: Duke University Press.

Christophers, Brett. 2011. "Follow the Thing: Money." *Environment and Planning D: Society and Space* 29, no. 6: 1068–84.

Constantinou, Marios. 2009. "Badiou's Topology of Action as an Ethical Epistemology of the Event." *Environment and Planning D: Society and Space* 27, no. 5: 771–82.

Constantinou, Marios, and Norman Madarasz. 2009. "Being and Spatialization: An Interview with Alain Badiou." *Environment and Planning D: Society and Space* 27, no. 5: 783–95.

Cook, Ian, et al. 2004. "Follow the Thing: Papaya." *Antipode* 36, no. 4: 642–64.

Cook, Ian, and Michelle Harrison. 2007. "Follow the Thing: 'West Indian Hot Pepper Sauce.'" *Space and Culture* 10, no. 1: 40–63.

Cook, Ian, and Divya Tolia-Kelly. 2010. "Material Geographies." In *The Oxford Handbook of Material Culture Studies,* edited by Dan Hicks and Mary C. Beaudry, 99–122. Oxford: Oxford University Press.

Crang, Philip. 2014. "Material Geographies." In *Introducing Human Geographies*, edited by Paul Cloke, Philip Crang, and Mark Goodwin, 277–91. London: Routledge.

Dewsbury, J. D. 2007. "Unthinking Subjects: Alain Badiou and the Event of Thought in Thinking Politics." *Transactions of the Institute of British Geographers* 32, no. 4: 443–59.

Eagleton, Terry. 2016. *Materialism*. New Haven CT: Yale University Press.

Gregson, Nicky, Mike Crang, Farin Uddin Ahamed, Nasreen Akhter, and Raihana Ferdous. 2010. "Following Things of Rubbish Value: End-of-Life Ships, 'Chock-Chocky' Furniture and the Bangladeshi Middle Class Consumer." *Geoforum* 41, no. 6: 846–54.

Hannah, Matthew G. 2016. "State Knowledge and Recurring Patterns of State Phobia: From Fascism to Post-Politics." *Progress in Human Geography* 44, no. 4: 476–94.

Harman, Graham. 2009. *Prince of Networks: Bruno Latour and Metaphysics*. Melbourne: re.press.

———. 2016. *Immaterialism: Objects and Social Theory*. Cambridge: Polity Press.

Harvey, David. 2006. "Editorial: The Geographies of Critical Geography." *Transactions of the Institute of British Geographers* 31, no. 4: 409–12.

Heidegger, Martin. 2001. *Poetry, Language, Thought*. New York: HarperCollins.

Jackson, Peter. 2000. "Rematerializing Social and Cultural Geography." *Social & Cultural Geography* 1, no. 1: 9–14.

Kirsch, Scott. 2012. "Cultural Geography I: Materialist Turns." *Progress in Human Geography* 37, no. 3: 433–41.

Lacan, Jacques. 2017. *Talking to Brick Walls: A Series of Presentations in the Chapel at Sainte-Anne Hospital*. Translated by Adrian Price. Cambridge: Polity Press.

Latour, Bruno. 2004a. *Politics of Nature: How to Bring the Sciences into Democracy*. Translated by Catherine Porter. Cambridge MA: Harvard University Press.

———. 2004b. "Why Has Critique Run out of Steam? From Matters of Fact to Matters of Concern." *Critical Inquiry* 30, no. 2: 225–48.

———. 2005a. "From Realpolitik to Dingpolitik or How to Make Things Public." In *Making Things Public: Atmospheres of Democracy*, edited by Bruno Latour and Peter Weibel, 14–41. Cambridge MA: MIT Press.

———. 2005b. *Reassembling the Social: An Introduction to Actor-Network-Theory*. Oxford: Oxford University Press.

———. 2006. "On Recalling ANT." In *Actor Network Theory and After*, edited by John Law and John Hassard, 15–25. Oxford: Blackwell.

———. 2007. "Can We Get Our Materialism Back, Please?" *Iris* 98: 138–42.

———. 2012. "Paris, Invisible City: The Plasma." *City, Culture and Society* 3, no. 2: 91–93.

———. 2013. *An Inquiry into Modes of Existence: An Anthropology of the Moderns*. Translated by Catherine Porter. Cambridge MA: Harvard University Press.

Latour, Bruno, and Emilie Hermant. 1998. *Paris, ville invisible*. Paris: Les Empêcheurs de penser en rond.

MacCannell, Juliet Flower. 2009. "Eternity or Infinity? Badiou's Point." *Environment and Planning D: Society and Space* 27, no. 5: 823–39.

Madarasz, Norman. 2009. "The Regularity of Non-Being: Space and Form in Alain Badiou's System." *Environment and Planning D: Society and Space* 27, no. 5: 796–822.

Mould, Oli. 2009. "Parkour, the City, the Event." *Environment and Planning D: Society and Space* 27, no. 4: 738–50.

Noys, Benjamin. 2012. *The Persistence of the Negative: A Critique of Contemporary Continental Theory*. Edinburgh: Edinburgh University Press.

Pfaff, Julia. 2010. "A Mobile Phone: Mobility, Materiality and Everyday Swahili Trading Practices." *cultural geographies* 17, no. 3: 341–57.

Plotnitsky, Arkady. 2012. "Experimenting with Ontologies: Sets, Spaces, and Topoi with Badiou and Grothendieck." *Environment and Planning D: Society and Space* 30, no. 2: 351–68.

Pohl, Lucas. 2018. "Angsträume—Lacan und die Leere des Schauplatzes." *RISS—Zeitschrift für Psychoanalyse, Sonderausgabe Ent-täuschung des Subjekts: Angst in Philosophie, Psychoanalyse und Kultur*: 65–83.

Ruda, Frank. 2015. *For Badiou: Idealism without Idealism*. Evanston IL: Northwestern University Press.

Shaw, Ian Graham Ronald. 2010a. "Sites, Truths and the Logics of Worlds: Alain Badiou and Human Geography." *Transactions of the Institute of British Geographers* 35, no. 3: 431–42.

———. 2010b. "WALL-E's World: Animating Badiou's Philosophy." *cultural geographies* 17, no. 3: 391–405.

———. 2012. "Towards an Evental Geography." *Progress in Human Geography* 36, no. 5: 613–27.

Thrift, Nigel. 2008. *Non-Representational Theory: Space, Politics, Affect*. London: Routledge.

Tolia-Kelly, Divya. 2011. "The Geographies of Cultural Geography III: Material Geographies, Vibrant Matters and Risking Surface Geographies." *Progress in Human Geography* 37, no. 1: 153–60.

Weibel, Peter, and Bruno Latour. 2007. "Experimenting with Representation: *Iconoclash* and *Making Things Public*." In *Exhibition Experiments*, edited by Sharon Macdonald and Paul Basu, 94–108. Malden MA: Blackwell.

Zemeckis, Robert. 2015. *The Walk*. TriStar Pictures.

Žižek, Slavoj. 2014. *Absolute Recoil: Towards a New Foundation of Dialectical Materialism*. London: Verso.

Coda
A Void More Placed

Paul Kingsbury and Anna J. Secor

It is about a minute into Shavasana or "corpse pose," as it is known in yoga. I am lying on my back with my limbs slightly spread, palms face up, and eyes closed. Then suddenly I have this beautiful epiphany: I am so blissed right now that it would be completely fine if I was abducted by aliens. More than this, it dawned on me that I *wanted* to be abducted and taken onto the flashy spaceship and zip off to some remote corner of the universe. "Yes," I thought, "I surrender. Take me. I will leave everything behind for this trip." About a month later, back in the studio and corpse pose again, I had another epiphany: it is not about wanting to be abducted. It's already happened. The yoga studio is the inside of the spaceship.

It might be his Mars in Pisces, you know, his roundabout way of doing or writing things, the clash of activity and passivity, love of detailed fantasies . . . , but the epiphanies home in on the idea of being in the "now." And so, dear reader, if we may, this is precisely where we want you: right now, in the Void (we capitalize this word for maximum effect). For the now is a perennially missed encounter, a lost half-second; perception and intention, like trauma, arrive "after the fact." The present is a zero-dimensional knife's edge splitting the past and the future. So, go on then, enter this unborn now. Get ready for the abduction: observe thoughts from another place, become an operator with no location.

And now, reader, where should you be now? Where should you be, having traversed the pages of *A Place More Void*? More to the point, where do *we* want you to be? Where do we want the book to take you, and what do we want it to do to you? Dear reader, permit us to speak plainly: we would like you to die. You should be dead like Julius Caesar. No, not that kind of death. It is not violent or unethical. And please know, we are not alone in considering your death or speaking to the living about death and the deceased (Maddrell 2013). And we would not dare wish a brutal assassination if you turned us down, gave us too much pause, or walked out on our proposal. We're talking about a completely different kind of death. To return to the *Tibetan Book of the Dead*, which Chogyam Trungpa Rinpoche likened to a "Book of Space," we are thinking of your death in terms of Voidness (*Śūnyatā* in Sanskrit):

> Thy body being a mental body is incapable of dying even though beheaded and quartered. In reality, thy body is of the nature of voidness; thou needst not be afraid. The Lords of Death are thine own hallucinations. Thy desire—body is a body of propensities, and void. Voidness cannot injure voidness; the qualityless cannot injure the qualityless. Apart from one's own hallucinations, in reality there are no such things existing outside oneself as Lord of Death, or god, or demon, or the Bull-headed Spirit of Death. Act so as to recognize this. (Lopez 2000, 258–60)

But it is precisely because of our bold invitation to our readers to embrace the Lords of Death as mere hallucinations that a vague fear stirs our editorial conscience. Who are we to tell you to take a leap of faith into the Void? Do we not risk making this coda, which really should be a diminutive passage (the word *coda* derives from the Italian for "tail") into a big bloated belly of a piece that is stuffed with imperial appetite and colonial palate? Perhaps in our editorial striving and textual violence we're actually channeling another kind of Void: a tidal disruption event (as astrophysicists call it) wherein a supermassive black hole (yes, that is us) feasts on its nearby stars (that is you), tears them apart with the gaping craw of its gravitational field, and spits out half of its starry stuff at the speed of light (Mattila et al. 2018).

Or maybe our demand for your negation is less bloodthirsty than it is an ethico-political call. Yes, of course, that is it! Truly, it is an invitation to

KINGSBURY AND SECOR

an "emancipatory project based on the self-sacrificing enjoyment of the death drive" (McGowan 2013, 2). After all, the status quo is a catastrophe; the angel of history travels blindly, leaving destruction and barbarism in her wake (Benjamin 1968). Our desire strikes out blindly, acquisitive and unsatisfied; it keeps us trapped, gorging ourselves in cul-de-sacs while a rapacious necropolitics (dis)orders the land. Our call to become impassive may seem obdurate, but refusal and negation are the revolutionary ethics of the Void (Edelman 2004). Fellow abductees or "experiencers" (as ufologists call them when consent and bilateralism are involved), we join forces with all those who are part of the system without having a place within it: the ones without papers, the uncounted, the parts of no-part, the non-all. For it is only as such an unincorporated excess that we can hope to puncture and intervene in the established order (Badiou 1999; Rancière 2010; Žižek 2017). Subtract yourself and join us in a "tiger's leap" (Benjamin 1968, 261) into the Void because this is the event, the rupture that is politics, which is a prerequisite for upending the deadening traditions and teleologies of our current historical conjuncture. We are on the shores of Hades. Let us place the coins on your eyes; we seek collective passage to the other side.

Or maybe when we invite you to become a casualty of the Void, we are unconsciously channeling what every good graduate student knows (or at least did back in the late 1990s, when he with his Mars in Pisces studied in the "deconstruction citadel" of geography at the University of Kentucky): the author is quite dead, and alacritous editors are no exception (even she with her Sun in Phoenix-like Scorpio). For it is in exercising these inky symbols designed and set in Minion Pro by L. Auten that "the author enters his own death, writing begins" (Barthes 1977, 142). But as is so often the case, it is only through the charring action of death that a bright birth can occur. In our fast-fading partnership with you, we find that "the true locus of writing is reading," and we desire "to restore writing its future . . . the birth of the reader must be ransomed by the death of the Author" (Barthes 1977, 148). Enticing you, then, with the nonexistence of the Lords of Death, beckoning you to let go of the cold railings and plunge into our warm but deadly arms, turns out to be nothing more than a reversal: with the invitation of death we offer your birth, we champion your future. But please know that you, creature of nothingness, have always been our distant starry beloved and addressee ever since we drafted and sent out that AAG CFP back in 2016. If anything, the CFP was a love letter to the future, for the time when your eyes could fall upon these words. In any case that was a long time ago (we thank the contributors for their patience), but it was a time, like now, when our hands could tap across the keyboard, when we were still alive. Perhaps the ultimate contribution of this book, then, is its status as a *memento mori*? At any rate, remember this: we're all going to die. And what better piece of advice to emerge from *A Place More Void*, what better material for our dear and beloved readers? As John Keats (2009, 378), knowing that his end was near, wrote in late 1819 (or thereabouts) to his beloved reader:

> This living hand, now warm and capable
> Of earnest grasping, would, if it were cold
> And in the icy silence of the tomb,
> So haunt thy days and chill thy dreaming nights
> That thou wouldst wish thine own heart dry of blood
> So in my veins red life might stream again,
> And thou be conscience-calm'd—see here it is—
> I hold it towards you.

See, we hold our hands toward you, beloved reader, and offer you this book and its chapters written by those many other warm and capable hands. We offer you this coda, this very sentence, this punctuation mark (!) so that they all might haunt your days and chill your dreaming nights. We desire that you desire your own heart be dry of blood, so you'll want to die with us in this cornered cage, snapped up with final words. But only so you can rise again with your veins streaming again with new red life and capable of making other places more Void. Take us.

References

Badiou, Alain. 1999. *Manifesto for Philosophy*. Translated by Norman Madarasz. Albany: State University of New York Press.

Barthes, Roland. 1977. *Image Music Text*. London: Fontana Press.

Benjamin, Walter. 1968. "Theses on the Philosophy of History." In *Illuminations: Essays and Reflections*, edited by Hannah Arendt, translated by Harry Zohn, 253–64. New York: Schocken Books.

Edelman, Lee. 2004. *No Future: Queer Theory and the Death Drive*. Durham NC: Duke University Press.

Keats, John. 2009. "This living hand, now warm and capable." In *Keats's Poetry and Prose*, edited by Jeffrey N. Cox, 378. New York: W. W. Norton.

Lopez, Donald S. 2000. *The Tibetan Book of the Dead: or, The After-Death Experiences on the Bardo Plane, according to Lāma Kazi Dawa-Samdup's English Rendering*. Compiled and edited by W. T. Evans-Wentz. Oxford: Oxford University Press.

Maddrell, Avril. 2013. "Living with the Deceased: Absence, Presence and Absence-Presence." *cultural geographies* 20, no. 4: 501–22.

Mattila, S., M. Pérez-Torres, A. Efstathiou, P. Mimica, M. Fraser, E. Kankare, A. Alberdi, M. Á. Aloy, T. Heikkilä, P. G. Jonker, et al. 2018. "A Dust-Enshrouded Tidal Disruption Event with a Resolved Radio Jet in a Galaxy Merger." *Science* 361, no. 6401: 482–85.

McGowan, Todd. 2013. *Enjoying What We Don't Have: The Political Project of Psychoanalysis*. Lincoln: University of Nebraska Press.

Rancière, Jacques. 2010. *Dissensus: On Politics and Aesthetics*. Edited and translated by Steven Corcoran. New York: Bloomsbury.

Žižek, Slavoj. 2017. *Incontinence of the Void: Economico-philosophical Spandrels*. Cambridge MA: MIT Press.

Contributors

Carmen Antreasian is an artist and scholar whose work has primarily focused on the critical intersections between Lacanian psychoanalysis, feminist theories, queer studies, and theories of dance and movement. Her academic background includes human geography at Indiana University and performance studies at New York University. She currently uses her dynamic expertise in the Political Science Department at Barnard College, Columbia University, and as a creative writer in the worlds of perfumery and Argentine tango.

Luke Bergmann is associate professor and Canada Research Chair in GIS, Geospatial Big Data and Digital Geohumanities in the Department of Geography at the University of British Columbia. His research interests include critical-computational and social-theoretical geographies.

Kai Bosworth is a geographer and political ecologist, currently assistant professor of international studies in the School of World Studies at Virginia Commonwealth University. His interdisciplinary research examines new political formations emerging in contemporary environmentalism, especially concerning pipeline opposition movements in the central United States.

Sarah de Leeuw is Canada Research Chair in Humanities and Health Inequities and is a professor in the Northern Medical Program and the Geography Program at the University of Northern British Columbia. She is an award-winning creative writer and researcher whose work focuses on colonial geographies and health humanities.

Harriet Hawkins is professor of geohumanities at Royal Holloway, University of London. She researches the geographies of art works and art worlds. Building on previous work on the arts of global environmental change, her recent research focuses on sensing and imagining subterranean spaces, including caves, grottos, caverns, and holes. Alongside publications, she regularly collaborates with creative practitioners to produce a range of work, from installations to exhibitions, artists books, and performative works.

John Paul Jones III is Don Bennett Moon Dean of the College of Social and Behavioral Sciences and professor of geography in the School of Geography, Development and Environment at the University of Arizona. His research interests include social and spatial theory and methodology.

Mikko Joronen is a Finnish Academy research fellow at the Tampere University, Finland. His research focuses on the politics of vulnerability in the occupied Palestinian territories, space and political ontology, and geographical theory. His recent publications deal with questions of waiting, governing, and everyday resistance in Palestine, and the relationship between ontology, space, and politics.

Oliver Keane is a PhD student in the Department of Geography at Simon Fraser University. He is researching the present-day cultural geographies of cryptozoology across the Cascades, where an increase in the number and scale of Sasquatch conferences and expeditions since the 1990s has spawned a cultural renaissance.

Paul Kingsbury is professor of geography and associate dean of the Faculty of Environment at Simon Fraser University. His most recent scholarship uses psychoanalysis to investigate the cultural geographies of paranormal investigations.

Nick Lally is assistant professor of geography at the University of Kentucky. His research interests include speculative cartography, critical computation, and technologies of policing.

Contributors

Jess Linz is a PhD candidate in the Department of Geography at the University of Kentucky. Her current research is on urban displacement in Mexico City, with a focus on affective politics emerging from post-earthquake gentrification.

Yahya M. Madra is associate professor of economics at Drew University, New Jersey, and is a psychoanalyst-in-training at the National Psychological Association for Psychoanalysis in New York City. His research explores the relations between the Marxian and the Freudian fields of critique and analysis. He is a coeditor of the journal *Rethinking Marxism*.

Morgan Meyer holds a PhD in sociology (University of Sheffield), is director of research at the Centre for the Sociology of Innovation (i3, Mines ParisTech, Paris Sciences Lettres, CNRS), and has been a visiting professor/researcher at the universities of Vienna and Edinburgh. His current research concentrates on three topics: participation and coproduction of knowledge; new configurations and communities in biology; and intermediation, translation, and representation of knowledge.

Alison Mountz is professor of geography and Canada Research Chair in Global Migration at the Balsillie School of International Affairs at Wilfrid Laurier University, where she directs the International Migration Research Centre. Mountz's recent scholarship contends with detention and asylum seeking on islands and with U.S. war resister migration to Canada, asking what kinds of safe haven people seek, find, and forge.

Ceren Özselçuk is associate professor in the Department of Sociology at Boğaziçi University, Istanbul. She is an editorial member and managing editor of the journal *Rethinking Marxism*.

Flora Parrott graduated from the Royal College of Art in 2009. Her work looks at notions of the subterranean, the restructuring of the senses in the dark, and conceptions of reality and fiction. Previous exhibitions include Tintype Gallery, Wysing Arts Centre, Norwich Castle Museum and Art Gallery, and the Royal Geographical Society.

Lucas Pohl is a postdoctoral research fellow in the Department of Geography at Humboldt University Berlin. He currently works for a collaborative research project on geographical imaginations of security and insecurity that is part of the research center "Re-Figuration of Spaces." More generally, he works on the interstices between geography, philosophy, and psychoanalysis with a focus on social and spatial theory, built environments, and political action.

Mitch Rose is a senior lecturer in the Department of Geography and Earth Sciences at Aberystwyth University. His research interests are in cultural geography, cultural and political theory, and the history, politics, and culture of Egypt and the Middle East.

Anna J. Secor is professor of human geography at Durham University, UK. Her work draws on psychoanalytic, feminist, and poststructuralist thought in an effort to understand the dynamic entanglement of difference, politics, and space in everyday life.

Ulf Strohmayer teaches geography at the National University of Ireland in Galway, where he is currently professor in the School of Geography, Archaeology and Irish Studies. His research interests are rooted in social philosophies, historical geographies of modernity, and urban planning.

Kira Williams is a postdoctoral fellow at Wilfrid Laurier University. They specialize in statistical programming, mathematical statistics, policy analysis, and social theory, with research on international migration, global governance, and analytical methodology.

Keith Woodward is associate professor of geography and social theory at the University of Wisconsin–Madison. His research interests include social theory, site ontology, and theories of affect, as well as radical geographies and metaphysics.

John Wylie is professor of cultural geography at the University of Exeter, UK. His research seeks to address a range of concerns, including landscape theory, spectral geographies, literary geographies, phenomenology, and nonrepresentational geographies.

Index

—Works: *Black*, 291; *Logics of Worlds*, 292
Balibar, Étienne, 271–72, 274–275, 281n5
Baltard, Victor, 34, *35*, 36–37, 43
being, 2, 5–7, 9, 11, 16, 21; and conceal-
    ment, 249–50, 260–61; and finitude,
    21, 249–51, 254, 257, 263; human, 90,
    255–56, 258; impotentiality of, 21, 250,
    259, 261–63; moment of (*Augenblick*),
    250, 252; mystery, 257–59, 261; and
    oblivion, 155, 258; openness of, 252–53,
    257–60; plenitude of, 11, 21, 249–51,
    253–57, 259, 261–63, 294; presencing,
    153, 255–57; receptivity of, 71, 250–53,
    255, 258–60; refuge of, 199, 257; reveal-
    ing of, 249–50, 253, 255–59, 261–62;
    shrine of nothing related to, 256–59
Benjamin, Walter, 95, 200, 204–5, 208;
    angel of history, 305; and catastrophe,
    209, 305; dialectical image, 159, 201;
    and shock, 210; tiger's leap, 305; on
    waking, 204
Bennett, Jane, 48, 50–52, 298n4
Bergmann, Luke, 19, 167–68, 178
Berlant, Lauren G., 199, 201; active pas-
    sivity, 202; attachment, 199; crisis, 199;
    encounter, 208; impasse, 202, 207. *See
    also* affect; encounter; impasse
Berlin. *See* Germany
Bigfoot, 213, 215, 224, 228; Field Research
    Organization, 216. *See also* Sasquatch;
    Yeti
black hole, 2, 44, 88, 304. *See also* space;
    wormhole
body, 106, 122, 190; cosmic, 12, 78, 87;
    and the earth, 55; human, 40, 54, 57,
    90, 119–21, 200, 209, 227; of matter, 79;
    mind and, 18, 71, 74, 122–24, 286, 304;
    and movement, 160; with objects, 48,
    95; out-of-, 74; and soul, 51, 71; and the
    void, 11, 304

Bol, Peter, 145
border, 7, 11, 31, 87, 177, 200, 206, 272–73
borderlinking, *187*, 188–89
borderspace, 186, *187*, 188–89, 195–96
Boston. *See* United States
Bosworth, Kai, 17–18, 48, 53–55
Bowman, Isaiah, 133–34, 138, 141, 143
British Columbia, 236–37. *See also*
    Canada
British Columbia Scientific Cryptozoo-
    logical Club, 216
Bryant, Page, 68, 77–79, 82, 82n3; *The
    Earth Changes Survival Handbook*, 77
Buck, Paul Herman (Dean), 142
Burgin, Victor, 9–10

Caesar, Julius, 1, 304
Cage, John, 104–5
Callard, Felicity, 14
Cambridge MA. *See* United States
Canada, 215; British Columbia, 235–36
Capital. See Marx, Karl
capitalism, 34, 38, 204, 274–76, 296–97;
    discourse, 21, 76, 268, 280, 281n2; and
    the economy, 34, 278; and logic of, 42,
    278–80; non-, 270, 276; opposition
    to, 41–50, 272, 276–77; systems, 44,
    225, 269; and the void, 12–13. *See also*
    Lacan, Jacques; Marx, Karl
Casey, Edward S., 11
caves, 17, 48; art and paintings in, 61,
    89; artificial, 88, 93–95; Black Hills,
    55–56; cracks/erosion/fracture, 52;
    definition of, 90; ecologies of, 58;
    and the environment, 49, 53, 57–58,
    60, 62; exploration and experience,
    56–58; genesis (speleogenesis), 12, 55;
    grottos, 55, 97; and humans, 97; and
    life force, 52; management/ownership
    of, 58; man-made, 96; mapping of,

55–56, *57*, 58; and politics, 49, 55, 62; reflection on death, 62; snow-, 95; and tourism, 55; and the void, 58, 60–62, 90, 95–96; and vortexes, 71; and water, 59; white nose fungus, 58; Wind and Jewel Caves SD, 49, 53, 55–56. *See also* Arizona; Native American peoples; U.S. National Park Service

caving, 18, 48, 56, 94; as an experience, 48–49, 59, 94; practices, 52, 61; and reflection, 62; requirements to perform, 57

Charlotte, Queen, 236–47

China, 114, 286

Christianity. *See* religion

claims, 82n2, 161, 237, 261, 290; by disciplines, 14, 48, 140–41, 224–26, 229, 247, 271, 292; by Freud, 79; of "God's eye view," 10; of geomagnetism, 74; and open systems, 50–51; of the self, 128–29; and subjectivity, 129; and the void, 119, 128, 252; of vorticism, 78

coda, 21, 303, 306

coherence, 61, 200, 208; space, 289, 291–93

Cold War, 136, 146

Colebrook, Claire, 51–52, 60

colonialism, 10, 20, 58, 177, 236–37, 304; anti-, 54; as settler, 54, 236

Conant, James B., 134–43

conscience, 6, 304, 306. *See also* Freud, Sigmund; Lacan, Jacques

consciousness, 69, 71, 79, 119–22, 124, 126, 145, 157, 167, 204, 268; higher, 71–72; human, 13; plateaus of, 122; self-, 120, 122, 127. *See also* unconscious

Copernican Revolution. *See* Freud, Sigmund

Copjec, Joan, 6, 62, 217

Cresswell, Tim, 145, 235

crevasse, 92

cryptozoology, 20, 214–16, 229–30; definition of, 214–15; movement, 215; "thing," 213–14, 218–26, 229

culture, 3, 14, 75, 103, 115, 122, 208, 213; appropriation, 67, 82n3, 236; and capitalism, 42; and nature, 49, 66; and place, 73; tribal, 67, 227

Custer, George Armstrong, 40

darkness, 62, 91, 93, 95, 97–98, 193, 202, 286; and matter, 291, 294, 296

Dasein, 249–57

Dean, Jodi, 49, 61

death, 1, 37, 39–40, 62, 118, 207, 304; of the author, 305; drive, 8, 305; and the ego, 3; Lords of, 304–5; and nothingness, 249, 251–53, 256–57; of the reader, 31; and symbolism, 209; and voidness, 304. *See also* Freud, Sigmund; Whittlesey, Derwent

de Leeuw, Sarah, 20, 235

Deleuze, Gilles, 7, 30, 52, 60, 200–201, 208; becoming-minor, 200, 202; burrows, 201–2, 205–6; intensity, 206; paradoxical element, 7. *See also* Guattari, Félix

Derrida, Jacques, 14, 16–17, 30, 32, 75, 133, 162

Descartes, René, 18, 78, 82, 83n11, 294–95, 298n8; and dotted subject, *81*; vortex theory of, 78–79, *80*

diachronic, 31, 60

différance, 8, 30

dimension, 10, 30–31, 54, 75, 169–71, 175, 177, 185, 193, 201, 218, 269, 303; and culture, 73, 146; enigmatic, 18–19, 119–20, 125–29; of extimacy, 273; and humans, 90; ontological, 116; parallel, 199

disappearance, 16, 19, 151–53, 156, 163, 224, 251–52

Latour, Bruno, 51; and actor-network theory, 287, 290–91; and material-ism, 288–89, 291, 294–95, 298n4; and nature, 49; plasma, 290–92, 294; the thing, 288–89, 293
—Works: *Paris, ville invisible*, 290–91; *Reassembling the Social*, 290–91
Lennon, John, 2
Lewis, George, 140
Linz, Jess, 20, 199, 204–5
literature, 68, 105, 119–24, 133, 136, 150–51, 213, 249
Logan, Richard, 138–39
London. *See* United Kingdom
Lonetree, Ben, 74–76
love, 111, 113, 142, 167, 181, 298n9, 303, 306; courtly, 184, 225; notion of, 75; primor-dial, 195; and solidarity, 207

MacDonald, Glen, 132
Macfarlane, Robert, 91
Madra, Yahya M., 21, 267
Magritte, René, 89
Malafouris, Lambros, 121–23
Manson, Johnny, 216, 226–27, 230nn2–3maps, 19, 61, 111, 119, 133, 214, 216, 245; of caves, 55–56, 57, 58; of energetic geometry, 78; and enfolding, 169–74, 178; and the European Renaissance, 10; and GIS, 168, 178; measures of distance, 175; 176–78; scientific, 48; of the void, 3; of vortexes, 70, 78, 79
Marcuse, Herbert, 145
Marx, Karl, 40; and capitalism, 34, 274–75; discourse-object unity, 271; impossibility of value, 275–78; and materialism, 271–72, 288; and political economy, 267–70, 274–76, 278, 280; and surplus labor, 270, 280; and surplus value, 267–68, 280; theory

of, 280. *See also jouissance*; Lacan, Jacques; materialism/materiality
—Works: *Capital*, 267–68, 274, 276–78; *Grundrisse*, 34
materialism/materiality, 7, 60, 287–89, 292; contemporary, 57; feminist, 16; and geography, 286–87, 295; historical, 269, 271–72; im-, 7, 17, 21, 89, 113, 285, 287, 292, 294, 296; and matter, 295; new, 16, 18, 48, 50–52, 60; role of, 122; of silence, 109, 115; and structuralism, 269; and the theory of everything, 286; of the void, 295; and the vortex, 69, 78. *See also* Badiou, Alain; environment; Latour, Bruno; Marx, Karl; ontology; presence; trace; world
McCartney, Paul, 22n2
McGreevy, Patrick, 10
McSweeney, Emmeline, 143–44
Meldrum, Jeff, 226–27, 229
memento mori, 306
memory, 53, 59, 71, 74, 132–33, 145, 147, 153, 155, 160
Merleau-Ponty, Maurice, 120, 160–61
Meyer, Morgan, 18, 103, 105
Miller, Iona, 74
Miller, Jacques-Alain, 268, 273, 281n1, 281n3.
mining, 246; and toxins, 54; uranium, 53, 59. *See also* Native American peoples
mood, 13, 161, 250–51, 253, 257; of curios-ity, 58, 133, 258, 262; of fear, anger, or shame, 250; *Gelassenheit*, 250, 258–62; of mindfulness, 258, 262; playful, 249–50, 259–60, 262–63. *See also* anxiety; uncanny; wonder
Morris, Rita, 133, 136–37, 140–41
Mountz, Alison, 19, 132, 134, 140, 145

Native American peoples, 40, 67, 227; Quinault Indian Nation, 227
necropolitics. *See* politics

negation, 224, 228, 235, 251, 257, 294, 304–5

New Ageism, 66

Neyrat, Frédéric, 50, 52, 59

Nietzsche, Friedrich, 6, 208; and nothingness, 6. *See also* forgetting

9/11. *See* September 11

Nixon, Richard, 40

oil, 246; crisis of 1973, 37

Olsson, Gunnar, 9, 316

ontology, 5, 8–9, 174, 176, 288, 292, 294; of absence, 18, 163; and change, 263; corporeal, 119–25; ecological, 50; and the existence of God, 78; geographical, 10, 178; and impasse, 199, 201, 207; and materiality, 16, 48–49, 52, 68, 115, 153, 287; negativity, 15; object-oriented, 16; of relationality, 50, 103, 105, 115; and sexual difference, 14; of silence and sound, 110, 114, 116; and voids, 13, 21, 249–51, 294, 296; and vortexes, 18, 69; Western, 14. *See also* being; caves; Sasquatch

Özselçuk, Ceren, 21, 267

palimpsest, 33, 67

Paris. *See* France

Parmenides, 5, 7–8, 52. *See also* Plato

Parrott, Flora, 86, 87, 89–90, 98n1, 99

Patterson-Gimlin (film), 215, 229. *See also* Bigfoot

Persinger, Michael A., 74

perspective, 59, 61, 160, 217, 228, 271; and absence, 9, 16; anthropocentric, 48; of being, 253–56; and Derrida, 16; dwelling, 120; first-person, 161; and the land, 152, 155–58, 162; partiality, 48, 52, 61; and politics, 61–62

phenomenology, 16, 48, 120, 152, 163, 287

Pile, Steve, 14–16

place, 1, 18, 20, 159, 214; attachment to, 158; empty, 7–8, 11, 16, 230, 267; and fullness, 11; and landscape, 14; of object *a*, 267, 271; physical, 73, 152, 203, 257; sense of, 158, 161, 208; and sound or silence, 105, 108, 111–15; and space, 14, 107; understanding of, 8; and void, 11, 17, 21, 181, 259, 285, 297, 303, 306. *See also* space; void

Plato, 8, 11, 72, 96–97, 295

poem, 5, 19–20, 150–52, 155–57, 160, 162–63, 236–47, 253–54, 260

poet, 9, 208, 253

poetry, 20, 235, 237

Pohl, Lucas, 21, 285

politics, 18, 20, 48, 199, 261–62, 288–89; bio-, 34; culture and, 75; economics and, 50; environmental, 48–49, 61–62; geo-, 177; impasse, 20, 199–212; of institutions, 136, 145; necro-, 305; and silence, 103–4; spatial, 206

presence, 201; and absence, 2, 16, 31, 39, 44n1, 110, 133, 153, 163, 279; coming-to-, 255–56; continuity of, 31; and cultural geography, 16; of ghosts, 15, 153; letting-, 255–56, 262; material, 152; new, 31; non-, 40; and sameness, 29; and the self, 128, 161; silence and sound, 104; spatial, 61–62; urbanism, 32; and void, 11; web and online, 74. *See also* absence; dream

production, 37, 66–67, 235, 274, 289; and art, 66, 82n4; associated, 276, 278; and capitalism, 269, 274–78. *See also* Marx, Karl; reproduction

Pusey, Nathan Marsh, 139–41

queer, 24, 135, 142, 146, 210; defamation of, 138–39; history of, 133, 140, 146; marginalization of, 200; and theory, 200, 205. *See also* Edelman, Lee; history; homophobia; homosexuality quietness, 103, 105–6, 109, 115–16

Quinault Indian Nation. *See* Native American peoples

railways, 155, 157, 168

Rancière, Jacques, 32, 41, 43, 305

reader, 19–20, 32, 151, 237, 303–5

relationality, 19, 50–51, 105, 114, 206, 209

religion, 3, 103, 230; Christian, 4, 49; Islam, 4; practice of, 68

reproduction, 89, 195, 269, 275; GIF, 205; meme, 205. See also *jouissance*; production

research, 1, 289; and conferences, 213–16, 222, 226–28; funding of, 138–40, 230; and gender, 217; at Harvard University, 133–34, 137, 140–43; method and theory, 1, 226, 230, 296; requirements for, 113; on silence, 104

response, 40, 121, 124, 138–39, 152, 190–91, 196, 287; and art, 191, 194; and culture, 73, 75; physical, 71, 154, 155; scientific, 90

response-ability, 260–63

retroactive, 214, 267, 269–70, 275–76

Rose, Gillian, 11, 14–15, 177

Rose, Mitch, 18–19, 73, 118, 249

rupture, 69, 90, 169, 204, 207, 305

Sanders, Pete A., 18, 71, 72–73, 74, 77

San Francisco. *See* United States

Sartre, Jean-Paul, 161–62

Sasquatch, 20, 213, 225–26; annual conferences, 213; and First Nations, 215; as human or non-human, 226–28; and images, 214, *219*, 220, *220–22*; and investigations, 213, 216–17, 223, 227, 229; publications, 215; sightings of, 216, 220–21, 224, 226; Summit, 20, 213–14, 216–18, 220–24, 226–30, 230n1. *See also* Bigfoot; cryptozoology; Yeti

Schenck, Hubert, 142

Schumann Resonances, 74

science, 3, 98, 107, 137, 226, 298n9; conventional, 20; and the development of knowledge, 29, 213; elimination of, 144; and experience, 30; fields of study, 137–38, 140, 142, 215, 226, 281n3; and the Other, 75–76; pseudo-, 215; scholars of, 49; social, 16, 30, 138, 140, 295; and spirit, 75; tenet of, 229–30; and the void, 90

sculpture, 92–93, 95, 169

Sebald, W. G., 19, 150–52, 154–63

—Works: *Across the Land and the Water*, 150; *Austerlitz*, 154; *Unrecounted*, 161; "Vanish," 162; *Vertigo*, 162

Secor, Anna J., 1, 20, 135, 176–77, 199, 205, 225–28, 274

senses, 71, 115, 119, 122, 127, 202

September 11 (9/11), 286, 297, 298n1

sexuality, 96, 193–94, 249; and females, 181–82, 194–95; hetero-, 14; identity, 185, 188; masculinity, 14; patriarchal view, 182; psycho-, 185, 188, 196; and relationships, 183; and sexual difference, 14–15. *See also* homophobia; homosexual; Lacan, Jacques; queer; sexuation

sexuation, 20, 181–95; Ettinger matrixial sexuation, 182–83, *184*, 185–86, 195–96; Lacanian sexuation, 182–86, 188, 195–96; 279; 183, 185, 267, 270–71, 273–74, 278–80. See also *jouissance*, objet *a*

Shavasana (corpse pose), 303

sifr. *See* zero (*sifr*)

sign, 18, 43, 55, 68, 220, 255; of absence, 68; and dimension of, 118–20, 123–29; and nonpresence, 16; role of, 128–29; systems of, 74, 87, 276; and the void, 11, 18–19, 127–28, 150. *See also* Kohn, Eduardo

Simpson, O. J., 225
Simpson, Paul, 121
Simpson Center for the Humanities, 178
Sinagua, 67
Sitting Bull, 40
skill, 121–22
Smith, Adam, 271
Smith, Neil, 132–35, 141
Smith, Robert, 12
solidarity, 20, 201, 206–7, 211; boycotts, 207; emergent, 210; self-effacement, 207
soothsayer, 1–2
space, 1–3; being of, 161; description or notion of, 168, 176; empty, 2–3, 8, 10, 79, 290, 293; as Euclidean, 9–10, 168, 171–73, 177–78; extent of, 8; as holes, 2, 4, 6, 10, 15, 17, 29–33, 37, 39, 40, 42, 88, 90, 161, 304; logic of, 34; and phenomena, 1, 76, 78, 168–69, 225; as relational, 19, 168; sense of, 107, 168; situated experience of, 9, 167–68; theory, 176; and time, 3, 79, 154, 202; understanding of, 8, 168–69, 173. *See also* earth; impasse; void; wormhole
Spinoza, Baruch, 82, 83n9
Stamp, Dudley, 138, 143
Stoics, 7–8, 11
Strohmayer, Ulf, 17, 29, 32, 44s
structuralism, 267–69, 271, 276, 279. *See also* Lacan, Jacques
subjectivity, 13, 18, 118–120; and an awareness of self, 128–29; configuration of, 120; and corporeal ontologies, 120–25; and engagement, 124–25; human, 79, 127, 217; relationships with, 185; and signs, 127–28
summons, 18, 93, 95, 118–20, 124–25, 127–29, 235
Śūnyatā (voidness), 304. *See also* void
supplement, 17, 32–34, 36–37, 41–43, 44n2

symbols/symbolism, 5–6, 20, 119, 155; and capitalism, 297; and death, 209; importance of, 113; influence of, 182; and maps, 168; and the other, 182, 184–86, 188, 195, 209, 214, 272; and paintings, 191–92; phallic, 183–84, 188–89, 195–96; representative of, 113–14; of social codes, 217, 271; sub-, 185–86, 188; and the vagina, 181–82, 188, 196; of voids, 73, 183, 220, 223–24. *See also* Ettinger, Bracha; Tolstoy, Leo
synchronic, 31, 60

terra incognita (*terrae incognitae*), 10, 13–14, 290, 294
theory, 2, 213, 267, 296; actor-network, 287; electromagnetic, 7; environmental, 49; of everything, 286; Gaia hypothesis, 51; human geographic, 168; limits of, 69; Marxian, 280; matrixial gaze, 190; psychoanalytic, 268; quantum field, 7, 200; queer, 200, 205; of sexuation, 182–83, 188, 195; social, 176, 290; spatial, 77; of the void, 2; and vortexes, 74, 78; and the womb, 181, 188
threshold, 15, 30–31, 122, 125, 177, 206; *Tibetan Book of the Dead*, 3, 304
tides, 240, 244–45, 258
time, 83n11, 175; diachronic, 60; of the earth, 9; in and across, 31; linear, 134, 208–9; "lost," 159; quasi-synchronic, 60; and space, 3, 34, 38, 74, 79, 94, 154, 167, 202. *See also* Heidegger, Martin
Tolstoy, Leo, 190–92, 195; *Anna Karenina*, 190–92
Tonto Apache, 67
topology, 176–77, 206, 249, 267, 275; Klein bottle, 206; Möbius strip, 91, 176–77, 201
tourism, 48, 55, 58, 66–67, 70, 126; alternative, 68

geography, 134–37, 145–46; his ghost, 19, 133, 145; and meticulousness, 143; obituary, 141. *See also* Harvard University; Kemp, Harold; Wright, William

Williams, Kira, 19, 132, 134, 145

Wilson, Matthew W., 140, 146

Wittgenstein, Ludwig, 5

wonder, 7, 13, 58, 111, 113, 147, 209–10, 257–58; -full geomorphology, 68; interpellation, 209, 281n3. *See also* Irigaray, Luce

Woodward, Keith, 18

world, 9; connectedness of, 48, 52, 174, 260; engagement with, 29, 121, 124, 127, 159; globalization of, 35, 59, 173, 245, 249, 296; material, 123–24, 127, 292; natural, 48–49, 106–8; and Plato, 295; relationship with the body, 120–23, 161; and scientific study, 13; and spirituality, 74–75; s-view, 52; and the void, 9–10, 128. *See also* caves; earth

World Trade Center, 37, 285–86

World War II, 136–37, 140, 151, 154

wormhole, 19, 167, *173*, 174, 201

Wright, John Henry, 97

Wright, John K., 13–14

Wright, Richard, 145

Wright, William, 132, 138; *Harvard's Secret Court*, 132

writing, 6–10, 62, 74, 106, 152, 178, 290, 303; act of, 6; and author comparisons, 30, 68, 151, 155, 281n2; and the void, 8, 10, 91

Wylie, John, 16, 19, 121, 150, 163, 249, 288, 313

Yavapai, 67

Yeti, 215. *See also* Bigfoot; Sasquatch

yoga, 303

zero (*sifr*), 4, 7, 203, 303; non-, 202; numbering systems, 3–4, 14, 210; story of, 3; and the void, 5

Žižek, Slavoj, 16, 183–84, 224–25, 295, 305; enjoyment, 226

Zola, Émile, 33

Topoi/Graphein: Mapping the Middle in Spatial Thought
Christian Abrahamsson
Foreword by Gunnar Olsson

Animated Lands: Studies in Territoriology
Andrea Mubi Brighenti and Mattias Kärrholm

Mapping Beyond Measure: Art, Cartography,
and the Space of Global Modernity
Simon Ferdinand

Psychoanalysis and the GlObal
Edited and with an introduction by Ilan Kapoor

A Place More Void
Edited by Paul Kingsbury and Anna J. Secor

Arkography: A Grand Tour through the Taken-for-Granted
Gunnar Olsson

To order or obtain more information on these or other University of Nebraska Press titles, visit nebraskapress.unl.edu.

CPSIA information can be obtained
at www.ICGtesting.com
Printed in the USA
LVHW030027110221
678953LV00001B/12

9 781496 223661